CATALOGUE

OF THE

COLLECTION OF

AMERICAN COLONIAL COINS
HISTORICAL MEDALS
UNITED STATES COINS
FRACTIONAL CURRENCY
CANADIAN COINS AND MEDALS

OF THE LATE

HON. GEORGE M. PARSONS

CATALOGUED BY

HENRY CHAPMAN

NUMISMATIST

TO BE SOLD AT PUBLIC AUCTION

AT PHILADELPHIA

JUNE 24th TO 27th, INCLUSIVE

1914

CATALOGUE

OF THE

MAGNIFICENT COLLECTION

OF

AMERICAN COLONIAL COINS
HISTORICAL AND NATIONAL MEDALS
UNITED STATES COINS
U. S. FRACTIONAL CURRENCY
CANADIAN COINS AND MEDALS, Etc.

FORMED BY THE LATE

HON. GEORGE M. PARSONS
COLUMBUS, OHIO

CATALOGUED BY

HENRY CHAPMAN
NUMISMATIST
No. 1348 PINE STREET, PHILADELPHIA, PA.

AND TO BE SOLD AT

PUBLIC AUCTION

BY

MESSRS. DAVIS & HARVEY
AUCTIONEERS
No. 910 WALNUT STREET, PHILADELPHIA, PA.

WEDNESDAY, THURSDAY, FRIDAY, SATURDAY,
JUNE 24, 25, 26, 27, 1914

COMMENCING DAILY AT 2 P. M.

PREFACE

It is a pleasure to have to offer to numismatists such a fine collection of the early coins and medals of America as are contained in this splendid old collection of the late Hon. George M. Parsons and others.

Among the Colonial Coins there are several coins which have not been offered for many years, and the student in this most interesting series must have been greatly impressed by the few real gems that have been offered for public competition in the past few years. The series of Historical Medals relating to the early history of our country is one that is highly interesting and records events of the greatest importance—it is a series that commands the attention of the historian as well as the collector.

The Pattern Collection is quite extensive, and one which is coming up fast in popularity. The collection of Washington Coins and Medals is one of the finest ever offered. United States Coins contain many examples of great beauty on account of their high state of preservation.

The superb example of that great rarity in the Canadian Series, the 1670 Quarter Crown, GLORIAM REGNI, will be a delight to the fortunate purchaser "across the border," as also the 1756 jeton in silver from hitherto undescribed dies. The United States Fractional Currency is one of the finest collections of this popular branch of collecting, which I hope will receive the attention it deserves.

I have endeavored to describe the coins as I see them, without favor to the seller or buyer, and so the description may not mislead the latter, have carefully noted the defects or evidences of wear that are on the coin. This great care is of value to the intending buyer, who, I am glad to be able to say, feels that he will get a coin meeting the description, hence, he bids its value to him and is not disappointed when those bought by or for him arrive.

Collectors desiring further information than the necessarily brief description incident to a public sale catalogue will please communicate with the undersigned, who will gladly make answer.

Bidders will please examine and compare their bids before sending them in, as mistakes made by them will not be borne by the cataloguer or auctioneers; also sign your name and address to your bid sheet. Forward your bids as soon as possible.

I will carefully execute bids entrusted to me for 5% *of the sum purchased*—no charge made on lots not bought.

The auctioneers will execute bids free of the above commission, but they are not numismatists and do not know the value of the lots, so simply execute the orders given, assuming no responsibility and requiring payment to be made in advance of their sending the goods.

Every coin, medal or note is sold so much each piece, except where lot or set or proof sets are stated.

Because this is a great sale do not let that fact deter the small buyer from sending in his bids—all are welcome and will be thankfully received—the large and the small; and here permit me to draw attention to there being such a varied offering that I believe there should be some item in the following 2,750 lots on which every one receiving this catalogue could make a bid. The cost of publishing this catalogue has been great, and I hope collectors will show their appreciation of my efforts at pleasing them, as well as making business for myself, by either sending in some bids or attending the sale in person or commissioning myself or others to represent them.

Any one who receives one of the catalogues and has no use for it, or subsequent catalogues, will confer a favor by returning it.

I appreciate greatly the loyal support given me in the past, and it is my aim to strive to merit a continuance of the same.

HENRY CHAPMAN,
Numismatist,
No. 1348 Pine Street,
Philadelphia.

Bell Telephone: Walnut 2019.

Registered Cable Address: "Moneta," Philadelphia.

THE CATALOGUE

Prior to June 27th, the plain catalogue may be obtained free of charge on application.

Prior to June 27th, the illustrated catalogue may be obtained on payment of $3.00. After the sale the illustrated catalogue may be obtained with a list of prices obtained bound in at the back on payment of $4.00.

After the sale a printed list of prices obtained at the sale may be had on payment of $1.00.

After the sale the plain catalogue with list of prices obtained bound in may be had for $1.25.

Expressage on all of the above prepaid by the publisher.

TERMS OF SALE

The sale is made for cash on delivery of the goods, which may be obtained at the termination of each day's sale, or at the end of the sale on the 27th.

The highest bidder to be the buyer.

Should a dispute arise and the disputant has a voucher and is willing to advance on the price at which the lot was stricken off, then the said lot is to be put up again and sold to the highest bidder.

The auctioneers reserve the right to refuse the bid of an individual if he declines to make a cash deposit or pay sum bid on their request to do so.

No lot is separated. All are sold subject to the catalogue description and by the catalogue numbers. Should any lot become misplaced, the buyer does not acquire any right in it if it is stricken off without the mistake being discovered, and such a lot must be returned to the auctioneers.

Every item is guaranteed genuine, and this holds good indefinitely.

Every lot sold so much each piece, except the proof sets.

No coins shown during the progress of the sale unless to oblige a special request. Any one wishing to see a lot will be given every opportunity to do if possible.

Collectors are requested to carefully examine the coins during the exhibition, marking their catalogue, thus being prepared, as the sale proceeds at the rate of about 200 lots to the hour.

ORDER OF SALE

Commence each day at 2 P. M.

Coins for the day's sale on exhibition at the auction room from 9.00 A. M. to 12.30 P. M.

First day—Nos. 1 to 560 inclusive.

Second day—Nos. 561 to 1278 inclusive.

Third day—Nos. 1279 to 2077 inclusive.

Fourth day—Nos. 2078 to 2756 inclusive.

SCALE.

4   8   12   16   20   24   28   32   36   40   44   48   52   56   60   64

CATALOGUE

SOMMER OR BERMUDA ISLANDS.

Men 50. — 1 (1616-1619?) Twopence. Wild hog standing to left, above II for value—2 pence. R. s I (Sommer Islands) at either side of a ship, which is very faint Obverse fine. R. Faint. Extremely rare. *Plate.* This denomination unknown to Crosby.

COINS OF THE BRITISH COLONIES IN NORTH AMERICA.
MASSACHUSETTS.

SILVER COINAGE.

NEW ENGLAND SHILLING.

White 62.50 2 (1652) Shilling. N E for New England in a punch mark nearly square on a plain planchet. R. XII for 12 pence or a shilling. Free from the usual bending and one of the finest examples I have seen. Fine. Very rare, and a coin that every American collector should strive to possess, being, as it is, *the first coin struck in North America. Plate.* Crosby, plate I, 3. *Eroded surface*

WILLOW TREE SERIES.

L 82.50 3 1652 Shilling. MASA(T)HVETS I (*part shows*) N Bushy tree with branches in loops. R. NEW EN(GL)AND (A)N DO(M) 1652 XII The letters in parenthesis do not show. Fine, slightly bent, but superior to those usually offered, and even then only once or twice in a decade. Extremely rare. *Plate.* Crosby, 3d-G 1.

NOTE.—From the C. I. Bushnell (1885) and J. G. Mills' Collections (1904).

OAK TREE SERIES.

Low 9.50 4 1652 Shilling. MASATIIVSETS.IN. Bushy tree with two lower limbs curved like horns. R. NEW ENGLAND.AN.DOM 1652.XII for 12 pence or a shilling. Die broken on top of obverse and along right side of reverse— Fine. Unusually even impression for this variety. *Plate.* Crosby, 2-D, plate 1, No. 9.

White   30.— 5 1652 Shilling. MASATHVSETS.IN. Bushy, spiny tree with shrub at either side of trunk. R. NEW ENGLAND.AN.DOM. 1652.XII Uncirculated. Planchet has nick on edge cutting into tops of NG on reverse. Slightly weak on obverse edge at N, otherwise very sharp even obverse, the reverse not quite even. Very rare. *Plate.* Crosby 3-D, rarity 4, plate 1, No. 8.

Straw Right   32.50 6 1652 Shilling. MASATHVSETS.IN. Very delicate skeleton-like tree with two shrubs. R. NEW.ENGLAND.AN.DOM. 1652.XII. Very fine. Even impression, slightly clipped. Pin head dent under first A bends it slightly. Rare. *Plate.* Crosby 6a-E¹.

Scan   12.50 7 1652 Shilling. MASATHVSETS.IN. Stately tree with few spiny limbs and two shrubs. R. NEW ENGLAND. AN DOM 1652 XII. Broad planchet showing rim outside of beading, except on left side of the top where the clipping invades the beading on both sides. Fine. Rare. *Plate.* Crosby 7-B, fig. 7, page 47.

           8 1652 Shilling. MASATHVSETS : IN: Finely formed, bushy tree with spiny limbs and two shrubs. R. NEW ENGLAND : AN DOM. 1652 XII. Fine. Slight defect in planchet on right arm of N on obv. Well centered. *Plate.* Crosby 9-H.

Vantybral   8.50 9 1652 Sixpence. MASATHV(SE)TS Bushy tree with center dot. R. IN NEW ENGLAND. ANO 1652 VI Good. Worn across SE and lower part of tree. The only sixpence with the legend so arranged. Rare. C. 6-F.

J.M.C.   27.50 10 1652 Sixpence. MASA(THVSET)S.IN. Bushy, spiny tree with two shrubs. R. NEW ENGLAND.ANO : 1652 VI for 6 pence. Obverse struck high, cutting entirely off the letters in parenthesis. Reverse perfect. Very good. Scratch across obv. Rare. *Plate.* Crosby 1b-D.

S. M.S   16.— 11 1652 Threepence. MASATHVSETS* Finely formed, sturdy tree with large shrub at right side and very light one on left. R. NEW ENGLAND* 1652 III. Very fine. Evenly struck. *Plate.* Crosby 5-B.

   22.— 12 1652 Threepence. MASAT(US)ETS:: Bushy tree with lattice-like trunk. R. NEW ENGLAND* 1652.III for 3 pence. Good. Excessively rare; believed but two others known. *Plate.* Crosby 6-C.

Wilson   17.00 13 1662 Twopence. MASATHVSETS.IN. Bushy tree, shrub at either side. R. NEW ENGLAND* 1662 II for 2 pence. Uncirculated. Evenly centered, which is unusual with this coin. Rare. *Plate.* Crosby 1-A¹.

PINE TREE SERIES.

LARGE SPREAD SHILLINGS.

C   )2 _ 14 1652 Shilling. MASATHVSETS IN Bushy tree finely formed, many
                 spines, trunk split. R. NEW ENGLAND. AN. DOM. 1652 XII. Un-
                 circulated. Crack in from lower edge to beading. Evenly
                 struck. Rare. *Plate.* Crosby 1ᵇ-D, fig. 13, page 54.

C   3. –15 1652 Shilling. MASATHVSETS IN. Wide tree, trunk very narrow
                 from second branches. R. NEW ENG(L) AND AN DOM (1)652 XII.
                 Very weakly struck on the ins. Short crack in on upper edge.
                 Fair. *Plate.* Crosby 2ᵃ-A¹.

White 32.50 16 1652 Shilling. MASATHVSETS IN Tall compact tree with very
                 spiny branches. R. NEW ENGLAND.AN.DOM. 1652 XII. Uncircu-
                 lated. Well and evenly struck. Rare. *Plate.* Crosby 4-F, fig.
                 15, page 58.

C   /:– 17 1652 Shilling. MASATHVSETS.IN. Natural, finely formed tree. R.
                 NEW ENGLAND.AN.DOM 1652 XII. Broad flan with border out-
                 side of beading only invaded in three places. Two pin point
                 dents. Planchet not even top nor bottom, and slight crack in
                 on lower edge. Very fine. Rare. *Plate.* Crosby 5-B², plate
                 VII, 1.

White 34 18 1652 Shilling. MASATHVSETS. IN* Small natural tree with four
                 long roots to r. R. NEW ENGLAND : AN : DOM* 1652 XII. Uncir-
                 culated. Even and sharply struck. Shows faint XII incused un-
                 der tree. Reverse die broken. Uncirculated. One of the most
                 beautiful of the Pine Tree Shillings, and a remarkable example.
                 Rare. *Plate.* Crosby 12-I, fig. 16, page 58.

Hines 7 —19 1652 Shilling. Duplicate of last. Uncirculated. Bad defect in
                 edge at top as if a small piece were broken out, but it was in the
                 planchet before coin was minted. Uncirculated. *Plate.*

SMALL, COMPACT COINAGE.

Winthrop 10.50 20 1652 Shilling. MASATHVSETS ·:· IN ·:· Tree with heavy stiff limbs.
                 R. NEW. ENGLAND.AN.DO. 1652 XII. Very fine. Well struck.
                 C. 14-R, fig 17, page 62.

White 16.– 21 1652 Shilling. MASATHVSETS IN Bushy tree with heavy roots.
                 R. NEW ENGLAND AN.DO 1652 XII. Very fine. Tops of HVSE off on
                 obverse, reverse even. Slight scrape in obverse field . C. 18-L.
                 Very rare. *Plate.*

22 1652 Shilling. MASATHVSETS IN. Finely formed tree with spiny
limbs. IN faintly struck. R. NEW ENGLAND.AN.DO. 1652 XII.
Extremely fine. The lightest planchet I have ever met with, as
it weighs only 56 grains. Probably unique of this weight. *Plate.*
C. 21-L, pl. II, 14.

23 1652 Shilling. Same dies as last, on a regular planchet, weighing 67½ grains. Very fine. Very light pin scratches in field to
left of tree. *Plate.*

24 1652 Shilling. MASATHVSETS IN. Fine, small tree. R. NEW
ENGLAND AN . DO. 1652 XII. Fine, but surface very lightly
eroded. *Plate.* Crosby 22-L, plate II, 13-14.

25 1652 Shilling. (M)ASATHVSETS (IN) NEW (faint) ENGLAND - AN
(DO) 1652 XII. Large, bushy tree with spiny limbs. Very good;
lower part so weak as to efface the inscription. *Plate.* Crosby
24-N, rarity 4! plate II, 8.

26 1652 Sixpence. MA(SATHV)SETS - IN. Fine tree of few limbs.
R. NEW ENGLAND ANO 1652 VI. Obverse off, as always. R. Even.
Fine. Rare. *Plate.*

27 1652 Threepence. (MA)SATHVSETS R. NEW ENGLAND 1652 III.
Obverse off, as usual, the MA not showing and tops of SETS off.
Very good. Very rare. *Plate.* Crosby 1-A².

28 1652 Threepence. MASATHVSETS Finely formed small tree. R.
NEW ENGLAND 1652 III. Uncirculated. Tops of HVS off. Rare.
Plate. Crosby 2ª-B.

MARYLAND.

29 (1659) Shilling. CÆCILIVS : DNS : TERRÆ - MARIÆ : &CT.+.
Bust of Cecil Calvert, Lord Baltimore, eldest son of George Calvert, first Lord Baltimore, to whom in 1632 Charles I of England
granted the province of Maryland; which was so named in honor
of Henrietta Marie, Queen Consort of Charles I. R. CRESCITE:
ET : MVLTIPLICAMINI (*Increase and be multiplied*). Arms of
Lord Baltimore crowned and dividing XII = 12 pence. Not
struck up fully on the hair, but evenly centered. Extremely fine,
and one of the best examples of this highly interesting and very
rare coin. *Plate.* Crosby, plate III, No. 1.

NEW JERSEY.

Coins probably struck in Dublin, Ireland, 1678, during the reign of Charles II, and not meeting with favor there were brought in quantity to America, 1681, by an immigrant, one Mark Newby, who settled in New Jersey, and by an Act of May 8, 1682, they were made to pass current in this Colony of New Jersey. On one is found an 8 below the figure of St. David, and Dr. Nelson thinks this probably denotes the year of 1678, for they were specifically mentioned in Act of the Isle of Man, June 24, 1679, wherein their circulation was ordered to cease.

30 (1682) Farthing in silver. King David kneeling on the ground to left, playing a harp; before him FLOREAT, above a crown, and at right : REX : (May the King Flourish). R. QVIESCAT PLEBS : St. Patrick, robed and mitred, a nimbus around his head, standing facing three-quarters left, his right hand extended; in his left and resting on his arm is a Metropolitan cross, while before him the reptiles flee, and behind is a church. Borders milled. Edge milled. Very good. *Unique.* Pictured by Dr. Nelson, plate II, No. 13, and page 18, where it is given as in the Caldecott Collection, and from which collection it passed to the present. *Plate.*

31 (1682) Farthing in silver. Type as last, but no ground under King David, and without the nimbus around the head of St. Patrick. No stop after PLEBS. Very fine. Very rare. *Plate.*

32 (1682) Farthing. Type as last. Very good. Maris 2-B.

33 (1682) Farthings. Different dies. With and without the ground under St. David. On one the brass has dropped from the crown, leaving a depression; one dented. Fair.   4 pcs.

34 (1682) Half penny. FLOREAT REX: (May the King Flourish). King David kneeling to left, playing on a harp; above a crown with brass inset before striking to make it a golden crown. FLORE before crown, AT between crown and King's head. 16 cords to harp. R. ECCE GREX (Behold the flock!) St. Patrick standing, mitred, a trefoil or shamrock in his right hand, and by which he is illustrating the Holy Trinity—Three in One—to the multitude standing before him, a crozier rests in his left arm; behind or to his left the arms of the City of Dublin—six castles. Very fine, remarkably so for this coin. *Plate.* Crosby, plate III, 8. Maris 1-A.

1 — 35 (1682) Half penny. Type as last, but legend larger—the word FLOREAT before the crown and between the crown and head of David is . * . 14 cords to harp. Poor. Rare.

VIRGINIA.

4 25 36 1685-1688 $\frac{1}{24}$ of a real. IACOBVS . II . DG . MAG . BRI . FRAN . ET . IIIB . REX. Equestrian statue of King James II r. R. VAL : 24 PART . REAL . HISPAN. Four shields cruciform of England, Scotland, France and Ireland crowned; a chain of three links each binds them together. Edge milled. Pewter. Uncirculated. Bright. Superior example. *Plate.*

6 — 37 1773 Penny, so called from its large size, 17½. GEORGIVS III. REX. No period after GEORGIVS Bare bust of the King, laureated facing r. R. VIRGINIA 1773 Arms of Great Britain crowned. Superb bronze proof. Broad, even heading on both sides. Rare. *Plate.* Crosby, plate IX, 10.

. 2 J 38 1773 Half penny. Type as last, but with period after GEORGIVS. Border of serratures. Ex. fine, light olive. Size 17. Crosby, pl. IX, 12.

1.50 39 1773 Half penny. Type as last. No period after GEORGIVS Mere trace of milling. Size 16. Leaf points to center of I and center of A Uncirculated. Brilliant red. Rare variety. Crosby, plate IX, 11.

1. . 40 1773 Half penny. Type as last. Nose points below R. Period after GEORGIVS as are all following. R. Leaves point to left of I and center of A. Uncirculated. Bright red.

1. 41 1773 Half penny. Type as last. Nose points at R. R. Leaf points at right side of I and center of A. Uncirculated. Bright red.

7. 42 1773 Half penny. As last. Uncirculated. Partly red.

1 — 43 1773 Half penny. Type as last. R E X widely spaced. R. Leaves touch V point to left side of I and center of A. Nose points to R. Uncirculated. Bright red.

1. — 44 1773 Half penny. Type as last. Legend evenly spaced. R. Leaves point at center of I curls into frame under V and left arm of A which is double cut. Uncirculated. Bright red.

3.50 45 1773 Half penny. Type as last. No period after GEORGIVS the REX very widely spaced, the X close to curl. R. Leaf points to right side of I and right arm of A. Proof. Light olive. Rare dies.

CAROLINA.

Whit 13 00. 46 1694 Half penny. Elephant standing on the ground, facing left. R. GOD : PRESERVE : CAROLINA : AND THE : LORDS : PROPRIETERS. 1694 in six lines. Edge plain, borders milled. Proof. Beautiful light olive color; traces of original color in the letters on the reverse. Weight, 142½ grains. A superb piece and the finest of the three known. It is truly remarkable the condition this coin is in, and it has excited the admiration of collectors when exhibited. Of the three known, one has been forever withdrawn from competition, being in the Appleton Collection, donated to the Massachusetts Historical Society; the other in the Parmelee Collection was sold in 1890, but its present whereabouts is unknown to the writer. Crosby, page 338, speaks of knowing but the Appleton and Parmelee specimens; where or when Mr. Parsons obtained this no information accompanied it. This coin with PROPRIETERS (Sic) must not be confounded with that which follows with the word changed in the die and made PREPRIETORS. *Plate.* Crosby, plate IX, No. 1.

47 1694 Half penny. Obverse as last. R. GOD PRESERVE CAR(OLIN)A AND TH(E LOR)DS PROPRIETOR(S) 1694. Good, but slightly eaten by corrosion on obverse and on reverse. The letters in parenthesis do not show. Extremely rare.

THE ROSA AMERICANA SERIES.

Issued by William Wood under a charter of George I, June 16, 1722, and the patent was passed by the English Parliament July 22, 1722.

48 (1722) Twopence. GEORGIUS . D : G : MAG : BRI : FRA : ET . HIB : REX. Laureated bare bust of George I facing r. R. . ROSA - AMERICANA . Below within a scroll UTILE . DULCI In the center a full-blown rose. Uncirculated. Sharp, even impression. *Plate.* Crosby, plate III, 15.

49 1722 Twopence. Same type as last, but different dies and with addition of the *date on reverse.* ROSA AMERICANA 1722. Uncirculated. Sharp, even impression. A very slight granulation spot on edge of obverse. *Plate.* Crosby, plate IV, 1.

50 1722 Penny. GEORGIUS . DEI . GRATIA . REX. Laureated, bare bust

of Geo. I r. Curl terminates over E. R. ROSA . AMERICANA *
VTILE . DVLCI . 1722 v's instead of U's as all that follow. Full-
blown rose in center. Extremely fine. Cleaned, now golden
color. Rare. *Plate.* Crosby, plate IV, 3.

2.6 ¢ 51, 1722 Penny. As last, but curl terminates over G Fine. Rare.

5 . -- 52 1722 Penny. GEORGIUS . DEI . GRATIA . REX Laureated, bare bust
of Geo. I r., nose points to I. R. ROSA AMERICANA . UTILE . DULCI .
1722 * Fleur de lis points at . before UTILE Uncirculated. A
very superior example. *Plate.* Crosby, plate IV, 5.

1.10 53 1722 Penny. Same type. Nose points between IA. R. Fleur de
lis points between . U. Very good.

1.12 54 1722 Penny. Same type. Period after X before bust nearly
touches the bust. R. Fleur de lis points at 7; another at . before
UTILE Very good.

2.50 55 1722 Penny. Type as last, but a star before UTILE, as all that fol-
low. Period after REX far from bust. R. Fleur de lis points at
D. Uncirculated. Sharp, even imp. *Plate.* Crosby, plate
IV, 4.

2.25 56 1722 Penny. As last. Diff. dies. Period evenly spaced between
bust and X, nearly on line with top of X. R. Almost identical
with last. Fleur de lis points between DU. Very fine.

1. - 57 1722 Penny. As last. Diff. dies. Fleur de lis points at 7. Good.

1. -58 1722 Penny. As last. Diff. dies. Fleur de lis points at D and 7.
Good.

. 60 59 1722 Penny. As last. Diff. dies. Good. Oxidized surface.

9.50 60 1722 Half penny. GEORGIUS . D : G : REX. Laureated, undraped
bust r. R. ROSA AMERI : UTILE . DULCI. 1722. Full-blown rose
in center. Uncirculated. Sharp imp. Beautiful specimen and
very rare. *Plate.* Crosby, plate IV, 7.

4.50 61 1722 Half penny. GEORGIUS . DEI . GRATIA . REX. Laureated, undraped bust r. Period after X nearer that letter than the bust.
R. ROSA . AMERICANA . UTILE . DULCI . 1722. Full-blown rose in
center. Point of fleur de lis points between 72. Fine. *Plate.*
Crosby, plate IV, 8.

2.25 62 1722 Half penny. Same type as last. Period evenly spaced between X and bust. R. Point of fleur de lis points before 7. Very
good. Pin scratch from chin to E.

3.0 63 1722 Half penny. Type as last. Point of fleur de lis points at 7.
Fair.

Hult 130. 64 1723. Twopence. GEORGIUS . D : G : MAG : BRI : FRA : ET . IIIB : REX.
against auction Laureated, bare bust of Geo I right, the nose points between ET.
to after Pl.. R. ROSA . AMERICANA . 1723 on a scroll below UTILE . DULCI, in the
center a full-blown rose crowned, top of the crown almost
touches the R. No period after date. The scroll rises to level of
point on either side of rose. Thin planchet weighing 143½
grains, whereas the regular one following weighs 227½ grains.
Proof. *Copper.* Probably the pattern from which the following were made. *Unique.* Plate.

Ruv 6 65 1723 Twopence. Type as last. Top of head close to legend.
T x. far from bust; nose points between T.II. R. Top of crown
points between RI. Date close to AMERICANA—wide space between date and scroll, which is very long, coming up well above
points on either side of rose. Very fine. Brown color. Rare.

SH C 22·1 66 1723 Twopence. Type as last. Top of head far from legend.
e Nose points between T.II. R. Top of crown directly under I.
Very good.

C . 80 67 1723 Twopence. Type as last. Nose points at I. x. close to
bust. R. Top of crown under I, date nearly equally spaced between A and end of scroll. Poor.

C /.— 68 1723 Twopence. Type as last. Bust with double profile. Nose
points at E. R. Top of crown between RI, date close to A. Good.

Row 3 69 1723 Penny. Type as last. Top of cross directly under upright
of R. Very fine.

Hines /.— 70 1723 Penny. Type as last. Different dies. Margin outside of
beading. Good.

C . 5¹ 71 1723 Penny. Type as last. Top of crown under center of R.
Poor.

(Boston . 6º 72 1723 Half penny. Type as last. Good, but spots of corrosion on
both sides. Crosby, pl. IV, 14.

WOODS' COINAGE FOR IRELAND.

Failing to meet with approval there, brought to America in large
quantities and circulated here.

London /05. 73 (1722) Pattern for a farthing. GEORGIUS . DEI . GRA. Laureated,
C but bare bust of George I (1714-27) to r., same as on the Rosa
Against auction Americana, with ROSA SINE SPINA reverse. R. Female figure
in bidsy?rn seated to left, holding in right hand a large orb, her left sup-

ports a sceptre and rests upon a shield bearing a rose and thistle; behind the shield a harp. Yellow bronze. Extremely fine. Excessively rare, and I believe the first time offered in this country. Plate. Nelson, No. 18, and pl. V, No. 3A.

74 1722 Half penny. GEORGIUS . DEI .GRATIA . REX. Laureated, undraped bust of Geo. I r. Nose points to I. R. HIBERNIA . 1722. Seated female facing, head turned to left, at which side is a harp. Fine. Very rare.

75 1722 Half penny. As last, but different dies. Nose points to A. Extremely fine. Dark olive.

76 1722 Half penny. Similar obv., neck long, nose points between TI. R. HIBERNIA . 1722. Seated female figure facing left, a palm branch (short, and ends on right side of N) in right hand, her left resting on a harp. Milling not even. Very fine. Brown color.

77 1722 Half penny. Similar obv., nose points at I. R. Small palm branch, ending under middle of N. Fine. Oxidized.

78 1722 Half penny. Similar obv. x. close to bust. R. As last. Very fine. Dent on edge. Brown color.

79 1722 Half penny. Similar obv. R. Palm branch terminates to right of I. Date far from harp. Very fine. Brown color.

80 1723 Half penny. Same design as last. *Period before* HIBERNIA. Palm branch heavy and terminates between NI. Uncirculated. Deep, even milling. Bright red. Extremely rare with the period. Plate.

81 1723 Half penny. Same design, but without period, as are all following. Palm branch not so large, and terminates to right of N. Uncirculated. Considerable red color.

82 1723 Half penny. Same type. Palm branch terminates under N. Slightly granulous on cheek. Uncirculated. Traces of red.

83 1723 Half penny. Small type. Palm branch long, terminating under I. Die broken along upper edge. Uncirculated. Traces of red.

84 1723 Half penny. Same type. Palm branch terminates just right of N. Very fine.

85 1723 Farthing. Same type as last. x. far from bust. Last leaf in laurel wreath points to . R. Palm branch under N. Over head of Brittania A. Extremely fine.

86 1723 Farthing. Same type. Last leaf in laurel wreath touches

I. R. I above head; palm branch under R. 3 touches harp. Very fine. Scarce.

Kean 55 87 1723 Farthing. Same type. Leaf of wreath to right of I. R. Palm branch below N above head, right part of A and the . Good.

London 62.50 88 1723 Pattern farthing. GEORGIUS . D : G : REX. Laureated undraped bust r. Similar obverse, but not same dies as Crosby, plate IV, 7. R. Similar to last. A above head, palm branch under N. Uncirculated. Sharp, even impression. Beautiful light olive color. Excessively rare, and I believe first time offered in this country. Plate. Nelson No. 6 and plate IV, obverse 10, rev. 13.

Hines . 45 89 1724 Farthing. Same type as regular 1723. DEI close to head. R. Palm points to I. Fair.

Prikall 30 90 1724 Farthing. Same type. Good. Dent near edge on both sides. Scratch on neck. Rare.

THE VOCE POPULI COINAGE.

Struck in Dublin, but not finding acceptance there brought to America and circulated here.

White 6.25 91 1760 Half penny. VOCE POPULI. Laureated, bare bust right of Hely Hutchinson, provost of Dublin College, and the P in field before face stands for Provost no doubt. R. HIBERNIA 1760. Hibernia seated facing l., palm in right and staff in left hand, harp behind her. Uncirculated. Sharp. Light olive. Finest example I have seen. Plate.

Boston 90 92 1760 Half penny. Type as last, but bust short and without P. R. HIBER before Hibernia. Very fine.

" , 30 93 1760 Half penny. Similar to last. Head with very narrow neck. R. HIBE before Hibernia. Fair.

PITT TOKENS.

Hines 2.75 94 1766 Pitt half penny. THE RESTORER OF COMMERCE 1766 NO STAMPS. Bust of Pitt l. R. THANKS TO THE FRIENDS OF LIBERTY AND TRADE Ship sailing to r., at bow AMERICA indicating she was sailing to that country. Extremely fine.

Hessltn 1.50 95 1766 Pitt half penny. As last, but has the tin coating put on before striking. Extremely fine.

LOUISIANA.

Boston   .5 96   1767 Sou. SIT NOMEN DOMINI BENEDICTUM 1767. Three fleur de lis within a wreath, crown above. R. COLONIES FRANCOISES L XV Crossed sceptres, below A. Paris mm. Fine.

   4.0 97   1767 Sou. As last, but C. S. RE (Republique Francaise) under the Republic. Fine.

COINS OF THE STATES.

PROVINCE OF MASSACHUSETTS.

Smith   57   98   1776 Pattern half penny. PROVINCE OF (M)ASSA. (The letters VINCE OF worn off almost entirely—trace shows.) Nude Indian standing to left (head not struck up) in the act of using his bow. R. D . . RATIS probably for DEFENSOR LIBERATIS Seated figure of Liberty to left, a globe at her right, against which she leans, a right arm extended, while she supports a staff of Liberty in her left; before her in the field a dog; beneath 1776. Poor or rather rudely struck over a half penny of George II for Ireland. The II above the bow are the numerals after GEORGIUS II. *Unique!* The rest of the set of these patterns for the coinage of the Province of Massachusetts are pictured in Crosby, plate VII, Nos. 7 and 8, the former being in the Appleton Collection, and the latter sold at my Stickney Collection Sale; on this Janus head half penny the word MASSA. is spelled same as on this coin, and on the former there is a figure of Liberty just the same, even to the dog at her feet, and this dog is on all three. Crosby speaks of them on page 303. They are evidently of native manufacture, and their crudeness more than likely precluded their issuance as money, and also accounts for there being but one example known of each die. NOTE.—This coin was discovered by Mr. Howland Wood, and first brought to public notice in The Numismatist, June, 1911, page 228, where it is pictured, and is not part of the Parsons Collection. While the property of Mr. Wood, he has placed no limit upon it, and orders it sold to the highest bidder. *Plate.*

MASSACHUSETTS.

Hines   / 7.5 99   1787 Cent. COMMONWEALTH Indian with bow and arrow standing. R. MASSACHUSETTS 1787 Eagle with shield inscribed CENT on breast, olive branch in right and arrows in left talon. Very fine. Dark olive. Nick on rev. Crosby 2b-A. All the following are of this type.

Whitfield 4.25 100 1787 Cent. Very good. C. 2b-E, rarity 6! Seldom has this extremely rare variety been offered.

Hines 4.25 101 1787 Cent. Extremely fine. Sharp, even impression. Brown color. C. 3-G.

C .50 102 1787 Cent. Good. C. 6-G. Rare.

C .87 103 1787 Half cent. Poor. C. 1-D, rarity 4!

Smith 5.— 104 1787 Half cent. Uncirculated. Sharp, even impression. Splendid light olive, and one of the most beautiful specimens of these very rare dies. Plate. C. 4-B, rarity 5!

Hines 2.25 105 1787 Half cent. Uncirculated. Not quite sharp on body of the Indian, otherwise sharp. Beautiful light olive color. Plate. C. 4-C.

Boston Drive 1.10 106 1787 Half cent. Very good. C. 5-A. Scarce variety.

2.00 107 1787 Half cent. Very good. C. 6-D, rarity 5!

J. H.C 2.25 108 1788 Cent. Uncirculated. Sharp impression. Planchet slightly granulous on edge. Olive color. Plate. C. 1-D.

C .50 109 1788 Cent. Good. C. 2-B, rarity 3!.

C .80 110 1788 Cent. Very fine. Light olive color. C. 3-A-//-K

C .25 111 1788 Cent. Good. Slightly corroded. C. 3-G. //FRS

Early Italy 2.10 112 1788 Cent. Very good. C. 4-G, rarity 2.

C 2.10 113 1788 Cent. No period after MASSACHUSETTS Fine. C. 6-N, rare.

C .30 114 1788 Cent. Fine. Surface eroded. C. 8-C, rarity 2.

Shaw 2.75 115 1788 Cent. Very fine. Light pin scratches on obv. C. 9-M.

HC 1.10 116 1788 Cent. Extremely fine. C. 10-L.

C .35 117 1788 Cent. Good. C. 11-E.

C .35 118 1788 Cent. Good. C. 12-I.

C .25 119 1788 Cent. Very good. Two slight defects. C. 12-K.

Shaw 7.— 120 1788 Cent. Uncirculated. Superb impression. Light brown color. Plate. C. 12-M.

Hines 2.75 121 1788 Half cent. Uncirculated. Sharp impression. Light olive. Plate. C. 1-B.

RHODE ISLAND.

Boston 2.— 122 1778-1779 Medalet. View of Island with four columns of troops crossing; at left three men of war, at right thirteen boats filled with troops. *D'Vlugtende* AMERICAAN^{EN} *van* ROHDE YLAND *aug*[t]

1778. R. Man of war to r., ornament below. DE ADMIRAALS FLAG *von* ADMIRAAL HOWE 1779. Brass. Fine. Scarce when complete as is this. Betts 563.

Boston R2   *2.50* 123 1778-1779 Medalet. As last, but in pewter. Complete. Very fine. Very rare.

4.70 124 1778-1778 Medalet. As above, but a word (traces of letters remain) removed from below ship at the time of issue. Brass. Fine. Betts 562.

PENNSYLVANIA OR "BUNGTOWN COPPERS."

A proclamation by order of Council, dated Philadelphia, July 14, 1781, prohibited the use of the coins which follow, and the use of which in the community had become a nuisance, as they were without authority. See Crosby, pages 172-174.

Phila   *1.40* 125 "1696" Half penny. Bust of man l. H-L. R. Shield, NON - PROGUL - DIES 1696. Not struck in 1696, but later. Good.

7.30 126 1777 Half penny. BRUTUS SEXTUS Bust l. R. BET ON 1777 Poor.

70 127 1796 Half penny. COLONEL KIRK Bust l. R. NORTH WALES 1796 Harp. Very fine.

2.75 128 1797 Half penny. ADMIRAL JERVIS Bust r. R. RULE BRITANNIA 1797 Britannia seated, ships' masts before her. Extremely fine. Rare.

.35 129 Half penny. ALFRED Bust of Alfred the Great r. R. BRITONS GLORY Female with harp. Very good.

.30 130 Half penny. GULIELMUS SHAKESPEAR Bust l. R. As last. Fine.

.45 131 Half penny. ROMULUS Bust l. R. VIRTUS IVV NO DEFICIT I O XXX. Harp. Fine.

.35 132 1756-97 Half pennies. Various curious legends. Different. Very poor, as usual.   20 pcs.

.05 133 177? Farthing. GRAGORY - II - PON. Bust l. R. BRITAIN RULES 177? Poor. Very rare.

.55 134 1771 Farthing. GLOROIVS . DUNCAN R. As last. Poor. Very rare.

.70 135 Farthing. GEORGE RULES Bust r. R. BRITANNIAS ISLES. Poor. Very rare.

.35 136 George II, III half pennies, 26. Farthings, 5. Counterfeits of the time. Very poor, as usual.   31 pcs.

MARYLAND.

COINAGE OF I. CHALMERS, GOLDSMITH, ANNAPOLIS.

137   1783   Shilling. I. CHALMERS ANNAPOLIS in center within a wreath two hands clasped. R. ONE SHILLING 1783 In center within a beaded circle are two birds pulling a worm (short), above a lattice fence, and above that a snake to right. Very light pin scratch across two-thirds of reverse. Very fine. Rare. Plate.

138   1783   Sixpence. I. CHALMERS. A all that shows on obv. R. I. C. SIX 83 and part of cross all that shows on rev. Very poor. Very rare.

139   1783   Threepence. I CHALMERS ANNAPS * Clasped hands. R. THREE PENCE 1783. In center an olive branch within wreath. Sharp imp. Plate. Very rare.

140   1783   Threepence. Same as last. Slightly weak in center of left side, but extremely fine. Plate. Very rare.

COINAGE OF STANDISH BARRY, SILVERSMITH, AT BALTIMORE.

141   (17)90   Threepence. BALTIMORE.TOWN.JULY.4.90. Bust of a man in coat and queue facing left; by some thought to be meant for Washington, but while intended as a portrait it is unfortunately not yet identified. R. STANDISH BARRY each letter entwined in a beaded net work. Across center in two lines with bar above and below are the words THREE PENCE. Extremely fine. Pin point nick on rev. Sharp, even impression. Extremely rare. Plate. Crosby, page 330, fig. 72, plate X, 23.

VERMONT.

142   1785   Cent. VERMONTS . RES . PUBLICA . 1785. Range of hills, 7 trees along the top, sun rising from behind the hills; below a plow to left. R. QUARTA . DECIMA . STELLA. The 14th star (referring to Vermont) in the American Constellation. Eye of Providence in center of a double circle of double rays, the points interspersed with 13 stars. Beaded border. Very fine. Two slight dents on reverse edge. Light olive color. Struck on a remarkably heavy planchet, and weighs 185 grains! (usually

110 grains). Believed to be unique as to weight, and for this coin, irrespective of this extraordinary weight, a superior example, as it is well struck and free of the usual defects. Plate.

143 1785 Cent. As last, but thin, regular planchet weighing 116 grs. Fine.

144 1785 Cent. VERMONTIS RES . PUBLICA . 1785 otherwise as last. Thin planchet, weight 91 grs. Good. Rare.

145 1786 Cent. VERMONTENSIUM . RES . PUBLICA . 1786. 7 trees on the hills, otherwise as last. Three slight planchet defects. Very good.

146 1786 Cent. As last, but 9 trees on hills. Extremely fine. Evenly and sharply struck. Brown color and far superior to those usually offered. Plate.

147 1786 Cent. As last. Good. Planchet defective on reverse, resembling bad streaks.

148 1786 Cent. AUCTORI VERMON Bust r. "Baby Head" R. INDE* ET : LIB : 1786 Liberty seated to l. Fair. Rare. C. 1-A.

149 1786 Cent. VERMON AUCTORI Bust l. R. INDE ET LIB 1786 Liberty seated l. Poor. Planchet slightly defective. C. 2-B, rarity 6!

150 1787 Cent. Bust r., otherwise as last. Two scratches on head. Fair. C. 2-A.

151 1787 Cent. Bust r. R. BRITANNIA R. Very poor, as always. C. 3-C.

152 1788 Cent. As last. Good. C. 1-A.

153 1788 Cent. Type as last. C. 3-A. Good.

154 1788 Cent. Type as last. Broad planchet. Grilling on neck. R. Slightly corroded. Good. C. 3-B, rarity 3.

155 1788 Cent. Type as last. Extremely fine. Steel color. Plate. C. 4-C.

156 1788 Cent. Type as last. Die broken across obverse. Poor, but all shows. C. 6-B, rarity 5!

157 1788 Cent. GEORGIVS . III . REX. Bust of Geo. III r. R. INDE + ET . LIB . 1788 Good. Two small dents on each side. One of the coins no doubt struck by Atlee at Newburg, N. Y. Spoken of by Crosby, pages 191, 192.

CONNECTICUT.

Remarkable for the high state of preservation in which they are in. The coinage of this State was generally weakly struck, hence easily worn.

158 1785 Cent. AUCTORI : CONNEC : Mailed and laureated bust r. The face has a smiling expression. R. INDE ET LIB : 1785. Liberty seated facing left. Shows the three grape vines on the shield. Very fine. Light olive. Plate. C. 2-A.

159 1785 Cent. Same type, but a very different expression on the face—the eye large and features small. Very fine. Light olive. Slight granulation spot on edge. Plate. C. 3-F.

160 1786 Cent. Similar. Large head with break in die on chin. R. ET LIB INDE 1786. Deep serratures. Good. Rare. C. 1-A.

161 1786 Cent. Similar. The variety with a large head. R. INDE ET LIB 1786. Good. Slight depression on edge in the planchet. Very rare. Plate. C. 3-D, plate V, No. 7.

162 1786 Cent. Similar, but bust faces left. A semicircular part with central dot on front of armor. The reverse not given by Crosby, as after INDE it has a fleuron and no other punctuation. This probably unique coin was weakly struck on upper half of head and corresponding part of reverse—the lower part of Liberty, otherwise extremely fine. Light olive. Plate. C. 5. New reverse not given by him.

163 1786 Cent. Similar to last, but without the semicircular front to armor around the dot. R. Semicolon and four dots after INDE, and period between ET . LIB. Very fine. Slight granulation around eye. Light brown color. Plate. Very rare. C. 5-I, plate V, 8.

164 1786 Cent. Similar, but without punctuation, except period after LIB. Fine. Rare. C. 4-G, rarity 3.

165 1787 Cent. AUCTORI CONNEC Bust in armor r., head small. R. ET LIB INDE 1787. Liberty seated to left. Serratures only half on, but an unusually fine example of this rare variety. Plate. C. 1-A.

166 1787 Cent. AUCTORI CONN(E)C Mailed bust, laureated right. The large head known as the Mutton head. R. INDE . ET LIB 1787 Large figure of Liberty l. Slightly off center, and slight chip off planchet on edge. Weakly struck in center, but I think one of the finest examples I have ever seen. Extremely fine. Light olive. Very rare. Plate. C. 1-C.

2

C   *2 —167*   1787 Cent. Bust facing left, and the die which is generally broken
                            from the armor upwards like a horn, while this example was
                            struck before the die broke. Fine. Very rare. C. 4-L.

C   */ – 168*   1787 Cent. As last, but die broken—the "horn" prominent.
                            Very fine. Slight oxidation adhering. Steel color. C. 4-L.

Wilson   *10.50 169* 1787 Cent. Similar type—the profile outlined. Extremely fine.
                    4   Heavy, deep, even serratures on both sides. Light olive. A
                            splendid example. Plate. C. 6-M.

White   *<3 – 170* 1787 Cent. Very fine, and probably one of the finest examples
                            known of this extremely rare variety. Slight chip off reverse
                            edge of planchet. Light olive. Plate. C. 8-O, rarity 5!

C   *2—171*   1787 Cent. Very fine. Not quite evenly centered. Light olive.
                            C. 11-K.

Smith   *2, 172*   1787 Cent. Extremely fine, practically uncirculated. Even im-
                    6   pression, with milling around obverse and reverse. Reverse die
                            cracked across which accounts for its extreme rarity. Light
                            olive. Plate. C. 12-Q, rarity 5!

White   *3.50173* 1787 Cent. Fine. Reverse not evenly struck, nearly all of INDE
                            off. Rare variety. C. 13-D.

**   *3.50 174* 1787 Cent. The variety with pheons before, through and after
                            inscriptions and at each side of date. No other like this. Fine.
                            Well struck. C. 14-H.

**   *3.50 175* 1787 Cent. AUCTORI CONNECT. Only one with this obverse. Good,
                            and singularly free from the usual planchet defects. C. 15-F*.

4   *3.50 176* 1787 Cent. Large letters in the ins. Obverse not quite even
                            nor struck up sharp in center. Very fine. Brown color. Rare.
                            C. 16-M.

r.   *2. 50 177* 1787 Cent. Unusual punctuation marks. Fine. Light color.
                            Very rare. C. 19-G, rarity 3.

4   *3.50 178* 1787 Cent. New variety, unknown to Crosby, similar to his No.
                            23, but with + before AUCTORI. R. Similar to Crosby C. Ex-
                            tremely fine. Light olive. Plate.

C   */ — 179*   1787 Cent. Fine. Well struck. Dent in field and forehead.
                            Brown color. C. 32-X.

White   *26. – 180* 1787 Cent. Crosby 33-Z. Termination of : * after AUCTORI far
                            from head. Uncirculated. Sharp, even impression. Splendid
                            example in every way, as the surface is lustrous and the color a
                            rich brown. One of the finest specimens known. Plate.

                 181   1787 Cent. Crosby 33-Z. The rose or star touches hair on fore-

head. Extremely fine, but not sharp in center and some of the
roughness in the copper showing on the neck. Light olive.

182 1787 Cent. Crosby 33-z. Differs from last. Very fine. Bold,
even imp. Slight nicks on edge. Light olive.

183 1787 Cent. Crosby 33-z. Die cracked across obverse! Very
good. Very rare.

184 1787 Cent. Crosby 33-z. Differs from last. Perfect dies. Fine.
Bold imp. Light olive.

185 1787 Cent. Unusual punctuations. Not struck up in center.
Very slightly off center. Very fine. Brown color. Rare. C. 37-I.

186 1788 Cent. Bust facing right. Slight granulation on edge at
top. Extremely fine. Steel color. Rare in this condition. Plate.
C. 2-D*, rarity 3.

187 1788 Cent. Similar to last. Poor, but extremely rare. C. 4-K.

188 1788 Cent. Bust faces left. Fine. Sharp, even imp. Cleaned.
C. 11-G, rarity 3.

189 1788 Cent. Uncirculated. Obverse very weak, curious tree-like
streaks up each field. R. Trace of original color. Not quite
even. Light olive. C. 12-E.

190 1788 Cent. Very fine. Evenly centered. Brown color. C. 12-F.

191 1788 Cent. CONNLC a curious error. Extremely fine, but the
planchet defective, as usual. One of the finest examples I have
seen of this rare die. Plate. C. 13-A.

192 1788 Cent. Very fine. Steel color. C. 15-D*.

193 1788 Cent. IN DE widely separated. Fine. Steel color. Extremely rare. C. 16-N, rarity 5!

194 1787 Cent. AUCTORI PLEBIS (By authority of the people). Bust
as on the Conn. cents to l. R. .INDEP : ET . LIBER. Female
seated l., globe, crowned lion and anchor, 1787 below. Good, as
usual. Crosby, pl. IX, 15.

195 No date. Cent. AUCTORI PLEBIS Bust to right. R. Blank. Good.

IMMUNE COLUMBIAS 1785.

196 1785 Cent. IMMUNE COLUMBIA (Free America). Liberty
seated on a box facing right; her right hand supports a staff of
Liberty with flag, while her left is extended and holds a pair
of balances. In exergue—1785—. R. NOVA CONSTELLATIO in
center the Eye of Providence, surrounded by a glory of thir-

teen points, which intersect a circle of 13 stars. Extremely fine. Sharp impression. Beautiful light olive color, and believed to be the finest known. Plate. Crosby speaks on page 314 of knowing only one example from these dies in copper as is this! Excessively rare. It is without any period after Nova and star after Constellatio. Crosby, figure 53, page 312, and plate VII, No. 31.

White
cypress Ryder

250. 197   1785 Cent. IMMUNE COLUMBIA Same obverse as last. R. Same design, but with a period after NOVA and a star after CONSTEL-LATIO. Extremely fine. Beautiful light olive color. Extremely rare. Plate. Crosby, figure 54, page 312, and plate VII, No. 30.

IMMUNIS COLUMBIA 1787.

',   32.50 198   1787 Cent. IMMUNIS COLUMBIA 1787. Liberty seated on a globe facing right; her right hand supports a staff of Liberty with flag; her extended left hand holds balances. R. * E * PLURIBUS * UNUM * Eagle facing, head to right, olive branch in right talon, arrows in left. Uncirculated. Light brown color. Sharp, even impression, with the date all on; a very unusual condition for this rare coin. Plate. Crosby, page 320, fig. 61, plate VIII, No. 8.

Kraft

7.50 199c   1787 Cent. IMMUNIS COLUMBIA As last. Fine. Well struck, date all on. Rare.

NEW YORK.

LIBER NATUS LIBERTATEM DEFENDO CENT.

Smith
Stickney 500
no bid ii nom.
an why auction

850.— 200   1787 Cent. LIBER NATUS LIBERTATEM DEFENDO * (Born free I defend liberty). Indian wearing war feathers standing, facing left, tomahawk raised in his right hand, while his left supports a bow, quiver on his back. R. NEO-EBORACUS 1787 (New York) EXCELSIOR Eagle with outstretched wings standing upon a section of a globe. Border serrated. Extremely fine. Smooth proof-like surface. Plum color. A finer specimen than lot No. 239 in my sale of the great Stickney Collection, sold June, 1907, where it fetched $850, and was bought by the late De Witt S. Smith. Excessively rare, about five known. Plate. Crosby, page 321, figure 64, and plate VIII, 7.

ARMS OF NEW YORK CENT.

17- 201 1787 Cent. Arms of New York. Eagle on top of globe faces *right;* shield with sun rising, at either side stand Liberty and Justice, below EXCELSIOR R. E * PLURIBUS UNUM * * 1787 * Large eagle displayed, faces right, U. S. shield on his breast, branch of olive in his right talon, a bundle of arrows in the left; about his head in a circle are 12 stars enclosing another, the thirteenth star. Good. Very rare, not in the great Stickney Collection. Plate. Crosby, pl. VII, 23.

NOVA EBORAC CENTS.

202 1787 Cent. * * NOVA EBORAC * (New York). Large male laureated and mailed bust facing r. R. * VIRT . ET LIB * (Virtue and Liberty). Liberty seated on a globe facing left; her right hand extended and holding an olive branch; her left supports a staff of Liberty, while resting against her at the back is a shield charged with the State arms—the sun rising from the hills, below 1787. Dies slightly sunken in center, which was the cause of so few being known from these dies. Uncirculated. Beautiful light olive. Proof-like surface. I fully believe this to be the finest example known of this very rare variety, which must not be confounded with the common varieties next following. Plate. Crosby, plate VIII, 9.

203 1787 Cent. Same type as last. Very fine. Light olive. Plate. Crosby, plate VIII, 11.

204 1787 Cent. Same obverse as last. R. Liberty seated facing right, otherwise as last. Curious planchet, having considerable brass mixed with the copper. Three defects in planchet on obv., but reverse struck from a perfect die without the usual break. Fair.

205 1787 Cent. As last, but from the die after it had broken from right side near date to top of B. Very good.

206 1789 Mott's Card, 1st American Store Card. Clock. R. Eagle. Long inscription. Pin scratches on reverse. Perfect die. Thick planchet. Good. Crosby, pl. IX, 17.

207 1789 Mott's Card. As last. Perfect die. Thin planchet. Very fine, as the inscription is all on.

208 1789 Mott's Card. Die broken at corner of the clock. Thin planchet. Fine, with the inscription clear.

L. F. *. 66* 209 1789 Mott's Card. Break in die larger. Two dents on edge. Very
      fine. Ins. clear.

Wilson *3 75* 210 1794 Cent. LIBERTY & COMMERCE. 1794 Liberty standing. R.
      TALBOT ALLUM & LEE ONE CENT A ship to r., above it NEW YORK.
      Edge, PAYABLE AT THE STORE OF. Small &'s on both sides. Proof
      Considerable original red color. Very rare. Crosby, plate IX,
      18.

Boston *. 30* 211 1794 Cent. Same as last. Good. Slight nicks.

   . 87 212 1794 Cent. Same dies as last, but reverse set upside down. Ex.
      fine.

Hines *. 20* 213 1794 Cent. Same type, but with a large & on reverse. Uncircu-
      lated. Traces of original color. Crosby, plate IX, 19.

Q? [illegible] *2.50* 214 1795 Cent. Obverse same type. R. AT THE STORE OF TALBOT
      ALLUM & LEE NEW YORK. Ship r. Edge, WE PROMISE TO PAY THE
      BEARER ONE CENT. Uncirculated. Crosby, pl. IX, 20.

CASTORLAND, NOW CARTHAGE, NEW YORK.

Wilson *1.10* 215 1796 Half dollar. FRANCO-AMERICANA COLONIA CASTORLAND 1796
      Head of female left, with veil and Mural crown. DUV below for
      Du Vivier the great die sinker. R. SALVA MAGNA PARENS FRUGUM
      (Hail, Mighty Mother of production). Beautiful figure of Ceres
      standing by a tree, cornucopia in right hand and auger in left
      hand. Sap running from a tap in the tree into a basin, in
      exergue a beaver and D. V. Milled edge. Bronzed proof. Struck
      slightly to one side. Possibly an original, as the edge is free
      from the word QUIVRE or BRONZE.

  2 ~ 216 1796 Half dollar. Same dies, but probably a restrike in silver
      from the original dies, which in this exhibit a sinking from edge
      to field on right side. Milled edge with ARGENT. Proof. Plate.

Bruce? *1 50* 217 1796 Half dollar. Same obverse die. New reverse die same de-
      sign. Edge milled and with ARGENT. Silver. Restrike. Proof.

  1 50/3 218 1796 Half dollar. Same design as last, but a new obverse die,
      the crown almost touches the C. R. Same die. Plain edge with
      ARGENT. Restrike. Brilliant proof.

  . 87 219 1796 Half dollar. Different obverse die, but reverse same die.
      1 of date touches beading. Bronzed proof. Restrike.

[illegible] *7.* 220 1796 Half dollar. Diff. die to last. Sand blasted bronze proof.

WASHINGTON—NEW JERSEY CENT.

221 (1785-1787) Cent. GEN . WASHINGTON. Bust of George Washington in uniform r. R. * E * PLURIBUS * UNUM * U. S. shield. Very fine. Light olive color. Small hole between w and A, not removing any of the letters on either side. This coin is evidently a pattern, as no issue was regularly coined bearing this remarkable obverse, but it was used in conjunction with two other reverses, as shown by Crosby on plate VII. This reverse was regularly used by the State of New Jersey in 1787, as Maris No. 6-C. This combination is Maris 4-C, where he speaks of it as only known in *one* example. So it was until this piece was discovered. Of great rarity, interest and value. The other known is fine, of a dark olive color and is forever out of the market, as it is in the Robert Garrett Collection at Princeton University, N. J. Plate.

NEW JERSEY.

Arranged and numbered according to the work by Dr. E. Maris' folio, published Philadelphia, 1881. The degrees of rarity of Dr. Maris were based on his knowledge of their scarcity, gained by collecting this series for a period from 1867-1881, and should prove of great value in determining the value of the coin. As Dr. Maris' Collection was sold as an entirety to Mr. T. H. Garrett, and is deposited at Princeton University, thus removed forever from sale, it should advance the degrees of rarity on the following as a financial possibility.

An unusually fine collection, one that it has required much time and expense to form and which it would be difficult to duplicate, so it seems a pity to dismember it without an opportunity being afforded of their being kept together, so it has occurred to me that if a bid of $250 is made (I consider this a low estimate of their value) the entire set from No. 222 to No. 302 will be started as an entirety.

222 1787 6-C, rarity 3. Very good. Broad, even serratures on both sides. Seldom obtainable.
223 1787 6-D. Fine. Even imp. Even serratures on obv.
224 1786 12-G, rarity 1. No coulter. Fair. Scarce.
225 1786 14-J. Fine.
226 1786 15-J. Good.

Jim   1.10 227   1786   15-L.   Fine.

Shaw   1.30 228   1786   15-T, rare.   Fine.

   1.30 229   1786   16-L.   Very fine.   Brown color.

Score   1.10 230   1786   17-B.   Very fine.   Two pin head spots of corrosion on obverse.

Kraft   1.80 231   1786   17-J, rare.   Slight crack in planchet behind head.   Very fine.

Stev   .70 232   1786   17-K, rare.   Good.

   .550 233   1786   18-M.   Extremely fine.   Deep, heavy serratures around both sides, but they are not quite even.   Light olive.

   7 — 234   1786   18-N, rarity 5!   Dr. Maris only knew of two of this variety, and this may be one of those two.   Good.   Slight dent on reverse edge.

Straw   2.25 235   1786   19-M, rarity 3!   Very good.   Slight nicks.   Light olive. Very rare.   Dr. Maris had seen "but four or five."

   .85 236   1786   20-N, rare.   Fair.   Slight nick on edge.

   5.1 237   1786   21-N.   Fine.   Scratch down bust.   R. Top of shield sunken in.   Slight chip off (in planchet) on edge.

   2.75 238   1786   21-O, rarity 4!   Dr. Maris had seen but five!   Fine.   Deep serratures.   Dark olive.

   4.5 239   1786   21-P.   Extremely fine.   Sharp impression, with serratures around obverse and reverse.   Light olive.   Plate.

   5.. 240   1786   23-P.   Die broken in two places on edge of the obverse. Fine.   Light olive.

   .25 241   1786   23-R.   Good.

Hins   .70 242   1786   24-P.   Very good.   Light olive.   Even impression.

Straw   7.25 243   1786   24-R, rarity 6!   Dr. Maris only knew of one example of this die!   Very good.   Deep, even serratures around both sides. Light olive.   Plate.

   .9. 244   1786   26-S, rarity 1.   Good.   Slight flake out of the planchet at A of NOVA.

   .5 245   1786   28-L.   Fine.   Slight nick on edge.   Brown color.

straw   1.10 246   1787   29-L, rarity 2.   Good.   Slight dent on edge.

Hines   .80 247   1787   30-L, rare.   Good.

Acre   .50 248   1787   31-L.   Very good.

   .95 249   1787   31-L.   Die broken across obverse, a circumstance which probably accounts for its scarcity.   Good.

   1.— 250   1787   32-T.   Very fine.   Brown color.

   .80 251   1787   33-U, rarity 1.   Very good.

Strew 2.75 252 1787 34-J. Perfect die. Fine. Blister in the planchet under front of plow beam. While Dr. Maris places this as common, I have never found it so, and as fine a specimen as this decidedly scarce.

C 1.50 253 1787 34-J. Die broken, covering the 8 of the date. Fine.

C .50 254 1787 37-J, rare. Fair. R. Poor. Nicks on edge.

C 5. 255 1787 37-X, rarity 5! Dr. Maris had only seen the one in his own collection. Poor obverse, reverse good.

C 1. 256 1787 38-C. Very fine, but slight planchet defects on the edge, as are usually found with this variety. Light olive.

C 1.20 257 1787 38-Y. Very fine. Defective planchet, as usual, shows in four places on reverse edge. Light olive.

lewy .70 258 1787 38-Z, rare. Good. Slightly off center. Light olive.
Perege 1.50 259 1787 39-a. Very fine. Small dent on edge. Light olive.
260 1.50 260 1787 40-b, rarity 4! Good. Broad planchet.

C .00 261 1787 43-d. Very fine. Two minute nicks on edge.

1.10 262 1787 43-e. Extremely fine, practically uncirculated. Off center, only half the serratures showing on either side. Light olive.

C 1.51 263 1787 44-d, rare. Fine. Brown color.

5. 264 1787 45-d, rarity 3! Fair. Slight edge dents.

.3 265 1787 45-e, rare. Poor.

1. 266 1787 46-e. Very fine. Die sunken above date. Brown color.

.5 267 1787 48-f, rarity 1. Fair. Defective striking for half an inch along edge on reverse.

.5 268 1787 48-g. Perfect die. Good. Light olive.

lucas .5 269 1787 48-g. Die cracked across shield. Extremely fine. Light olive.

2.01 270 1788 49-f, rarity 1. Bust of horse faces left. Fair. Far more rare than Maris's rarity 1 would indicate.

4. 271 1788 50-f, rare. Bust of horse faces left. Very fine. Sharp, even impression, with deep, even serratures around obverse and reverse. Very slight defect on edge. Steel color. One of the finest specimens I have ever seen of this rare variety. Plate.

Hew 2.10 272 1787 52-i. Extremely fine. Sharp impression. Light brown color.

C 1.80 273 1787 53-j. Very fine. Light olive.

C 1.— 274 1787 54-k. Long, curved neck to horse and sometimes called the "Serpent head." Fine. Brown color.

C .60 275 1787 55l, rarity 4! Fair.

Sears /.— 276 1787 55-*m*, rarity 2! Fine. Surface lightly eroded. Black.

Wilson . 60 277 1787 56-*n*. Fine. Struck over a Conn. cent. Brown color.

2.20 278 1787 56-*n*. Very good. Struck over a Conn. cent, showing a curious mingling of inscriptions—reading NOVA CÆREA ET LIR 1787 from the N. J., as also 1787 from the Conn. die. R. * E * PLURIBUS UNU *CONNEC. A curiosity.

Henry . 80 279 1787 56-*n*. Good. Similar to last, but reading NOVA CÆSAREA ET LIR 1787. R. AUCTO * E * PLURONNFC.*INUM

Hines , 60 280 1787 56-*n*. Good. Over a Vermont cent, showing on reverse UNERMON

Henry
Hoff? . 80 281 1787 56-*n*. Very fine. Traces of letters of a Regal ½ penny.

/.8 282 1787 58-*n*, rarity 2! Die cracked across obverse, which accounts for its being very rare. Fine. Holed between 8 and 7.

HC /.70 283 1787 59-*o*, rarity 2! Very good. With wonderful deep serratures all around obverse and reverse, and a margin outside of them. A rarity!

Straw 4.75 284 1787 60-*p*, rare. The error * E * PLURIBS * UNUM *. Very fine. Steel color. Seldom offered as fine as this.

C /.— 285 1787 61-*p*, rarity 2. The error * E * PLURIBS * UNUM *. Die broken behind head. Good. Slight granulation on neck of horse. Very rare.

C 2.50 286 1787 62-*q*. Extremely fine. Has probably been cleaned long since—now presents a dull red color. Sharp, even impression with deep serratures. Plate.

Straw /.50 287 1787 63-*q*. Perfect die. Very fine. Light olive.

. C 2.50 288 1787 63-*q*. Die broken at right corner of shield. Not struck up on horse's head around the eye. Very fine, with a lustrous surface. Even serratures around both sides. Light olive.

C . 80 289 1787 63-*r*, rarity 3! Fair. Very rare.

Rubull 35 290 1787 63-*s*. Very good. Steel color.

S 3- -291 1787 64-*t*. Very fine, the surface lightly eroded. The full die struck on a huge planchet, size 20! Showing broad margins outside the serratures on both sides. Steel color, and the largest N. J. cent I have ever seen. Plate.

C . 50 292 1787 64-*t*. Another broad planchet, size 19! Evenly struck, with deep serratures and slight margin outside of them. Fine. Brown color.

Hines /.20 293 1787 64-*t*. Planchet, size 18, the usual size. Very fine. Deep, even serratures around both sides. Light olive.

Shaw   2.10   294   1787   65-*u*. Very fine. Planchet slightly defective—a fine crack from nose to edge—two slight granulation spots on reverse. Dark steel color. Rare.

8.50   295   1788   66-*v*, rarity 5! Dr. Maris had seen but 3 of this combination. Fine. Slight chip off of obverse surface above RE. I quite concur in the estimation of rarity placed on this piece by Dr. Maris, and have always considered it an exceedingly rare coin.

1   296   1788   67-*v*. Very fine. Light olive.

1.50   297   1787   68-*w*, rarity 4! Very good. Slight defect in planchet cuts off the 7 in the date. Reverse has two slight nicks on edge; perfect die. Very rare.

4   298   1787   73-*aa*, rarity 5! Dr. Maris had seen but three. Good. Die sunken at NOVA, which word it obliterates. Very slight crack in from edge. One of the rarest N. J. cents, a far superior specimen than that owned by Dr. Maris, as this shows the date, and with the exception of the one word noted above, all the inscription which is not confused as was his.

2.7   299   1787   75-*bb*, rarity 2! The rare variety, with a small horse preceding the legend on the reverse. Die broken along edge from cinquefoil at end of plow handles to near the date, and on reverse along the edge over UNV. Very fine. Light bronze color. Very rare. Plate.

1.10   300   1788   77-*dd*, rare. Small horse between cinquefoil and E. Very good.

3—   301   1788   78-*dd*, rarity 2! Obverse dies broken. Small horse on reverse, as last. Very fine for these dies. Plate.

1.10   302   Unique curiosity. Maris reverse *i* only; fully struck, and on its reverse with same design as obverse, but *incused*. Very good. Dent on edge.

KENTUCKY.

16—   303   (1791) Half penny. UNANIMITY IS THE STRENGTH OF SOCIETY Hand holding out a scroll inscribed OUR CAUSE IS JUST R. Pyramid of 15 stars, each charged with name of a State. *Edge engrailed.* Thin planchet. Extremely fine. Light color. Almost invisible pin scratch in field. Extremely rare. Mentioned by Crosby on page 343.

1.—   304   (1791) Half penny. As last. Edge plain. Extremely fine.

305   (1791) Half penny. As last. Thick planchet. Edge lettered

PAYABLE IN LANCASTER, LONDON OR BRISTOL. Uncirculated.
Light olive.

1.50 306 (1791) Half penny. As last, but inscription overruns, and N DON
is all there is of LONDON. Uncirculated. Light olive.

25. 307 1796 Cent. BRITISH SETTLEMENT KENTUCKY 1796 Hope presenting a male and female infant to Liberty, who stands ready to receive them, her right hand extended in welcome, the left supports a staff surmounted by a Liberty cap; between her and the
children lies a wreath from which springs an olive branch—
Peace. R. PAYABLE BY P. P. P. MYDDELTON. Britannia seated in
a dejected attitude, her spear inverted, while on the ground a
Liberty cap, fasces and scales. *Silver.* Brilliant proof. Very
rare. Plate for obverse. Crosby, plate IX, 22, figure 88, page
344.

27.— 308 1796 Cent. As last. Copper. Proof. Steel color, with traces of
original red around outlines. Very rare. Plate for reverse.

LOUISIANA.

.30 309 1798 U. S. cent, worn smooth. Counterstamped from an oval
die with RF. Only one I have ever met with.

22— 310 (1830?) New Orleans. Cut $¼ from a Spanish dollar. Coun-
terstamped with a round die inscribed NOUVELLE . ORLEANS in
center an eagle displayed with U. S. shield on his breast. R.
P. B. (Puech Bein & Co.) within a chain of 16 links, each enclosing a star. Sharp and perfect, which is remarkable for this
issue. Uncirculated. Very rare. Plate.

10.— 311 (1830?) New Orleans. Cut $¼ from a cast necessity dollar of
Zacatecas. The counterstamp with same wording as last, but
from different dies; the eagle not so well ordered, and the *P. B.*
high in circle. The inscriptions readable, but not up so sharp
as last. Good. Very rare. Plate.

1.10 312 1858 New Orleans. Medalet. Silver. Size of a $¼. SOCIEDAD
YBERA DE . BENEF^A MUTUA ANO 1858, N. O. Flags of U. S. and
France crossed. R. Same as obverse. Fine. Extremely rare.

MISCELLANEOUS.

.30 313 Ship sailing r., below W & B N.Y. (Wright & Bale, N. Y.). U. S.
flag. R. SHIPS COLONIES & COMMERCE. Fine. Corroded surface.
Wood, No. 1.

314 Ship r. Type as above, without engraver's initials. U. S. flag. Ex. fine. Wood, No. 2.

315 Ship r. Type as above. British flag. Blacksmith's. R. Slightly incused. Same as obv. Hole near edge. Unique. Wood, No. 3.

316 Ship r. Type as above. British flag (16), U. S. flag (2). Several var. Good to fine. 3 damaged.   18 pcs.

317 1781 NORTH AMERICAN TOKEN 1781 Hibernia seated. R. COMMERCE Ship l. Fine.

318 Columbia farthings. Bust r. and l., COLUMBIA R. Justice seated. Several rare. Unusually fine set, and seldom so many different are seen together.   9 pcs.

319 1794 Franklin Press cent. View of press. R. PAYABLE AT THE FRANKLIN PRESS LONDON. Perfect die. Very good. Crosby, pl. IX, 16.

320 1794 Franklin Press. As last. Die broken. R. Scratch across. Fine.

321 1776 Continental Currency dollar. Copper. Prof. Dickeson's struck copy.

322 1776 Continental Currency dollar. Bronzed. Prof. Dickeson's struck copy.

323 1776 Continental Currency dollar. Tin. Prof. Dickeson's struck copy.

324 1776-8 Seals as used on the Continental paper money of Feby. 17, 1776. Three different obverses. R. CONTINENTAL CURRENCY SEAL WHOLE AMOUNT ISSUED 60.965.269 APRIL 11th 1778. Issued by Dickeson. Bronze. Perfect. 24.   3 pcs.

325 1776 Seals. Four different obverses (1 dif. to last lot). R. Same as last. Tin. Proof. 24.   4 pcs.

326 1776 Seals. Mules of four obverses of above. 3 tin, 1 bronze. 24.   4 pcs.

EARLY PATTERNS FOR THE COINS OF THE UNITED STATES.

327 1776 Dollar. Sun dial, below MIND YOUR BUSINESS; enclosing this are double lines, between which FUGIO—the Sun, whose rays descend upon the dial, while below are E G FECIT for Edward Getz, engraver or maker. Around, outside and enclosing the above CONTINENTAL CURRENCY 1776. R. Thirteen circles interlinked, each charged with the name of one of the original thirteen States; in the center, AMERICAN CONGRESS WE ARE ONE, the field

between this device and the links being filled with rays. Borders beaded. Edge ornamented with twin olive leaves. Pewter. Uncirculated. Sharp impression. A superb example of this very rare and most interesting coin, which should be the starting coin of a United States collection. It is noteworthy that the *paper money* issued February 17, 1776, by the Continental Congress for $1/6, $1/3, $1/2, $2/3 bore the same devices on it, and the dollar values did not, this causing the inference to be drawn that it was their intention to issue a coin—this one for the dollar—to be in silver, but for lack of the metal printed that and other denominations on paper. Only two are known in silver, one of which I sold in the Earle Collection, 1912, for $2,200. Plate.

328   1776 Dollar. Same design as last, but different dies. Without B G FECIT. Currency spelled with two R's. Pewter. Very fine. Rare. Plate. Crosby, plate VIII, 16.

329   1776 Dollar. Same design, but different obverse die, the word currency spelled with one R. Die cracked up left side. Pewter. Extremely fine, splendid specimen. Rare. Plate. Crosby, plate VIII, 15.

330   1783 Cent. LIBERTAS * JUSTITIA . 1783. In center U. S. within a continuous wreath of twin olive leaves. R. NOVA . CONSTELLATIO* in center all seeing eye within a glory of thirteen groups of rays, each divided by a star. Extremely fine. Light olive. Plate. Crosby 1-A, rarity 3.

331   1783. Cent. Same type as last. Uncirculated. Sharp imp. Light olive color. Plate. C. 2-B.

332   1783. Cent. Similar obverse. R. NOVA CONSTELATIO Eye in center of double set of rays, which intersperse another set of larger heavy rays that are separated by stars. Extremely fine, practically uncirculated. Light olive. Plate. C. 3-C.

333   1785 Cent. LIBERTAS ET JUSTITIA . 1785. *U S* in large script letters intertwined, enclosed in an endless wreath of twin olive leaves. R. As last. Uncirculated. On a remarkably large planchet, being size 19, while the regular one is size 17. Broad margin outside of letters, and on reverse beading completely around the border. Light olive. Unique in this size. Plate. C. 1-B, rarity 3.

334   1785 Cent. As last, but smaller planchet, size 17. Very fine.

335 1785 Cent. Similar to last, but no period at either side of the date. R. NOVA CONSTELLATIO Eye in center of a glory of thirteen groups of fine thin rays, each divided by a star. No punctuation on either side. Uncirculated. Partly original color, and the finest example I have met with of this very rare variety. Plate. C, 2-A, rarity 4!

336 1785 Cent. Similar to last, but with a period at either side of the date. Uncirculated. Nearly full original red color, turning in places slightly steel color. A wonderful example, and like the last the finest I have seen. Plate. C. 3-B.

337 1785 Cent. Perfect die, very rare so. Very good. C. 3-B.

338 1785 Cent. Similar to last. Uncirculated. Steel color. Plate. C. 4-C, rarity 5!

339 1785 Cent. Similar to last. Very fine. Light olive. Plate. C. 4-D, rarity 6! His highest.

340 1785 Cent. Similar to last. Extremely fine. Light olive. Plate. C. 5-E, rarity 4.

UNITED STATES PATTERN PIECES.

AFTER THE ESTABLISHMENT OF THE MINT.

341 1792 Cent. Defiant eagle standing on a U. S. shield. R. TRIAL PIECE DESIGNED FOR UNITED STATES CENT 1792. Copper. Uncirculated. Very rare. This obv. should not be confused with the far more common one on which the eagle stands on half of a U. S. shield. Obverse die probably made in 1792, reverse about 1858, when this was issued by Dr. Dikeson, of Phila.

342 1794 Half dime. The regular dies, but struck in copper. Extremely fine. Of excessive rarity—probably only one other known. Plate. A. W. 16.

343 1804 Cent. So called restrike. Die of obverse cracked. R. As 1816. Copper. Bright red.

344 1804 Cent. Trial impression in lead of the obverse die, as last. Unique?

345 1805 Half eagle. Impression in brass from obverse die after it had become rusted. Probably restruck about 1860. Unique? Not in A. W.

346 1805 Half eagle. Impression on a large white metal planchet of the obverse die, as last. Unique? Not in A. W.

347 1807? Half dollar. Impression in white metal of reverse die. Unique?

H'ams 3.75 348 1816? .Cent. Impression in white metal of the reverse die used
with the 1804 cent. Uncirculated. Ex. rare.

⌐ 2θ— 349 1823 Cent. Perfect date. Die cracked. *Silver*. Restrike. Uncirculated. Extremely rare. Not in A. W.

Adams 2.75 350 1823 Cent. As last. Copper. Thick planchet. Restrike. Unc.
Not in A. W.

C 1.— 351 1836 Medalet. Liberty cap in rays. R. UNITED STATES FIRST
STEAM COINAGE FEB. 22. 1836. Original. Thick planchet. Very
fine. Rare.

C 1.— 352 1836 Same. Planchet a trifle thinner. Original. Very fine.
Rare.

C 1.— 353 1836 Same. Original. Brass. Good. Very rare.

C .50 354 1836 Same design, but date Mar. 23. Original. Thick planchet.
Very fine. Rare.

C .50 355 1836 Same. Thinner planchet. Original. Very fine. Rare.

C .50 356 1836 Same. Restrike. Very thick planchet. Bronzed.

C .25 357 1836 Same. Restrike. Thin planchet. Bronzed.

C .25 358 1836 Same. Restrike. Copper. Thick planchet. Proof.

C 10.— 359 1836 Two cents. Eagle on clouds l. Milled edge. Copper silvered before striking. A. W., type as No. 57, but metal unknown
to them. Rare.

Wilson 2.25 360 1837 Three cents. Arms of N. Y. 1837. R. FEUCHTWANGER'S
COMPOSITION THREE CENTS. Very fine.

" .4 361 1837 Cents. Eagle and snake. 1837. R. FEUCHTWANGER'S COM-
POSITION ONE CENT. Different obv. dies. Ex. fine and unc. 3 pcs.

" 3.75 362 1850 Three cents. Liberty cap in rays, 1850. R. UNITED STATES
OF AMERICA Palm branch enclosing III. Silver. Proof. Rare.
A. W. 110.

Call 8.50 363 1850 Ring cent. U S A ONE TENTH SILVER. R. CENT 1850. Composition. Very fine. A. W. 118.

" 6.75 364 1850 Ring cent. UNITED STATES OF AMERICA in center a wreath,
enclosing circle and blank space (which is generally cut out,
making this a ring cent). R. CENT . ONE TENTH SILVER Two circles in center. Silver plated before striking. Proof. Rare.
A. W. 123.

Jenkins .7 365 1850 Cent. As last, but center not cut out. Copper. Proof.
Rare. A. W. 123.

Call 4.80 366 (1850) Cent. ONE CENT in wreath. R. Blank. Copper, silver
plated before striking. Proof. Type A. W. 142.

Perkins .. 25 367 1851 Cent. Liberty seated, 13 stars 1851. R. 1 CENT in wreath. Copper. Proof. Brown color, traces of red. A. W. 148.

" 1.75 368 1851 Cent. As last. Proof. Light olive. Rare.

C. 3.- 369 1852 Ring dollar. UNITED STATES OF AMERICA 1852. R. DOLLAR and wreath. Copper-nickel. Proof. Rare. A. W. 168.

C 2 370 1853 Cent. Obv. as regular ¼ eagle die. R. ONE CENT in wreath. Nickel. Proof. Milled edge. Rare. A. W. 171.

C 2.-371 1854 Cent. Head of Liberty. R. UNITED STATES OF AMERICA . ONE CENT. Copper. Proof. Light olive. A. W. 186.

Walter .50 372 1854 Cent. As last. Cleaned. Fine.

Adams 3.75 373 1854 Cent. Same, but different metal, oroide? Proof. A. W. 188.

Henry 4.- 374 1854 Cent. Eagle flying l. R. As last. Copper. Proof. Steel color. Rare. A. W. 189.

_: 1.25 375 1855 Cent. Type as last. Copper. Ex. fine. A. W. 197.

1.10 376 1855 Cent. As last. Oroide. Proof smeared. A. W. 200.

M 1.10 377 1855 Cent. As last. Very fine.

C 2a- 378 1856 Cent. Eagle flying l., UNITED STATES OF AMERICA . 1856. R. Tobacco wreath enclosing ONE CENT Pure copper. Steel color. Extremely rare. A. W. 205.

Made 5.25 379 1856 Half cent. Regular dies in copper-nickel. Proof, hair-marked. A. W. 216-A, 217.

Adams 1.75 380 1857 $2½. Head of Liberty l. R. Eagle, UNITED STATES OF AMERICA 2½-D. Bronzed copper. Ex. fine. Rare. A. W. 219.

C 2.- 381 1858 Cent. Large eagle flying l., UNITED STATES OF AMERICA (small letters). R. Tobacco wreath, enclosing ONE CENT. Copper-nickel. Dull proof, spot on obv. As A. W. 242, but dif. metal.

C 2 - 382 1858 Cent. Same obv. R. Oak wreath. Copper-nickel. Proof. A. W. 243.

. . 4.. 383 1858 Cent. Same obv. R. Laurel wreath. Copper-nickel. Proof. A. W. 244.

1.3 384 1858 Cent. Same obv. R. Oak wreath, broad shield. Copper-nickel. Proof, finger smeared. A. W. 246.

Brown 3.- 385 1858 Cent. Small eagle flying l. R. Oak wreath, broad shield. Copper-nickel. Proof. Rare. A. W. 257.

... 2 3 386 1858 Cent. Small eagle. R. Oak wreath. Copper-nickel. Proof. Rare. A. W. 255.

. 2 .. 387 1858 Cent. Small eagle. R. Laurel wreath. Copper-nickel. Proof. Rare. A. W. 256.

3

388   1858   Cent.   Small eagle.   R. Tobacco wreath.   Copper-nickel. Proof.   Rare.   A. W. 259.

389   1858   Cent.   Indian head.   R. Oak wreath.   Copper-nickel.   Proof. A. W. 263.

390   1858   Cent.   Indian head.   R. Laurel wreath.   Copper-nickel. Proof.   The design adopted and used in 1859, thus by some collectors considered to be a regular issue.   A. W. 264.

391   1858   Cent.   Indian head.   R. Oak wreath, broad shield.   Copper-nickel.   Proof.   A. W. 268.

392   1858   Cent.   Indian head.   R. Tobacco wreath.   Copper-nickel. Proof.   A. W. 270.

393   1859 $20.   Pacquet design.   Liberty seated, supports fasces with left hand and the right rests on U. S. shield; eagle behind, above 13 stars.   R. UNITED STATES OF AMERICA 20 DOLLARS 1859.   Copper.   Proof.   A. W. 276.

394   1859   50c.   Similar obv.   R. Eagle.   UNITED STATES OF AMERICA HALF DOLLAR.   Copper.   Proof.   A. W. 292.

395   1859   50c.   Bust of Liberty r.   R. $\frac{1}{2}$ DOLLAR.   Copper.   Proof. A. W. 296.

396   1859   50c.   Bust of Liberty r.   R. 50 CENTS.   Copper.   Proof. A. W. 298.

397   1859   Cent.   Indian head.   R. Oak wreath, narrow shield.   Copper-nickel.   Proof.   A. W. 312.

398   1859   Cent.   Regular issue in red copper.   Thick planchet.   Proof. Extremely rare.   A. W. 315.

399   1860   Cent.   Regular issue in copper.   Thick planchet.   Proof. R. Stained.   Extremely rare.   A. W. 330.

400   1861   50c.   Obv. as regular issue.   R. With GOD OUR TRUST on a scroll above eagle.   1st issue of this motto on a U. S. coin.   Copper.   Proof.   Rare.   A. W. 348.

401   1861   Cent.   Regular issue in copper.   Thick planchet.   Proof. Extremely rare.   Unknown to A. W.

402   1862 $10.   Regular issue with GOD OUR TRUST on a label on reverse.   Bronze proof.   A. W. 355.

403   1862 $10.   As last.

404   1862 $10.   As last.   2 pcs.

405   1862 $10.   Regular issue with GOD OUR TRUST in the field. Bronzed.   Proof.   A. W. 356.

406   1862   50c.   Regular issue with GOD OUR TRUST in field.   Copper. Proof.   A. W. 361.

407   1863 $10. Regular issue with GOD OUR TRUST on label. Bronzed. Proof. A. W. 364.

408   1863   10c. POSTAGE CURRENCY ACT JULY 1 1862. in center 10 CENTS. 1863. R. EXCHANGED FOR U. S. NOTES. Shield on crossed arrows. Aluminum. Proof. Wt., 9½ grs. A. W. 381.

409   1863   10c. As above. Copper. Proof. Rare. A. W. 384.

410   1863   10c. As above. Tin. Slightly bent. Wt., 22½ grs. A. W. 385.

411   1863   10c. As above. Probably block tin. Wt., 21 grs. Surface rough. A. W. 385?

412   1863   3c. Type of large cent of 1857. Head of Liberty l. 13 stars 1863. R. UNITED STATES OF AMERICA, in center 3 CENTS. Copper. Proof. Thick planchet. Very rare. A. W. 395.

413   1863   3c. As last. Thin planchet. Copper. Proof. Very rare. A. W. 396.

414   1863   2c. GOD AND OUR COUNTRY 1863 Bust of Washington r. R. UNITED STATES OF AMERICA 2 CENTS. Copper. Proof. A. W. 408.

415   1863   2c. GOD OUR TRUST Shield 1863. R. UNITED STATES OF AMERICA Wreath enclosing 2 CENTS (curved). Bronze. Unc. Rare. A. W. 414.

416   1863   Cent. Regular issue in nickel. *Edge milled.* Unc. Rare. A. W. 420.

417   1863   Cent. As last, but thin planchet. Copper. Proof. Scarce. A. W. 423.

418   1863   Cent. Regular issue in *copper*. Thick planchet. Proof. Rare. A. W. 424.

419   1864   Two cents. IN GOD WE TRUST Same type as last, but different die. The boll on bottom of shield small and to left of 6 in date. R. Heavier and more evenly shaped wreath, spear of the cane points between D S. Type as regular issue. Copper-nickel. Proof. Extremely rare, A. W. 451 or 453.

420   1864   Two cents. IN GOD WE TRUST on ribbon. Shield, wreath, crossed arrows, date. R. UNITED STATES OF AMERICA, in tall wreath 2 CENTS (deeply curved), spear of sugar cane under s of STATES. Copper. Dull proof. Light brown. Rare. A. W. 455.

421   1864   Two cents. As last. Pure red copper. Brilliant proof. Rare. A. W. 452.

C.   7.25 422   1864 Two cents. As last, but different obverse dies, the boll larger and over 6. Type as regular issue. Copper-nickel. Proof. Extremely rare. Not in A. W.

Cull   10. 423   1864 Cent. Regular dies. Thick planchet. Red copper. Proof. Ex. rare. Wt., 62½ grs. Not in A. W.

Kraft   10.50 424   1864 Cent. As last. Copper-nickel. Thick planchet. Proof. Wt., 73½ grs. Not in A. W.

Call   10. 425   1864 Cent. As last. Copper-nickel. Thin planchet. Proof. Ex. rare. Wt., 47½ grs. A. W. 461?

straw   12.50 426   1864 Cent. As last. Oroide. Thin planchet. Uncirculated. Rare. Wt., 38 grs. Not in A. W.

smith   9. 427   1864 Cent. L on ribbon for *Longacre*. Copper. Thin pl. Proof, slightly smeared. Rare. Wt., 49½ grs. Not in A. W.

C.   6. 428   1865 Five cents. Type as adopted and used in 1866. Copper. Brilliant proof. Ex. rare. A. W. 507.

C   2.-429   1865 Three cents. Similar to regular issue. Copper. Rare. A. W. 518.

C   5= 430   1865 Two cents. Boll over 6. Type of regular issue on planchet silver plated before striking, hence having a brilliant proof surface. Very rare. Not in A. W.

Jenkins   1.30 431   1865 Two cents. Boll over space between 8 6. Pale copper. Unc. A. W. 520?

Beau   13. 432   1865 Cent. L on ribbon. Thin planchet. Nickel. Proof. Ex. rare. Wt., 33½ grs. A. W. 524?

Liverti   13. 433   1865 Cent. L on ribbon. Thin planchet. Nickel. Proof. Ex. rare. Wt., 32 grs. A. W. 524?

Jenkins   4.25 434   1866 Five cents. UNITED STATES OF AMERICA 1866. Bust of Washington. R. IN GOD WE TRUST. Slender wreath, enclosing 5 CENTS. Nickel. Proof. A. W. 541.

C   2.- 435   1866 Five cents. Shield with boll dividing date; above IN GOD WE TRUST. R. 5 in rays and stars, as on regular coins. Copper. Proof. Very rare. A. W. 565.

C   2.50 436   1866 Five cents. Same obv. R. UNITED STATES OF AMERICA. Large, heavily-shaded 5 in laurel wreath with prominent berries. Nickel. Proof. Rare. A. W. 567.

Abbey   6.50 437   1866 Five cents. As last. Copper. Proof. Very rare. A. W. 569.

C   6. 438   1866 Five cents. Adopted obv. R. As adopted, but *without rays*. Nickel. Brilliant proof. Excessively rare. A. W. 570.

439 1866 Five cents. As last, but copper. Brilliant proof. Excessively rare. A. W. 572.

440 1866 Five cents. Same obv. R. 5 in slender, wide wreath. Nickel. Proof. Very rare. A. W. 575.

441 1866 Five cents. Same type, but boll above date, latter small and close. R. 5 upright. Nickel. Proof. Very rare. A. W. 578.

442 1866 Five cents. As last, but copper. Proof. Very rare. A. W. 580.

443 1867 Five cents. As regular issue without rays. Copper. Proof. Rare. A. W. 623.

444 1867 Five cents. UNITED STATES OF AMERICA 1867 Head of Liberty with diadem l., 7 near end of hair. R. 5 CENTS (straight) in slender wreath, which occupies space near border; in minute letters above IN GOD WE TRUST. Nickel. Proof. Rare. A. W. 626.

445 1867 Five cents. UNITED STATES OF AMERICA 1867 Head of Liberty with feathers and ribbon UNION & LIBERTY. R. Large V on shield; IN GOD WE TRUST above. Aluminum. Plain edge. Proof. A. W. 630.

446 1867 Five cents. As last in every respect.

447 1867 Five cents. Head of Liberty l. R. 5 CENTS in wreath, above IN GOD WE TRUST in minute letters. Nickel. Proof. Very rare. A. W. 644.

448 1868 $10. Head of Liberty, 13 stars 1868. R. UNITED STATES OF AMERICA TEN D. Small eagle, with motto IN GOD WE TRUST above. Aluminum. Milled edge. Brilliant proof. Rare. A. W. 652.

449 1868 $5. International coin. UNITED STATES OF AMERICA 1868. Head of Liberty l. R. In wreath 5 DOLLARS 25 FRANCS. Aluminum. Proof. Plain edge. Rare. A. W. 655.

450 1868 Ten cents. Type as 1857 large cent. Head of Liberty, 13 stars, 1868. R. UNITED STATES OF AMERICA, in wreath TEN CENTS. Nickel. Proof. Very rare. A. W. 669.

451 1868 Ten cents. As last, in copper. Proof. Very rare. A. W. 670.

452 1868 Ten cents. As last in every way. Proof. Very rare. A. W. 670.

453 1868 Five cents. Head of Liberty, with LIBERTY and star on dia-

dem. R. Large v, above IN GOD WE TRUST on ribbon. Nickel. Proof. A. W. 675.

1.20 454 1868 Five cents. Same, but copper. Proof. A. W. 676.

455 1868 Five cents. Similar, but *no star* on diadem. R. v in elaborate wreath, with blank scroll and star at top. Broad border. Copper. Proof. Extremely rare. A. W. 678.

2. 456 1868 Five cents. Similar obv. R. 5 CENTS in wreath; above in minute letters IN GOD WE TRUST. Nickel. Proof. A. W. 680.

457 1868 Five cents. Same, but with a broad edge. Nickel. Proof. Very rare. A. W. 684.

458 1868 Five cents. As last, but in copper. Proof. Very rare. A. W. 685.

2,25 459 1868 Three cents. Similar. Nickel. Proof. Broad border. Very rare. A. W. 688?

460 1868 Three cents. Similar, but date and letters larger. R. III in olive wreath. Nickel. Proof. A. W. 692.

2. 461 1868 Three cents. As last. A. W. 692.

5. 462 1868 Cent. Same type as Nos. 684, 688. R. Sugar cane wreath. Nickel. Proof. Broad margin. Very rare. A. W. 698?

1.50 463 1868 Cent. Similar, but narrow margin. R. Olive wreath. Nickel. Proof. A. W. 700.

1.50 464 1868 Cent. Duplicate of last.

465 1868 Cent. As last, but in copper. Proof. Extremely rare. A. W. 701.

466 1869 Standard silver set, $1/2, $1/4, $1/10, three of each denomination and three designs of each denomination, which are shown in A. W., Nos. 732, 738, 744. Silver. Milled edges. Brilliant proofs.   9 pcs.

1.25 467 1869 $1/2. Bust of Liberty with pointed diadem r. R. STANDARD SILVER 1869 50 CENTS. Silver. Proof. Plain edge. A. W. 744.

1.25 468 1869 $1/2. As last, but reeded edge. Silver. Proof. A. W. 745.

50 469 1869 $1/2. As last, but in copper. Proof. A. W. 747.

470 1869 $1/4. Bust with cap. R. STANDARD SILVER etc. Silver. Milled edge. Proof. A. W. 754.

70 471 1869 $1/4. Bust with pointed diadem. R. As last. Silver. Plain edge. Proof. A. W. 765.

50 472 1869 Dime. As last. Silver. Proof. A. W. 786.

10.50 473 1869 Five cents. Head of Liberty. R. Large v on ornamented shield, as No. 618. Nickel. Proof. Extremely rare. A. W. 802.

474 1869 Five cents. Obv. as last. R. v in wreath, scroll above with IN GOD WE TRUST. Nickel. Proof. A. W. 803.

475 1869 Five cents. Regular die struck in copper. Proof. Extremely rare, as four are all that were struck it is said. A. W. 804.

476 1869 Three cents. Head of Liberty l. R. III in laurel wreath. Nickel. Proof. A. W. 815.

477 1869 Cent. Small head l. R. III in wreath. Nickel. Proof. A. W. 820.

478 1869 Cent. Duplicate of last in every way.

479 1870 Dollar. Liberty seated to l., 13 stars, 1870. R. STANDARD. In beautiful wreath of corn, cotton, etc., is 1 DOLLAR. Silver. Plain edge. Proof. Extremely rare. A. W. 864.

480 1870 $½. Bust of Liberty with cap r. R. STANDARD SILVER 1870 in center 50 CENTS. Silver. Proof. Milled edge. Rare. A. W. 896.

481 1870 $½. Bust of Liberty with pointed diadem. R. As last. Silver. Proof. Milled edge. Rare. A. W. 908.

482 1870 Standard $½, $¼, $1/10. Three of each denomination and three designs of each; shown in A. W., Nos. 915, 920, 926. Milled edges. Silver. Brilliant proofs. (Cost $15 the set at the Mint in 1870.)   9 pcs. sold as 1 set.

483 1870 Standard $½. Beautiful bust of Liberty with star on forehead. R. As above. Copper. Plain edge. Proof. A. W. 923.

484 1870 Standard $½. Bust with pointed diadem. Copper. Plain edge. Proof. A. W. 929.

485 1870 Standard $¼. Bust with cap. R. STANDARD SILVER. Silver. Milled edge. Proof. A. W. 940.

486 1870 Standard $¼. As last, in copper. Proof. A. W. 942.

487 1870 Standard $¼. Bust with pointed diadem. R. STANDARD SILVER. Silver. Milled edge. Proof. A .W. 952.

488 1870 Standard $¼. Bust with star. R. STANDARD. Silver. Milled edge. Proof. A. W. 963.

489 1870 Standard $¼. As last, but copper and edge plain. Proof. A. W. 963.

490 1870 Standard $¼. Bust with pointed diadem. R. STANDARD SILVER. Copper. Milled edge. Proof. A. W. 969.

491 1870 Standard dimes. Types as above. Different. Silver. Proofs. Milled edges. A. W., Nos. 988, 994, 1000, 1005. 4 pcs.

! F. .45 492 1870 Standard dime. Bust with pointed diadem. R. STANDARD. Copper. Plain edge. A. W. 1013.

4.25 493 1870 Five cents. Regular issue in copper. Proof. Extremely rare. A. W. 1054.

Seale (— 494 1870 Five cents. Regular issue in nickel on a thin planchet. Proof. Extremely rare, probably less than five struck. A. W. 1056.

2.57 495 1870 Three cents. Regular issue in copper. Proof. Extremely rare, said to have been four struck. A. W. 1066.

6. 496 1871 Half dollar. As last, but 13 stars added. R. As regular issue. Copper. Proof. Milled edge. Rare. A. W. 1131.

5. 497 1871 Half dollar. Indian Queen seated on a globe, 1871 below, no inscription or stars. R. STANDARD In center 50 CENTS. Copper. Proof. Plain edge. Rare. A. W. 1140.

Kraft 1.60 498 1871 Five cents. Head of Liberty. R. V CENTS the right arm of the V shaded instead of the left, a curious error. Nickel. Proof. A. W. 1193.

1. 499 1871 Five cents. As last, but in copper. Rare. A. W. 1194.

1 500 1871 Five cents. Similar obv. R. 5 CENTS. Copper. Proof. Rare. A. W. 1198.

Straw 4.25 501 1871 Five cents. Same, but in aluminum. Proof. Extremely rare, as but four were struck it is said.

.3_ 502 1872 Commercial dollar. Liberty seated on globe, flags, etc. 13 stars 1872. R. UNITED STATES OF AMERICA . COMMERCIAL DOLLAR 420 GRS . 900 FINE. Copper. Brilliant proof. Milled edge. Extremely rare. A. W. 1246.

3.50 503 1873 Trade dollar. The six designs prepared—four with figure of Liberty seated, two with head of Liberty. Silver. Proofs, hairmarked. Milled edges. Rare. Illustrated in A. W. under Nos. 1297, 1302, 1307, 1312, 1317, 1323.   6 pcs.

Leas 2.45 504 1873 Trade dollar. Obverse adopted design. R. Small eagle. Silver. Proof, hairmarked. Milled edge. A. W. 1308.

4.- 505 1874 Twenty cents. Liberty seated l. 13 stars and date. R. UNITED STATES OF AMERICA TWENTY CENTS. Eagle. Copper. Proof. Plain edge. *Thick planchet.* Very rare. A. W. 1386.

Jenkins 6.25 506 1874 Twenty cents. As last, but a *thin planchet.* Very rare, and which of these two is the most rare I cannot say, but lean to the first. A. W. do not mention there being two thicknesses.

Sine 8. 507 1875 Ten dollars. Bust of Liberty l. 13 s. 1875. R. UNITED

STATES OF AMERICA TEN DOLLARS. Eagle similar to that used on the 20c., above which E PLURIBUS UNUM and below on a scroll IN GOD WE TRUST. Copper. Proof. Milled edge. Extremely rare. A. W. 1404.

508 1875 Five dollars. Same design as last. Copper. Proof. Milled edge. Extremely rare. A. W. 1407.

509 1877 Ten dollars. Beautiful head of Liberty with cap, E PLURI-BUS UNUM 1877. R. UNITED STATES OF AMERICA . TEN DOL. Eagle, as afterwards employed on the dollar of 1878, between the wings *In God we trust.* Copper. Proof. Milled edge. Ex. rare. A. W. 1502.

510 1878 Five dollars. Head of Liberty with Phrygian cap and long hair, above IN GOD WE TRUST Seven stars before and six behind head. R. UNITED STATES OF AMERICA FIVE DOLLARS Small eagle with large wings, E PLURIBUS UNUM between them. Copper, gold plated, proof. Milled edge. Extremely rare. A. W. 1549.

511 1878 Five dollars. Fine head of Liberty, with two broad bands binding hair. E PLURIBUS UNUM 1878. R. UNITED STATES OF AMERICA FIVE DOLLARS. Eagle with drooping wings facing, three large arrows in talon. Copper. Proof. Milled edge. Ex. rare. A. W. 1553.

512 1878 Five dollars. Same obverse. R. Large eagle with long, thin arrows in talon. Copper. Gilt. Unc. Ex. rare. A. W. 1555.

513 1878 Goloid dollar. Head of Liberty, with broad band on hair, above E PLURIBUS UNUM 1878 13 stars. R. UNITED STATES OF AMERICA ONE DOLLAR. In circle of stars GOLOID.1-G. 24-S. 9 FINE. 258 GRS. Copper. Milled edge. Proof. Very rare. A. W. 1566.

514 1878 Goloid dollar. Same obv. R. In center enclosed by an olive wreath 1 GOLD. 24 SILVER. 9 FINE. 258 GRS. Copper. Milled edge. Proof. Extremely rare. A. W. 1568.

515 1878 Goloid metric dollar. Head of Liberty l., above E PLURIBUS UNUM 13 stars and date. R. UNITED STATES OF AMERICA 100 CENTS, in center within circle of stars GOLOID METRIC I-G. 161-S. 19-C GRAMS 14.35. Goloid. Proof. Rare. A. W. 1570.

516 1878 Goloid metric dollar. As last. Proof, slightly hairmarked.

517 1878 Standard dollars. Designs submitted by Messrs. Barber and Morgan. Silver. Brilliant proofs. A beautiful pair, and very rare. A. W. 1559, 1562.   2 pcs.

C   *5.*   518   1878   Standard dollars. Same as last. Copper. Proofs. W. E. DuBois, Chief Assayer's pair—in envelopes bearing his initials. Extremely rare. A. W. 1560, 1563.   2 pcs.

Nile   *3.50* 519   1879   Metric dollar. Head of Liberty l. E PLURIBUS UNUM 13 stars. 1879. R. UNITED STATES OF AMERICA ONE DOLLAR, in center 895. 8 s. 4.2-G. 100-C. 25 GRAMS. Above DEO EST GLORIA. Silver. Proof. A. W. 1598.

Kroh   *3.75* 520   1879   Goloid metric dollar. Obverse type of 1878 goloid. R. UNITED STATES OF AMERICA 100 cents GOLOID METRIC DOLLAR. DEO EST GLORIA. In center 15.3-G 236.7-S. 28-C. 14 GRAMS. Goloid metric. Proof. A. W. 1606.

Real   *5.—* 521   1880   Stella. Head of Liberty with long hair. R. Star ONE STELLA 400 CENTS. Copper. Proof. Extremely rare of this date. A. W. 1631.

Jenkins   *2.75* 522   1881   Five cents. Head of Liberty, as afterwards used in 1883. UNITED STATES OF AMERICA 1881. R. v in cotton wreath. Copper. Proof. Extremely rare. A. W. 1649.

   2.00 523   1881   Five cents. As last, but aluminum. Proof. Extremely
Stacus   *5.50* 523a   rare. A. W. 1650. *two laws picture*

C   *2.70* 524   1882   Five cents. Head of Liberty UNITED STATES OF AMERICA 1882 R. v in cotton, corn, wreath, above E PLURIBUS UNUM. Nickel. Extremely rare. A. W. 1667.

Jenkins   *2.75* 525   1882   Five cents. Similar to last. Copper. Proof. Extremely rare. A. W. 1670.

Ely   *2.00* 526   1882   Five cents. IN GOD WE TRUST Head of Liberty l. 13 stars 1882 R. UNITED STATES OF AMERICA. E PLURIBUS UNUM, in wreath v. Nickel. Proof. Extremely rare. A. W. 1672.

cushium   *3 -* 527   1882   Five cents. As last, but aluminum. Proof. Extremely rare. A. W. 1674.

   5.50 528   1882   Five cents. As last, but without motto. Adopted design as used on first issue of 1883. Nickel. Proof. Extremely rare. A. W. 1675.

Lrim   *?.00* 529   1882   Five cents. As last, but in copper. Proof. Extremely rare. A. W. 1676.

Leon   *6.25* 530   1882   Five cents. Shield similar to type 1866, but without boll on end of shield. Nickel. Proof. Excessively rare. A. W 1678.

Jenkins   *3.25* 531   1882   Five cents. As last in copper. Proof. Excessively rare. A. W. 1679.

C.   *4 -* 532   1883   Five cents. Head of Liberty. 13 stars. 1883. R. UNITED STATES OF AMERICA . E PLURIBUS UNUM; in the center v with a

C.   *4.*   533 L   1881 1C *inden*

scroll across it inscribed CENTS. Were it not for this word cents across the V it would be same as adopted design. Nickel. Proof. Excessively rare. A. W. 1681.

533 1883 Five cents. Same, but aluminum. Proof. Excessively rare. A. W. 1683.

534 1883 Five cents. Same head. UNITED STATES OF AMERICA 1883 R. FIVE CENTS 13 stars, in wreath PURE NICKEL. Nickel. Proof. Very rare. A. W. 1686.

535 1883 Five cents. Same obverse. R. FIVE CENTS 13 stars, in center 50 N. 50 C. Nickel. Proof. Very rare. A. W. 1689.

536 1883 Five cents. Same obv. R. FIVE CENTS 13 stars, in wreath 33 N. 67 C. Nickel. Proof. Very rare. A. W. 1694.

537 1883 Five cents. Same head. LIBERTY above. 13 stars, 1883. R. Same as regular issue without CENTS. Nickel. Proof. Extremely rare. A. W. 1696.

538 1883 Five cents. As last, but in aluminum. Proof. Extremely rare. A. W. 1698.

539 1884 Ring cent. UNITED STATES OF AMERICA 1884. R. ONE CENT Inverted U. S. shield with olive branch at either side. Hole in center. Nickel. Proof. Extremely rare. A. W. 1704.

540 1896 Five cents. E . PLURIBUS . UNUM. 13 stars 1896, in center U. S. shield on crossed Liberty staff and pole with eagle, across center a ribbon with LIBERTY R. UNITED STATES OF AMERICA A branch of olive forms a wreath and encloses 5 CENTS. Nickel. Proof. Very rare. A. W. 1735.

541 1896 Five cents. As last, but aluminum. Proof. Very rare. A. W. 1736.

COMMEMORATIVE MEDALS OFTEN CALLED "DOLLARS."

542 1876 Centennial of the Declaration of Independence. Official medal issued by the Commission under an Act of Congress. THESE UNITED COLONIES ARE AND OF RIGHT OUGHT TO BE, FREE AND INDEPENDENT STATES. Female kneeling with sword, thirteen stars and rays above; below 1776. R. BY AUTHORITY OF THE CONGRESS OF THE UNITED STATES IN COMMEMORATION OF THE HUNDREDTH ANNIVERSARY OF AMERICAN INDEPENDENCE 1876. Silver. Proof, slight dent on edge. 24.

543 1876 Centennial. LET GOD BE WITH US AS HE WAS WITH OUR FATHERS. Soldier of 1776 and 1876 presenting arms to the Liberty bell; above CENTENNIAL. R. MADE FROM NEVADA ORE AT

INTERNATIONAL EXHIBITION * ALL FOR OUR COUNTRY *. View
of mine, R. R. train, mountains, etc., above NEVADA. Silver.
Proof, slightly hairmarked. Rare. 24.

544 1876 California. WASHINGTON THE GREAT FOUNDER OF THE
UNITED STATES OF AMERICA JULY 4TH. 1776. Scene of a stage
coach, post boy, ship, mountain scenery, above bust of Washington in wreath, 13 stars, pine tree and U. S. flags, 1776-1876,
A.KUNER.F (who cut the dies for 1855, Kellogg & Co., $50,
1855). R. PROGRESS OF TIME AND FREEDOM TO ALL MANKIND JULY
4TH. 1876. CALIFORNIA. View of R. R. train, miners, steamship,
etc., above arms of Cal. Silver. Proof. Very rare. 26.

545 1898 Nebraska. TRANSMISSISSIPPI EXPOSITION OMAHA 1898.
Beautiful female bust l. R. Indian hunting a buffalo, 1848.
Silver. Very fine. Rare. 22.

546 1904 St. Louis. LOUISIANA PURCHASE EXPOSITION. Busts left of
Napoleon I and Pres. Jefferson. R. Map, LOUISIANA TERRITORY
1803 etc. Silver. Fine. 22.

547 1906 Pike. ZEBULON MONTGOMERY PIKE . 1779-1813. Bust r. R.
COLORADO 1806-1906 etc. View of Pike's Peak. Silver. Proof. 22.

548 1907 Virginia. TER-CENTENNIAL OF THE SETTLEMENT OF JAMES-
TOWN 1607-1907 Bust of Pocahontas l. R. LANDING OF THE
EXPEDITION UNDER CAPN. JOHN SMITH MAY 13 1697 Ships r.
Silver. Extremely fine. Rare. 22.

SATIRICAL PIECES ON BRYAN CAMPAIGN—1896-1900.

549 823 GRAINS OF SILVER $\frac{900}{1000}$ FINE THE EQUIVALENT OF ONE GOLD
DOLLAR IN VALUE SEPT 14 1896. R. SIZE OF GOVERNMENT DOLLAR
CONTAINING 412½ GRAINS OF SILVER $\frac{900}{1000}$ FINE. Near edge,
TIFFANY & CO. Silver. Original. Very rare. 32½.

550 A GOVERNMENT DOLLAR CONTAINS 412½ GRAINS COIN SILVER $\frac{900}{1000}$
FINE. THIS PIECE CONTAINS 823 GRAINS COIN SILVER IN VALUE THE
EQUIVALENT OF ONE GOLD DOLLAR SEPT 16TH 1896. GORHAM MFG
CO. SILVERSMITHS. R. Wheel, inscribed on rim SIZE OF A GOV-
ERNMENT DOLLAR CONTAINING 412½ GRAINS OF SILVER $\frac{900}{1000}$ FINE.
Silver. Ex. fine. 33.

551 Same obverse. R. Blank. Silver. Very fine. 33.

552 1896 IN GOD WE TRUST IN BRYAN WE BURST 1896 Head of Liberty
r. R. IN GOD WE TRUST FOR THE OTHER 47¢ Eagle, 16 TO 1. 10
stars. Nickel. Scratches on check. Nick on edge. Cast. Extremely rare. 50.

/. 553 1896 Head of Liberty, LIBERTY l. 13 stars, 1896. R. UNITED STATES OF AMERICA 16 TO 1 NIT Eagle, olive branch and three arrows in talons. Lead. Cast. 56.

/. 554 1896 Same design. Plain diadem, and serratures raised instead of incused, as on last. R. Same, but two staffs with three leaves at termination. Lead. Cast. Very fine. Pin hole at top. 56.

/. 555 1896 Head of Liberty l., diadem of stars. 1896. 13 stars. R. UNITED STATES OF AMERICA 16 TO 1 NIT Eagle, with three arrows in left and olive branch in right, semi-olive wreath tied with a bow below. Raised border. Cast in type metal. Very rare. 55.

/. 556 1896 Head of Liberty l., BRYAN'S MONEY 1896 8 stars. R. BRYAN'S IDEA OF COINAGE 16 TO 1 ABER NIT Cast in type metal. 54.

l. 557 1896 FREE SILVER ONE DIME NOT 1896. R. SIXTEEN TO ONE and list of 16 names from BLUSTER TO LUNACY Cast in hard metal. 29.

('558 1896 UNITED SNAKES OF AMERICA . IN BRYAN WE TRUST Goose, P. O. P. with Jackass's head. R. FREE SILVER ONE DAM 1896. Struck in tin. Holed. Rare. 29.

/ 559 1896 VOTE FOT A 100c DOLLAR AND M^{C}KINLEY. R. FREE SILVER ONE DIME 1896. Struck in lead. Uncirculated. Extremely rare. 32.

/ 560 1900 A GOVERNMENT DOLLAR CONTAINS 412½ GRAINS OF SILVER $\frac{900}{1000}$ FINE THIS PIECE OF SILVER IS THE SIZE AND WEIGHT OF A GOVERNMENT DOLLAR CONTAINING 412½ GRAINS OF SILVER $\frac{900}{1000}$ FINE AND ITS VALUE JULY 5TH 1900 WAS 48 CENTS. GORHAM MFG. CO. SILVERSMITHS R. MARKET VALUE JULY 5TH 1900 — 48 CENTS COINAGE VALUE AT THE RATE OF 16 TO 1 100 CENTS? Silver. Edge milled. Very fine. Rare. 24.

WASHINGTON COINS.

Arranged and numbered according to the book, Medallic Portraits of Washington, by W. S. Baker, Philadelphia. 1885.

Lowg 9.75 561 No. 1 1783 Cent. WASHINGTON & INDEPENDENCE 1783 Draped and laureated bust facing l. R. UNITY STATES OF AMERICA Wreath enclosing ONE CENT Below bow $\frac{1}{100}$. Uncirculated. Sharp, and I believe the finest example I have met with. *Plate.*

Need .3 562 No. 2 1783 Cent. Obverse similar to last. R. UNITED STATES Liberty seated l., holding olive branch in right hand and Liberty staff in left. Extremely fine.

Long 2.75 563 No. 3 1783 Cent. Type as last. Restrike. Silver. Engrailed edge. Rare.

70 564 No. 3 1783 Cent. As last. Bronze proof.

80 565 No. 3 1783 Cent. As last. Copper proof.

150 566 No. 3a 1783 Cent. Type as last, but letters and date smaller, more like No. 2. Plain edge. Restrike. Bronze proof. Very rare.

Nilan. 325 567 No. 4 1783 Cent. WASHINGTON & INDEPENDENCE 1783. Bust laureated and in uniform left, head small. R. UNITED STATES. Liberty seated to left, olive branch in right and Liberty staff in left hand; below the base line T . W . I . E.8 Very fine.

Kessler 60 568 No. 4a 1783 Cent. Larger back to the head. Dif. dies. Liberty cap between TA and touching A. Very good. Scarce.

569 No. 6 (1783) Cent. WASHINGTON. Bust laureated and in uniform l. R. ONE CENT Bust as on obv. Extremely fine.

570 No. 7 1783 Cent. GEORGIUS TRIUMPHO Undraped bust r. R. VOCE POPULI 1783 Liberty behind a trellis. Good.

C 2.70 571 No. 14 1789 GEORGE WASHINGTON PRESIDENT 1789 Bust in uniform l. R. Eagle displayed. Copper. Proof. Published about 1863 by A. S. Robinson, of Hartford. Rare.

572 No. 15 1791 Cent. WASHINGTON PRESIDENT 1791 Fine bust in uniform to left. R. Large eagle displayed, above ONE CENT. Edge, UNITED STATES OF AMERICA Semi-proof. Original bright red color. This and next lot came from the same family, and no doubt had been kept together and handed down since their birth. It seems a pity to separate them, and the cataloguer reserves the right to offer them together first. *Plate.*

Jones 12 *ea.*

573 No. 16 1791 Cent. Same as last, but without date. R. Heraldic eagle with eight stars about his head, and above a band of clouds from wing to wing, above which ONE CENT Beneath the eagle 1791. Edge as last. Semi-proof. Mostly original red color. This and next preceding are, I believe, the finest pair of these cents I have seen. *Plate.*

574 No. 18 1793 Half penny. Same obv. as last. R. HALF PENNY 1793 Ship sailing to r. Edge, PAYABLE IN ANGLESEY LONDON OR LIVERPOOL Very fine. Light olive.

White 48.— 575 No. 59 1792 Cent. WASHINGTON PRESIDENT 1792. Bust of Washington in uniform facing l. R. *GENERAL OF THE AMERICAN ARMIES 1775 RESIGNED 1783 PRESIDENT OF THE UNITED STATES 1789.

Edge plain. Very fine. Extremely rare. *Plate.* Crosby, plate X, No. 11.

576 No. 60 Cent. GEO. WASHINGTON BORN IN VIRGINIA FEB. 11. 1732. Bust in uniform to left. R. °GENERAL OF THE AMERICAN ARMIES 1775 RESIGNED 1783 PRESIDENT OF THE UNITED STATES 1789. Edge plain. Extremely fine. Slight dent on edge. Beautiful specimen. Very rare. *Plate.*

577 No. 29 1795 Grate cent. Bust r., with four large buttons on coat. G. WASHINGTON . THE FIRM FRIEND TO PEACE & HUMANITY R. Fire grate. Extremely fine. Rare.

578 No. 29a 1795 Grate cent. As last, but with five small buttons on coat, other differences, too. Very fine.

579 No. 30 (1795) Penny. GEORGE WASHINGTON. Bust in costume l. R. LIBERTY AND SECURITY Shield, with eagle above. Edge, AN ASYLUM FOR THE OPPRESS'D OF ALL NATIONS. Uncirculated. Partly original color. Splendid example.

580 No. 31 1795 Half penny. GEORGE WASHINGTON. Bust in uniform, as on grate cent. R. LIBERTY AND SECURITY 1795 Eagle and shield. Edge, BIRMINGHAM REDRUTH & SWANSEA. Good. Extremely rare.

581 No. 31 1795 Half penny. As last, but edge lettered PAYABLE AT LONDON LIVERPOOL OR BRISTOL. Good. Extremely rare.

581a 1795 Reverse of last combined with IRISH HALFPENNY 1795 Hope standing. Edge, PAYABLE AT LIVERPOOL LONDON OR BRISTOL. Good.

582 No. 34 GEORGIVS WASHINGTON. Bust in costume l. R. NORTH WALES Harp, crowned star above. Good.

583 Washington Inaugural Button. Eagle displayed MEMORABLE ÆRA MARCH THE FOURTH Brass. Shank off. Vg. Rare.

584 Washington Inaugural Button. *G.W.* in script in center, around LONG LIVE THE PRESIDENT Outer border of links each enclosing the initial of one of the 13 Original States. Brass. With shank. Perfect. 22.

585 Washington Inaugural Button. G W (script) Enclosed by LONG LIVE THE PRESIDENT Outside of this a glory of rays and plain band, outer border of stars. Copper. Perfect. With shank. The only one I have seen. 21.

586 Washington Inaugural Button. G W in oval in center; above in sunken tablet LONG LIVE THE PRESIDENT. Copper. With shank. Fine. Rare. 22.

WASHINGTON MEDALS.

Arranged and numbered according to Baker's Medallic Portraits of Washington.

Closing number refers to size in 16th of an inch.

All in bronze and in perfect condition, unless the contrary is stated.

587 No. 47 1776 Washington Before Boston, 1776. Bust r. R. Washington and his Generals viewing the departure of the British fleet from the harbor. Paris Mint. *Original.* Very fine. Rare. 43.

588 No. 47 1776 The obverse only in steel, apparently made by the ruling machine. From I. F. Wood's Collection.

589 No. 48 1776 Same design as last. One foot less to horse. Paris Mint restrike. 43.

590 No. 50 1776 Equestrian statue l. R. SIEGE OF BOSTON 1775-6. Copper. 20.

591 No. 50 1776 As last. Brass. Rare. 20.

592 No. 50 1776 As last. Tin. Unknown to Baker in this metal. 20.

593 No. 52 1776 Equestrian statue l. R. Bust of Washington. Copper. 20.

594 No. 53. 1776 Signing of the Declaration of Independence. Bust of Washington, nude, facing left, GEORGE WASHINGTON R. View of the signing of the DECLARATION OF INDEPENDENCE JULY 4TH 1776. Bronze. Ex. fine. Very rare. 56.

595 No. 53a 1776 Same as last, but in block tin. From the Bushnell sale (1882), No. 1273, and believed to be unique. 56.

596 No. 55 1834 Bust l., in uniform, surrounded by ins. R. Eagle, with shield and scroll inscribed ALL MEN ARE CREATED EQUAL JULY 4. 1776. Above INDEPENDENCE Below 1834. Tin. Very fine. Rare. 32.

597 No. 58 1783 Peace. Busts of Washington and Franklin jugate to l. R. Section of the globe inscribed UNITED STATES Above eagle with thunderbolts issuing from talons, olive branch in his beak; above 1783. Silver. Proof. Very rare. 26.

598 No. 61 1790 Manly medal. Aged bust of Washington l., *Brooks f.* GEO. WASHINGTON BORN VIRGINIA FEB. 11.1732. R. GENERAL OF THE AMERICAN ARMIES 1775. etc. Sharp. Extremely fine. Rare. 30.

599 No. 61 1790 As last, but gold plated, of the time. Very fine. Rare. 30.

600 No. 62 1790 Manly medal. Similar to last. GEO. WASHINGTON NATUS VIRGINIA - BP.W M.C. 11 FEB. O. S. 1732. 30.

601 No. 64 1789 GEORGE WASHINGTON OF VIRGINIA. Bust r. R. GENL. OF THE AMERICAN ARMIES 1775 RESIGNED THE COMMAND 1783. ELECT PRESIDENT OF THE UNITED STATES 1789, in two concentric lines; in center pyramid of 15 cannon balls with crossed sabres below. *Silver.* Restrike, 21 made. Dies destroyed. Extremely rare. 21.

602 No. 64 1789 As last. *Brass.* Restrike, 21 made. Extremely rare. 21.

603 No. 64 1789 As last. Copper. Restrike, 21 made. Extremely rare. 21.

604 No. 65 1789 Twigg medal. GEORGE WASHINGTON. Very fine bust in uniform r. TWIGG on arm. R. GENERAL OF THE AMERICAN ARMIES etc. Tin. Brilliant example of this rare medal. The edge below bust rough from not being struck up full in the die. 22.

605 No. 66 1797 Presidency Resigned. GEORGE WASHINGTON Bust in uniform l. WYON on arm. R. GENERAL OF THE AMERICAN ARMIES. 1775. RESIGNED THE COMMAND 1783 ELECTED PRESIDENT OF THE UNITED STATES 1789. RE-ELECTED, 1793. RESIGNED 1797. Tin. Very fine. Rare. 24.

606 No. 67 1797 Resumed Command. GEORGE WASHINGTON DIED 14. DECEMBER 1799. AGED 68. R. GENERAL OF THE AMERICAN ARMIES 1775. RESIGNED THE COMMAND 1783. ELECTED PRESIDENT OF THE UNITED STATES 1789. RE-ELECTED 1793. RESIGN'D 1797. RESUMED THE COMMAND OF THE ARMIES 1798. (Above reverse inscription in *twelve* lines.) Tin. Extremely fine. Excessively rare, I believe but four examples are known—two forever withdrawn from trade, being in the cabinet of the U. S. Mint, and W. S. Baker's gift of his collection to the Historical Society of Pa. *Plate.*

607 No. 68 1796 But with a unique edge. GEORGE WASHINGTON 1796. Bust r. R. GENL. OF THE AMERICAN ARMIES 1775 etc., in three concentric lines; in center scroll REPUB AMERI, a cannon, fasces, caduceus. Edge, (Payable) IN LONDON LIVERPOOL OR ANGLESEY Fine, but slightly dented on edge. Unknown to Baker with this edge, and I have never heard of a duplicate. 21.

608 No. 68 1796 Same, but plain edge. Good.

4

C   . 50 609 No. 69 1799 Similar to last. Tin. Proof. 21.

(Wilson   575 610 No. 70 1797 Presidency Relinquished. GEORGE WASHINGTON
                   PRESIDENT OF THE UNITED STATES. Bust in civilian dress r. On
                   arm, HALLIDAY . S. R. COMMISSION RESIGNED. PRESIDENCY RE-
                   LINQUISHED. 1797 Sword, fasces and wreath laid on the Altar of
                   his Country. Unusually fine proof of this very rare medal. 34.

,   2.25 611 No. 71 1797 Type as last, legends abbreviated. *Silver*. Ex-
                   tremely fine. *Original*. Very rare. 26.

Purball   . 30 612 No. 71 1797 As last. Tin, silver plated. Original. Ex. fine.
                   Rare. 26.

"   . 50 613 No. 72 1797 As last. U. S. Mint reproduction. 26.

C   . 50 614 No. 73 1797 As last, but larger die. Bronze. 29.
Purball

Ivry   15 615 No. 73 1797 As last. White metal. 29.

Ivry   130 616 No. 74 1799 George Washington. Bare head of l. W.P^T. at
                   edge WRIGHT & BALE. R. Oak wreath, enclosing BORN FEB. 22^D
                   1732 CHOSEN COMMAND^R IN CHIEF JULY 1776. CHOSEN PREST
                   1789. DIED DEC^R. 14 1797. AGED 68 YEARS. Tin. Fine. Very
                   rare. 28.

Ivry   . 4 617 No. 75 1799 Similar to last. WRIGHT & BALE partly erased. R.
                   Same wording as last, but a different die. Bronze. 28.

         40 618 No. 75 As last. Tin. 28.

         1/ 619 No. 76 Bust ¾ l. R. GEN. OF THE AMERICAN ARMIES etc. Brass.
                   Copper (thick and thin planchets). Brass. 12.   4 pcs.

Kraft   . 3x 620 No. 77 Bust l. Border of eagles, stars and semicircles. R. His-
                   tory. Brass. Copper. Tin. 21.   3 pcs.

Ilery   350 621 No. 78 (1778?) G^E. WASHINGTON E^R. GENERAL OF THE CONTIN^L.
                   ARMY IN AMERICA. Head r. R. WASHIN. REUNIT etc. Cannon,
                   drum, mortar, etc. Proof, slightly hairmarked. The rare medal,
                   known as "the Voltaire medal." 25.

Purball . 25 622 No. 81 1775 Bust r., by *Westwood*. GEORGE WASHINGTON ESQR.
                   R. WITH COURAGE etc. Holed at top. Good. Abused. Possibly
                   used as an Indian Peace Medal. 25.

Ivry   21/— 623 No. 84 1803 Fame medal. WASHINGTON. BORN FEBRUARY 11 1732
                   DIED DECEMBER 21 1799. Very fine bust in civilian dress to right.
                   R. WISDOM VIRTUE & PATRIOTISM Fame flying over land and sea,
                   blowing her trumpet and holding out a wreath, in exergue
                   MDCCCIII . Superb proof. Excessively rare. *Plate*. 24.

C   5. 624 No. 85 1805 Eccleston medal. GENERAL WASHINGTON INSCRIBED
                   TO HIS MEMORY BY D. ECCLESTON . LANCASTER. MDCCCV Magnifi-

cent bust in rich armor in high relief r., by *Webb.* R. In center
Indian standing, THE LAND WAS OURS, around in three concentric
lines HE LAID THE FOUNDATION OF AMERICAN LIBERTY IN THE
XVIII CENTURY. INNUMERABLE MILLIONS YET UNBORN WILL VENER-
ATE THE MEMORY—OF THE MAN WHO OBTAINED THEIR COUNTRY'S
FREEDOM. Superb exámple of this great medal. 48.

625 No. 87 Hero of Trenton. GEORGE WASHINGTON Bust in military
costume r. Border of deep serratures on both obverse and reverse. R. In seven lines THE HERO OF TRENTON PRINCETON GLOU-
CESTER YORKTOWN etc. Low relief, and I judge it to be the work
of C. Wylie Betts. Lead. 30. Baker only knew of one example,
that in the McCoy Sale, 1864, No. 2348, and this may be that example, as I have never met with another. *Plate.*

626 No. 88 1799 WASHINGTON. Head r. within wreath, below M (for
Merriam, Boston). R. THE HERO OF AMERICAN INDEPENDENCE,
in wreath DIED DEC. 14. 1799 Below MERRIAM BOSTON. Brass,
Copper. Tin. 17.   3 pcs.

627 No. 89 1799 GEORGE WASHINGTON BORN FEBY 22 . 1732. * DIED
DEC^R 17. 1799.* R. A MAN HE WAS TO ALL HIS COUNTRY DEAR,
within a wreath; eye of Providence above casting rays over the
inscription. Bronze. 24.

628 No. 89 1799 As last. Copper. Tin. 24.   2 pcs.

629 No. 89 1799 As last. Lead; thick planchet. Very rare. 24.

630 No. 89 1799 Same obverse. R. Oak wreath, blank center. Unknown to Baker with this rev. White metal. 24.

630a No. 91 GEORGE WASHINGTON. Head r. R. Wreath enclosing TIME
INCREASES HIS FAME. Silver, bronze (thick and thin planchets),
copper. 18.   4 pcs.

631 No. 92 WASHINGTON. Bust l., by *J. A. Bolen.* R. HE LIVED FOR HIS
COUNTRY. Copper. Rare. 18.

632 No. 94 1799 PATER PATRIÆ 1732 Bust l., by *Key.* R. "PROVI-
DENCE LEFT HIM CHILDLESS THAT THE NATION MIGHT CALL HIM
FATHER" 1799 Copper, white metal. 18.   2 pcs.

633 1799 As last, but the bust enclosed by a tombstone-like line, as
B 211. R. Line between FATHER and 1799. Unknown to Baker.
White metal. 18.

634 No. 95 GEORGE WASHINGTON BORN 1732 DIED 1799 Bust l. R.
PATER PATRIÆ Bust l. Silver. Copper. Bronze. 18.   3 pcs.

635 No. 98 Equestrian fig. R. WASHINGTON in rays and stars. Tin. 20.

8.— 636 No. 96 GEORGE WASHINGTON. Undraped bust l., by *Wright*. R. SI QUÆRIS MONUMENTUM CIRCUMSPICE within a glory enclosed by thirteen rings, each enclosing initials of one of the original thirteen States. Tin, unknown to Baker in this metal. 40.

.2b 637 No. 97 Head r., between branches of olive and palm. R. WASHINGTON in a glory of rays and 13 stars. Copper. Wm. 20. 2 pcs.

5.25 638 No. 99 Bust undraped l. Exquisite work. R. Star in rays. Silver. Extremely rare. Plate. 7.

11.50 639 No. 100 Note. Very fine undraped bust l. in wreath, by C. C. Wright. R. THOUGH LOST TO SIGHT TO MEMORY DEAR enclosed by a band with 13 stars. Silver. Extremely rare, probably unique, Mr. C. I. Bushnell said they were. 18.

7.— 640 No. 100 Note. As last. Copper. Extremely rare, if not unique.

.50 641 No. 100 Note. As last. Tin. Extremely rare, if not unique.

12.— 642 No. 104 Note. Obverse as last. R. WHOM ALL DO HONOR MUST BE GREAT. Silver. Extremely rare, if not unique. 18.

7 — 643 No. 104 Note. As last. Brass. Extremely rare, if not unique. 18.

6.— 644 No. 104 Note. As last. Copper. Extremely rare, if not unique. 18.

4 — 645 No. 104 Note. As last. Tin. Extremely rare, if not unique. 18.

.50 646 1856 Mt. Vernon. Circular steel engraving—bust of Washington—Mt. Vernon, Tomb, etc., by Am. Bank Note Co. Set in a frame made of wood from Mt. Vernon. As 1 lot. 52.

1.40 647 No. 111 GEORGE WASHINGTON. Bust l., by F. B. Smith and Hartmann, N. Y. R. RESIDENCE OF WASHINGTON MOUNT VERNON, VIRGINIA View of the mansion. Tin. Scarce. 40.

.25 648 No. 113 Mt. Vernon. Bust r. R. WASHINGTON'S RESIDENCE AT MOUNT VERNON. Copper. Wm. 22. 2 pcs.

.85 649 No. 113a Same head as last, but enclosed by a wreath of laurel leaves. R. Blank. Wm. Very rare. 22.

.35 650 No. 114 Mt. Vernon. Equestrian fig. R. THE HOME OF WASHINGTON MOUNT VERNON. Bronze. Brass. Copper. 20. 3 pcs.

1.50 651 No. 117 Same obv. as last. R. Tomb. Tin. Scarce. 40.

.55 652 No. 126 Statue Richmond. R. Tomb. Copper. 18.

.35 653 No. 122 GEORGE WASHINGTON BORN FEBRUARY 22. 1732. Head r., by *Merriam*. R. Tomb. Copper. 20.

1.— 654 No. 124 GEORGE WASHINGTON. Draped bust r. R. Washington's tomb, Mt. Vernon, Va. View of tomb. Copper. Rare. 18.

1 — 655 No. 128 Bust l. R. Tomb, ornamental border. Copper. Unknown to Baker. Very rare. 12.

656 No. 129 Death. GEN[L] GEORGE WASHINGTON. Bust in civil dress l. R. BORN FEB 22[D] 1732. DIED DEC[R] 14 1799. Fine. Tin. Very rare. 28.

657 No. 130 GEORGIUS WASHINGTON Head with curly locks right. R. NATUS VIRGINIAE etc. Series Numismatica. 1819. Tin. Unknown to Baker in this metal! Excessively rare. 26.

658 No. 131 GEORGIUS WASINGTON the H omitted from WASHINGTON. Bust l. R. as last. Rare. 2-G.

659 No. 133 GEORGE WASHINGTON Fine bust, undraped, to left O.C.W. f. (C. C. Wright.) R. BORN IN VIRGINIA FEB. 22. 1732. DIED IN VIRGINIA DEC. 14. 1799 within heavy oak wreath. Silver. Excessively rare, as but two were struck. I. F. Wood said, C. C. Wright made this splendid head of Washington from a drawing made by the six-year-old daughter of Prof. Mapes, of N. Y. Plate. 40. •

660 No. 135 GEORGIUS WASHINGTON PRÆS PRIM. RER. CONF. AMER. MDCCLXXXIX. Head r., by Lovett, Phila. R. FIDELI CERTA MERCES MDCCCLX etc. Bronze. 33.

661 No. 135 As last. Tin. 33.

662 No. 135 As last. Brass. Unknown to Baker. Very rare. 33.

663 No. 136 Bust r. R. Born, etc. Copper. 20.

664 No. 137 Bust r. R. WASHINGTON, BORN, 1732. DIED, 1799. Copper. 18.

665 No. 140 Bust r. R. WASHINGTON BORN, 1732 DIED, 1799 in wreath. Copper. 18.

666 No. 141 Bust l., border of stars and semicircles. R. As last. Brass. Unknown to Baker. Very rare. 18.

667 No. 143 GEORGE WASHINGTON. Bust draped r. R. BORN 1732 DIED 1799 Shield in center, crossed branches above and below. Copper. 18.

668 No. 145-146 Obverses of each combined. Copper. Not in Baker. 18. 2 pcs.

669 No. 146 Washington statue. R. Shield. Copper. 18.

670 No. 147 GEORGE WASHINGTON. Bust draped r. R. Liberty cap, rays, stars, eagles. WASHINGTON NATVS 1732 OBIT 1799. Copper. 18.

671 No. 150 Washington statue. R. Liberty cap. Copper. 18.

672 No. 151 Head to left within a wreath. R. BORN FEB. 22. 1732 DIED DEC. 14. 1799 Wreath and border of stars. Silver. Extremely rare, if not unique. Plate. 18.

673 No. 151 Same as last. Brass. Extremely rare, if not unique. 18.
674 No. 151 Same as last. Copper. Extremely rare, if not unique. 18.
675 No. 151 Same as last. Tin. Extremely fine, if not unique. 18.
676 No. 155 Bust r. On bust P for *Paquet*. R. BORN 1732 DIED 1799 within a wreath. 12.
677 No. 156a Bust r. On bust P. R. Same as 156. Not in Baker. Thick and thin planchets. Bronze.   2 pcs.
678 No. 155a Similar, but without P Around border of obverse slanting milling. Copper. Not in Baker. 12.
679 No. 156 Bust of Washington in civilian dress. Silver. Bronze. Copper. 12.   3 pcs.
680 No. 155a Similar, but with AP on edge of bust. R. as B 156. Silver. Not in Baker. 12.
681 No. 157 Bust in uniform r., stars around edge. R. Fac simile of signature. Silver, gilt. Ring in top. Very rare. 7.
682 No. 158 Equestrian figure r. GEORGE WASHINGTON. R. BORN FEB. 22D 1732 PRESIDENT 1789-1796 DIED 1799 Border of stars and liberty caps. Copper. Rare. 18.
683 No. 160 Medallion, with bust of Washington r., held by an eagle, glory above, ribbon below with PATRIAE PATER R. STRUCK & DISTRIBUTED IN CIVIC PROCESSION FEB[RY] 22ND 1832 THE CENTENNIAL ANNIVERSARY OF THE BIRTH OF WASHINGTON BY THE GOLD & SILVER ARTIFICERS OF PHILAD Silver. *Original.* Proof, and rarely seen in this condition and metal. 20.
684 No. 160 As last. Original. Silver. Loop and ring attached to edge. Very fine. 20.
685 No. 160 As last. Tin. Original. Fine. Rare. 20.
686 No. 160 As last. Restrikes in copper and tin.   2 pcs.
687 No. 161 Cent. of birth. GEO. WASHINGTON. FEB 22, 1832. Bust l. in sunken field. Tin shell distributed by the Tin and Iron Workers in the parade in Phila. Rare. 26.
688 No. 161a As last, but inscription smaller letters and not on a raised band as last. Tin. Very rare. 26. Not in Baker.
689 No. 162 WASHINGTON. Bust in uniform to right, below CONRADT 170 N. FOURTH S. R. THE FATHER OF HIS COUNTRY FEBR 22D 1832 in six lines, enclosed within a wreath composed of a branch of oak and a branch of olive, crossed at ends, and on point of crossing is a star, below this *Phila.* Tin. Very fine. Small hole at top. Plate. 23. But one other specimen is known of

this medal, and that was sold in the Mickley Collection in 1878, where it was bought for Wm. S. Appleton, of Boston, and is now given to the Mass. Hist. So. So it is forever withdrawn from trade. This great rarity should command a large price. Mr. Baker had never seen one, and his description is erroneous in consequence in the spelling out of the word February.

Ratified 2.75 690 No. 165 Funeral. HE IS IN GLORY THE WORLD IN TEARS Bust in uniform left, within a wreath. R. History in four concentric lines, a skull and cross bones below. Holed at top, as usual. Silver. Fine. Very rare. 19.

C .3 691 No. 166 Funeral medal. Obverse as last, but a different die. R. Abbreviated history. In center a funeral urn. Silver. Small hole at top, as usual. Extremely fine. Very rare. 19. There being several varieties of this medal, I will endeavor to mark the easily noticed varieties, as shown by the following: Obverse, two berries almost directly beneath N of IN and the shoulder is rather far from the leaf. R. No period after s in U s and 89 clear of base on which urn rests.

C .50 692 No. 166 Funeral medal. Obv. as last. R. s of U s farther from top of urn and 9 touches corner of platform. Pewter. Holed. Good. Rare. 19.

C 2 693 No. 166 Funeral medal. Obverse differs from last—two berries, one points to right arm of N, the other to field to right of N, a leaf nearly touches the shoulder. R. As last. Silver. Holed at top. Very good. Rare. 19.

L 1 694 No. 166 Funeral medal. As last. Pewter. Fine, but slight edge dents. Rare. 19.

C 4. 695 No. 166 Funeral medal. Obverse as first, No. 166. R. Period after s in U s., and the 9 merges into the platform. Silver. Holed. Uncirculated. Remarkably fine example. Very rare. 19.

cont? 1.2 696 No. 166 Funeral medal. As last. Pewter. Holed. Ex. fine. Rare. 19.

Hilm. 1.—697 Nos. 170, 171, 172 Season medals. Indian Peace Medals. Perfectly made copper, silver plated *electrotypes*, in appearance equaling the originals. The three designs. Perfect. 30. 3 pcs.

Im .91 698 No. 175 Valley Forge. Equestrian fig. R. WASHINGTON'S HEAD QUARTERS VALLEY FORGE. Gilt. Bronze. Both unknown to Baker. 20. 2 pcs.

Imy   . 5̃0 699 No. 175 As last. Brass. 20.

  6̃0 700 No. 178 Tappan. Obv. as last. R. WASHINGTON'S HEAD QUARTERS
     AT TAPPAN. Gilt. Bronze. Brass. 20.   3 pcs.

Rikule .2̃5 701 No. 180 Headquarters Tappan. Head r. R. View of house. Wm.
     Very fine. 22.

. *Milm* .40 702 No. 181 Newburg. Obv. as No. 178. R. THE OLD HASBROOK HOUSE.
     NEWBURG, N. Y. Bronze. 20.

Imy 1.0 703 Nos. 184 to 192 Headquarters. Lovett's Series. Bust left, border,
     shields and spears. R. Views of Headquarters. Silver. Very
     rare. 18.   10 pcs.

C? .25 704 Nos. 184 to 192 As last. Copper. Proofs. Lacks No. 4. 9 pcs.

C 2— 705 Nos. 184, 194 The obverse dies of these two numbers struck to-
     gether. Copper. Not in Baker. Unique? 18.

C.' 40 706 No. 194 Headquarters. Lovett's Series 1 to 10. Bust of Wash-
     ington left, border of semicircles and stars. R. View of head-
     quarters. Copper. Rare. 18.   10 pcs.

1.lfc 2.70 707 No. 196 Washington. Lafayette. Kosciusko. Heads accolated to
     l. TO THE HEROES OF LIBERTY THE FRIENDS OF THE PEOPLES
     INDEPENDENCE. R. Three wreaths, above, history of each of
     above. A splendid medal by Rogat. Bronze. Rare. 32.

Wilsn 3.25 708 No. 197 Washington-Lafayette. Heads vis-a-vis, by Wright &
     Bale. R. PAR NOBILE FRATRUM in wreath. Silver. Rare. 17.

⊏ 2— 709 No. 197 As last. *Nickel,* a metal not given by Baker. Ex. rare.
     17.

Acay .60 710 No. 197 As last. Copper. Scarce. 17.

Mulyfad. 85 711 No. 198 Washington-Lafayette. 1824. Head on either side. Sil-
     ver. With struck loop on edge. Very fine. Rare. 9.

Imy .40 712 No. 200 Washington-Lafayette. Busts on either side. Wood's
     Series. Silver. Copper (unknown to Baker). Bronze. 20.
     3 pcs.

Mlm .— 713 No. 201 Washington-Franklin, by Bale. Bust on either side. Sil-
     ver. Tin. Copper. Scarce. 13.   3 pcs.

⊏. 2— 714 No. 202 Washington-Franklin. Busts vis-a-vis, by Bale. R.
     PAR NOBILE FRATRUM. Silver. Scarce. 17.

Wlsn 1.10 715 No. 202 As last. Brass. Unknown to Baker. Very rare. 17.

C.' 5̃0 716 No. 202 As last. Copper. Scarce. 17.

Q 70 717 No. 205 Washington-Franklin. Busts on either side. Copper.
     Rare. 18.

Im-y .6̃t 718 No. 205 Same. Bronze, not given by Baker. 18.

719 No. 208 George and Martha Washington. Busts on either side.
　　Brass. Nickel. Copper. Tin. 13.　　　　　　　　5 pcs.
720 No. 211 Washington-Webster. Bust on either side. Wm. 18.
721 No. 214 Washington-Everett. Busts on either side. Bronze.
　　Wm. 20.　　　　　　　　　　　　　　　　　　2 pcs.
722 No. 220 Washington-Forrest. Busts on either side. Wm. 18.
723 No. 221a Eight Presidents. Busts of the first eight Presidents.
　　Without name of the engraver. R. Names of the Presidents.
　　Bronze. Rare. 29.
724 No. 221a Same. Tin. Rare. 29.
725 No. 222 Washington-Jefferson. Busts on either side, by Bolen.
　　Tin. Holed. 16.
726 No. 223 Washington-Jackson. Busts on either side. Silver.
　　Bronze. 12.　　　　　　　　　　　　　　　　2 pcs.
727 No. 223a Washington-Jackson. No P on bust. Border of slanting
　　lines on obv. Otherwise as last. Wm. Unknown to Baker. 12.
728 No. 224 Washington-Jackson. Small bust of Washington. Sil-
　　ver. 12.
729 No. 225 Washington-Jackson. Equestrian figures. Brass. Un-
　　known to Baker. Very rare. 18.
730 No. 225 Same as last. Tin. Unknown to Baker. Very rare. 18.
731 No. 225 As last. Copper. 18.
732 No. 240 Bust r. FIRST IN WAR etc. R. REVERSE LINCOLN. Bust of
　　Lincoln l. Tin. 18. Rare, and a remarkable production, stat-
　　ing that Lincoln was not first in war, peace or the hearts of his
　　countrymen.
733 No. 245a Washington-Lincoln. On bust of LINCOLN *Paquet.* Sil-
　　ver. Very rare. 12.
733a No. 245b Washington-Lincoln. No initial on either bust. Not
　　in Baker. Silver. Very rare. 12.
734 No. 246 Washington-Lincoln. Silver. Bronze. 12.　　2 pcs.
735 No. 251 Washington-Grant. Busts on either side. Copper. Tin.
　　18.　　　　　　　　　　　　　　　　　　　　2 pcs.
736 No. 252 Washington-Grant. Silver. 12.
737 No. 252a Washington-Grant. On bust of Grant W B (Wm. Bar-
　　ber). Bronze. Not in Baker. 12.
738 No. 256 Washington. PATER PATRIÆ. Bust. R. Grant. GENERAL
　　U. S. GRANT. Brass. Copper. Only 10 made of each. Very
　　rare. 13.　　　　　　　　　　　　　　　　　2 pcs.
739 No. 257 Letter to Hamilton. Bust l., by *Bolen.* R. "I HOPE THAT

LIBERAL ALLOWANCES WILL BE MADE, FOR THE POLITICAL OPINIONS OF EACH OTHER," etc. Bronze. Extremely rare, as only 10 were struck. 36.

740 No. 257 As last. Tin. Only 14 struck. Very rare. 36.

741 No. 258 GEORGE WASHINGTON. Bust l., by *Bolen*. R. AVOID THE EXTREMES OF PARTY SPIRIT Copper. Rare. 18.

742 No. 259 Bust r., by *Bolen*. R. THE UNION IS THE MAIN PROP OF OUR LIBERTY. Bronze. Copper. Tin. Rare. 16.   3 pcs.

743 No. 259 As last. Brass. Unknown to Baker.

744 No. 261 Bust r. R. "MAY OUR COUNTRY NEVER WANT PROPS, TO SUPPORT THE GLORIOUS FABRIC" G. W. 1786. Border of rays and stars. Copper. Rare. 18.

745 No. 261a Busts of Washington on either side. Copper. Proof. Very rare. 18.

746 No. 265 Success to U. S. Fine bust in costume r. GEORGE WASHINGTON. R. SUCCESS TO THE UNITED STATES Eye in a glory of rays and 15 stars. Edge engrailed. Perfect die. Brass, gold plated before striking. Proof. Believed to be the only example known in this superb condition. *Plate*. 16.

747 No. 265 Success to U. S. As last, but die cracked across. Edge plain. Brass. Vg. Unknown to Baker with plain edge.

748 No. 266 Success to U. S. Smaller and better formed face than on last. Good. Brass. 16.

749 No. 267 Success to U. S. Small-size, otherwise as last. Nick on edge. Brass. Very fine. Rare. 12.

750 No. 268 GEORGE WASHINGTON. Bust r. R. PRO PATRIA. Copper. 20.

751 No. 268 Same as last, but tin. Unknown to Baker. 20.

752 No. 268 Same obverse. Blank rev. Unknown to Baker. Copper. 20.

753 No. 271 Bust l. Ornamental border. R. PRO PATRIA etc. Brass. Bronze. 13.   2 pcs.

754 No. 272 THE FATHER OF OUR COUNTRY. Bust in civil dress, three-quarter face left. R. LIBERTY AND INDEPENDENCE Liberty seated, holding a cup to an eagle. In her left she holds a Liberty staff, and under her elbow is a U. S. shield; ship and sea in distance. Tin. Holed at top, as usual. Extremely fine, and very rare. 21.

755 No. 275 Bust l., border of stars and semicircle. R. UNITED STATES OF AMERICA * LIBERTY, etc. Liberty cap in rays. Brass. Rare. 18.

Invy / 25 756 No. 275 As last, but tin, a metal not given by Baker. Very rare. 18.

· . 141 757 No. 279 Mint Allegiance, 1861. Bust r. Silver. Thick planchet. 19.

Walker 38 758 No. 279 Same. Silver. Thin planchet. 19.

LF .50 759 No. 279 Same. Bronze. Thick planchet. 19.

○ .87 760 No. 279a Obverse as last. R. Wreath, blank. Silver. Very rare. 19.

C. . 40 761 No. 279a Same as last. Bronze. Very rare. 19.

C 10 762 No. 280 Bust r. FATHER OF HIS COUNTRY. R. Arms. Brass. Struck loop. 14.

Invy . 55 763 No. 281 Bust ¾ l. R. Trophy, 1864. Tin. Thick planchet. R. Struck to one side slightly. Very rare. 12.

Nelson 175 764 No. 282 Figure of Washington standing front face with scroll and sword in his hands. THE FOUNDER OF OUR UNION 1776, R. A DECISIVE WAR ONLY—CAN RESTORE PEACE AND PROSPERITY 1861. Die loop at top. Tin. Very rare, and a most curious medal. 16.

Invy 40 765 No. 284 GEORGE WASHINGTON Draped bust r. R. FAMILY ARMS OF GEORGE WASHINGTON. Copper. Rare. 18.

(· 4. 766 No. 288 Masonic. G. WASHINGTON PRESIDENT. 1797 Bust in costume l. Rope border. R. Blank (usually with Masonic rev.). Hole over head. Copper, silvered. Very good. Unique.

·. .20 767 No. 287 Fine bust l. GEORGE WASHINGTON 1732-1799. R. His book plate. Wm. 21.

Invy .50 768 No. 292 Masonic. Marvin 267. Bust l. R. Cherry tree scene. MAGNA EST VERITAS ET PRÆVALEBIT I CANNOT TELL A LIE 1876. Bronze. 32.

Invy . 40 769 No. 292 Same. Tin. Scarce. 32.

·. .40 770 No. 305 Masonic. Marvin 326. Bust r. R. Keystone and emblems. Brass. Rare. 6.

Invy .30 771 No. 305a Same obverse. R. Blank. Silver. Brass. Copper. Rare. 6.   3 pcs.

Henry .25 772 No. 304 Masonic. Marvin 307. SOLOMON'S LODGE PO'KEEPSIE N. Y. Bust. Brass. Copper. Tin. 22.   3 pcs.

Henry .50 773 No. 315 Statue, Richmond. GEORGE WASHINGTON. Bust r. R. View of statue. Copper. Rare. 18.

Wilson / 72 774 No. 317 Statue, N. Y. Medallion, head of Washington r., eagle above, scrolls at sides, trophy below. R. Statue, Union Square MDCCCLXI. Bronze. 32.

775 No. 317   As last. Tin. 32.

776 No. 318   Statue. Bust r. R. Washington statue, N. Y. Copper. Rare. 18.

777 No. 320   National Monument. Bust r. THE FATHER OF HIS COUN-TRY BORN FEB. 22. 1732. R. NATIONAL MONUMENT JULY 4 1848. Holed, as always. Tin. Proof, remarkably fine for this medal. 25.

778 No. 321   National Monument. *FIRST IN WAR AND IN PEACE * LAST IN SECURING—over to rev.—A MONUMENT etc. Uncompleted monument. Silver. Rare. 25.

779 No. 321   As last, thick planchet. 25.

780 No. 321   As last. Bronze, thin planchet. Tin. 25.   2 pcs.

781 No. 322   Similar to last, but the monument lined off as if blocks of stone. Brass. Bronze. Tin. 25.   3 pcs.

782 No. 323   Baltimore Mon. Bust l. R. View of MONUMENT AT BAL-TIMORE. Silver. Rare. 18.

783 No. 323   As last. Brass. Nickel. Copper (thin and thick plan-chets). Tin. Scarce. 13.   5 pcs.

784 No. 324   Balto. Bust. R. NORTH POINT AND FORT MCHENRY, SEPT. 12' & 13' 1814. Copper. Tin. 20.   2 pcs.

785 No. 325   Cabinet. Bust r. R. A MEMORIAL OF THE WASHINGTON CABINET MAY 1859. Silver. Bronze. Copper. (Last not men-tioned by Baker.) 14.   3 pcs.

786 No. 326   Cabinet. Bust r., by *Paquet.* R. WASHINGTON CABINET OF MEDALS, U.S. MINT INAUGURATED FEB. 22 1860. View of Cabinet. Silver. 38.

787 No. 326   As last. Bronze. 38.

788 No. 328   WASHINGTON TEMPERANCE SOCIETY Bust r. R. TEMPER-ANCE DECLARATION . etc. Tin. 26.

789 No. 329   Same obverse. R. HOUSE OF TEMPERANCE View of a happy family. Bronze. Tin. 26.   2 pcs.

790 No. 330   WASHINGTON TEMPERANCE SOC. Head r. R. UNITED WE STAND DIVIDED WE FALL. Brass. Very rare. 14.

791 No. 331   Same obv. R. Fountain. Holed. Tin. Rare. 14.

792 No. 332   WASHINGTON TEMPERANCE BENEVOLENT SOCIETY. Head r., by *Bale,* name BALE below wreath. R. WE SERVE THE TYRANT ALCOHOL NO LONGER. Silver. Rare. 13.

793 No. 332   Same. Bronze. Holed at top. Rare. 13.

794 No. 333   Similar. BALE under head. Silver. Holed at top. Very rare. 13.

! ƒ⁻ .⁴ᵗ 795 No. 334 WASHINGTON UNITED STATES OF AMERICA. Bust l. R. TO THE CAUSE OF TEMPERANCE TEN DOLLARS TO KING ALCOHOL NOT ONE CENT. Brass. Fine. 15.

.2⟨⁻ 796 No. 335 Temperance. Undraped bust r., in center of a seven-pointed star HONOR TEMPERANCE Below head S. SCHMIDT F. F below S. SCHMIDT. R. IN HOC SIGNO VINCES within which is a laurel wreath of two branches, crossed and tied with a ribbon, between and below which are the initials of the engraver, S. Schmidt, the whole of this device enclosed by a seven-pointed star. Silver. Believed to be unique. Baker never saw one, and the description here given shows he lacked several things that would have been apparent to him had he seen it. 12.

Inbacc /⁵ 797 No. 336 O. U. A. M. Bust r. R. HONESTY INDUSTRY AND SOBRIETY O. U. A. M. Compasses, etc. Gilt. Silvered. Copper. 16. 3 pcs.

l. F. *ƭₜ* 798 No. 339 LANCASTER CO. AGRICULTURAL SOCIETY 1858 THE FARMER OF MOUNT VERNON. Fine head r. R. AWARDED TO— Bronze. 28.

√ₙₗʲ . ᵧₜ 799 No. 339 As last. The edge neatly milled. Copper. 28.

800 No. 340 Bust l. THE PATTERN OF PATRIOTISM, INDUSTRY AND PROGRESS. R. UNION AGRICULTURAL SOC: OF RIDGEWAY & SHELBY. N. Y. In wreath ORGANIZED JULY 17TH. 1858. Silver. Very rare. 18.

·⁹!ʲ(·m 3 ₂ᵣ⁵ 801 No. 346 West Point. UNITED STATES MILITARY ACADEMY. Bust l. R. ACADEMIC MERIT. Bronze. Very rare. 17.

⁻ᶻᴵˢ˙〉 2 2⁵ 802 No. 347 Assay, 1876. Head r. R. YEAR ONE HUNDRED OF AMERICAN INDEPENDENCE 1776 ANNUAL ASSAY 1876. Bronze. Very rare. 21.

⟍⟍⁚ .⁵⁻ 803 No. 350 Undraped bust to r., around GEORGE WASHINGTON BORN 1732 DIED 1799. Below DAVIS BIRM. Above eagle FIRST IN WAR FIRST IN PEACE AND FIRST IN THE HEARTS OF HIS COUNTRYMEN. Stars at sides. R. Interior of a library, girl writing, SCIENTIA MORES EMOLLIT. Tin. Holed at top, as usual. Proof, and the finest example of this very rare medal which I have seen. 32.

Ｃ 4 804 No. 352 GEORGE WASHINGTON, THE CINCINNATUS OF AMERICA B. 1732 D. 1799 Bust l. R. INDUSTRY PRODUCES WEALTH. Tin. 20.

≠ℾↄ 5 25 805 No. 355 GEORGE WASHINGTON, FIRST PRESIDENT OF THE U. S. A. MDCCLXXXIX Undraped bust facing right. R. AWARDED TO Wreath of oak and olive branch tied by a bow, center blank. Scroll border on obverse, and dotted border on reverse, a fact not mentioned by Baker, and it is possible he never saw the

example he speaks of. Tin. Probably unique, as Baker knew of only the Edwards Collection specimen, and I have never met with another; so this is probably that example. 32.

806 No. 356 WASHINGTON TEMPERANCE SOCIETY Bust r. R. AWARDED TO. Tin. 26.

807 No. 357 GEORGE WASHINGTON . THE GREAT AND GOOD. Undraped bust left, on edge of which A C M. F (A. C. Morin). R. Wreath, composed of two cornucopiæ, completed at the top by branches of laurel and oak. Lead, surface lightly corroded. *Original,* and the only original impression that has come under my notice. Judging from the condition of the surface it is probable this medal was made about 1850, as Morin cut the dies for No. 361. 30.

808 No. 357 Same. Restrike. Tin. 30.

809 No. 358 GEORGIO WASHINGTON Bust r., by Lauer. R. Wreath. Brass. Dented. Good. Very rare. 358.

810 No. 358a Same obv. R. NUENBEERGE SPIE(L) & RECHEN PENNIG. German eagle. Holed over head. Brass. Unknown to Baker. 30.

811 No. 358b Obverse as last, reduced. R. SPIEL MARKE in wreath. Brass. Very fine. Unknown to Baker. 13.

812 No. 358c Obverse as last. R. German eagle. Brass. Very fine. Unknown to Baker. 13.

813 No. 361 Fair, N. Y. Bust l., by Morin. R. View of the Crystal Palace, N. Y., 1853. Bronze. Scarce. 32.

814 No. 361 As last. Tin. 32.

815 No. 362 Sanitary Fair, N. Y., 1864. Bust r. Brass. Nickel. Copper. Rare. 15.   3 pcs.

816 No. 362 As last. Struck on a large planchet. Lead. Double struck. Poor. Unique.

817 No. 363 Sanitary Fair, Philadelphia, 1864. Bust r. Silver. Copper. Gilt. Pure nickel. Copper-nickel. The last two unknown to Baker! 11.   5 pcs.

818 No. 364 Sanitary Fair, Nantucket, Mass., 1864. Bust as last. Copper. Rare. 15.

819 No. 365 Soldiers' Fair, Springfield, 1864. Bust l., by J. A. Bolen. Tin. Scarce. 18.

820 No. 369 Norwalk Memorial, 1869. Bust in uniform r. R. BOUGHT OF THE NORWAKE INDIANS etc. Silver. C, No. 1 (punched in with a die near bottom). 24.

821 No. 369 As last, but without the C, No. 1. Copper. Tin. 24.
2 pcs.

822 No. 371 Brooklyn S. S., 1876. Bust l. Copper. Wm. 20. 2 pcs.

823 Nos. 372, 373 Jersey City S. S. Bust l. Tin. Holed. 18.   2 pcs.

824 No. 373 Jersey City S. S. Bust l. THE PATTERN OF PATRIOTISM, INDUSTRY AND PROGRESS. R. As last. Silver. Rare. 18.

825 No. 373 As last. Bronze. Rare. 18.

826 No. 375 Bethany S. S., Phil. Bust r. R. 25th Anni. Tin. 22.

827 No. 380 First eight Presidents. Busts. R. Buchanan and Breck-inridge made by a buck leaping to r., below a cannon AND BRECK-INRIDGE Between the buck and cannon 1856, and around the buck thirty-two stars. Bronze. Rare. 29.

828 No. 382 First eight Presidents, as last. R. THE UNION MUST AND SHALL BE PRESERVED JACKSON. UNITED WE STAND DIVIDED WE FALL 1856. Bronze. Rare. 29.

829 No. 384 Lincoln. Bust of Washington l. REPRESENTED BY WM. LEGGETT BRAMHALL. R. ABRA - HAM LIN - COLN HONEST ABE OF THE WEST. Copper. Rare. 12.

830 No. 384 Lincoln. As last. Copper-nickel. Rare. 12.

831 No. 385 Calendar. Bust r., by True. Corroded, and central disc gone from reverse. Rare. Brass. 23.

832 No. 386 Calendar. Full length of Washington, standing on a battlefield, orderly with horse in background. R. Movable calendar. Worn. Good. Rare.

833 No. 387 Calendar. Equestrian fig. R. Movable calendar. Bright. 23.

834 No. 388 Bust r., border of cavalry and infantry. R. Signing of the Declaration of Independence, 1776. Heads facing. Tin. Very rare. 26.

835 No. 389 As last, but heads in *profile*. Bronze. Tin. 26. 2 pcs.

836 No. 391 Obv. as last. R. Signature of *John Hancock*. Tin. 26.

837 No. 392 Bust r. R. Independence Hall. Copper (badly scratched). Tin. 24. 2 pcs.

838 No. 395 Bust r. R. Independence Hall. Copper. Brass (un-known to Baker). 11. 2 pcs.

839 No. 396a Obv. as 155, but no initial. R. As 396. Copper. Tin. 11. 2 pcs.

840 No. 400 Bust. R. Liberty bell. Copper, holed. No. 401 similar. Silver. Oroide. 11. 3 pcs.

841 No. 402 Bust r. R. Bell. Oroide. Copper. Tin. No. 403 similar. Silver (holed), unknown to Baker. Oroide. Copper.
Tin (damaged). 11.   7 pcs.

842 No. 404 Bust r., 1776. R. AMERICAN COLONIES. 1776. View inside a fort. Bronze. 24.

843 No. 407 GEORGE WASHINGTON 1876 Bust l. R. IN MEMORY OF THE
CENTENARY Shield. Brass. Holed. Good. Very rare. 16.

844 No. 409 Washington and Grant at either side of U. S. arms. R.
DEDICATED TO etc. Tin. Ring. 26.

845 No. 411 Bust in costume l. TO AID 'ST. JOHN'S—GUILD'—FLOATING
HOSPITAL. (Wood's Series, "C" NO. 5.) R. CENTENNIAL RECEP-
TION, BALL & TEAPARTY FEBY 22ND 1876. ACADEMY OF MUSIC,
"N. Y." Bust of Martha Washington l. Silver. This one
struck before the die broke, and nearly all showed the crack in
the die. Excessively rare, only 10 struck. 18.

846 No. 411 As last. Showing the crack in die. Only 10 struck in
any metal or condition. Silver. Excessively rare. 18.

847 No. 411 As last. Tin. Only 10 struck from die. Excessively
rare. 18.

848 No. 412 Bust r., undraped, otherwise similar to last. Silver.
Copper. Tin. Rare. 18.   3 pcs.

849 No. 413 Bust r. R. Bust Martha Washington, 1876. Tin. Rare.
18.

850 No. 414 Bust l. FATHER OF OUR COUNTRY. R. As last. Brass.
Copper. Very rare, 10 struck. 18.   2 pcs.

851 No. 415 Same bust as last. R. 1876 DEDICATED TO THE CHILDREN
OF AMERICA. Bronze. Copper. Tin. 21.   3 pcs.

852 No. 416 Same obverse. R. DELPHOS UNION SCHOOL JULY 4, 1876,
etc. Tin. 21.

853 No. 417a Mule. Two obverse dies combined, B 240 and 417. Tin.
Rare. 18.

854 No. 417b Mule. Obverse as B 240. R. B 417. Tin. Not in
Baker. 18.

855 No. 418 Bust l. R. THE BOYS & GIRLS OF AMERICA 1876. Copper.
Tin. Rare. 18.   2 pcs.

856 No. 421 Cape May. Bust r. R. Stockton Hotel, etc., 1877. Copper. Oroide. Tin. 11.   3 pcs.

857 No. 425 Union for Ever. Bust r. R. International Exhibition at
Philadelphia, 1876 UNION FOR EVER. Silver. Unknown to
Baker. 25.

858 No. 425 As last. Brass. Bronze. Tin. 25.   3 pcs.

859 Nos. 426, 427 Centennial, 1876. Medallion head, cupids, eagle, etc. R. Group of beautiful females. Tin. 33. Different. 2 pcs.

860 No. 427 Centennial, 1876. As last, but with LET US HAVE PEACE. Silver. Very rare in this metal.

861 No. 428 Centennial, 1876. Bust l. A CENTURY ADDS LUSTRE TO HIS NAME. R. Two females. SEE HOW WE PROSPER. Bronze. Tin. 28.   2 pcs.

862 No. 429 Centennial, 1876. Half length, in civil dress r. 1776-1876 etc. R. Memorial Hall. Tin. Holed. Very rare. 27.

863 No. 430 Centennial, 1876. UNITED STATES OF AMERICA 1776. Bust l. R. CENTENNIAL MEMORIAL BUILDING, PHILADELPHIA, 1876, between this last word and view of Memorial Hall is COPYRIGHT SECURED which Baker omits, as he probably never saw this medal. Brass. Obv. vg. R. Fair. Holed. Probably unique, as this is the Wood specimen which Baker refers to. 23.

864 No. 432a *Centennial*, 1876. Bust ¾ f. r. GEORGE WASHINGTON ***1776*** R. EXHIBITION PHILADELPHIA CENTENNIAL 1876. Memorial Hall. Brass. Holed. Extremely rare. 17.

865 No. 435 7th Regt. N. Y. to Centennial E'xh. 1876. Bust of Washington on a pedestal. Vf. Tin. 28.

866 No. 436 Washington Elm, Cambridge. Bust r. R. Elm. Bronze. Tin. 25.   2 pcs.

867 No. 437 Mule. 1775-1875. Head of Washington either side. Also obv. of B 240 and 436 combined. Copper. Rare. 18. 2 pcs.

868 No. 438 Assumed Command, 1775. Bust in egg-shaped field. R. Crossed swords, etc. Silver. Gold plated. Bronze. Tin (scratch). Rare. 18.

869 Nos. 440 to 447 Battles of Rev. Bust r. Bronze. 21.   8 pcs.

870 Nos. 440 to 447 As last. Tin. 21.   8 pcs.

871 No. 449 Valley Forge, 1778-1878. Bust r. Bronze. 26.

872 No. 451 Yorktown, 1781-1881. Bust ¾ l. Bronze. Tin. 21.   2 pcs.

873 No. 452 Yorktown, 1781-1881. Busts accolated of Washington and Lafayette r. R. Surrender. Bronze. 32.

874 No. 452 Yorktown. Same. Copper. Unknown to Baker. 32.

875 No. 452 Yorktown. Tin. Slightly hairmarked. 32.

876 No. 453 Yorktown. Busts of Washington, De Grasse, Lafayette. Tin. 21.

877 No. 454 Yorktown. Busts of Washington, Lafayette, De Grasse, Rochambeau. R. PRESENTED BY THE STATE OF PENNSYLVANIA etc. Tin. Rare. 21.

878 No. 455 Newburgh, N. Y. Headquarters. Bust. Tin. Holed. 20.

879 No. 456 Newburg. Same head, no ins. R. Headquarters. Bronze. Tin. 17.   2 pcs.

880 No. 456a Newburgh. Head as last, but with 35 stars. R. Headquarters, as last. Bronze. Unknown to Baker. 17.

881 No. 458 New York, Evacuation. Busts of Washington, Knox, Clinton. Bronze. Tin (holed). 22.   2 pcs.

882 No. 458a Same event. Bust in high relief l. Tin. 28.

883 No. 460 Same event. Bust r. Bronze. Tin. 20.   2 pcs.

884 No. 461 Same event. Bust r. Tin. 20.

885 No. 462 Same event. Washington horseback. Holed. Tin. 25.

886 No. 463 Same event. Bust r. Silver. Bronze. Gilt. 10. 3 pcs.

887 No. 463a Same obverse. R. Lord's Prayer. B 464 holed, and two similar. R. Bell. R. Lord's Prayer. Last two not in Baker. Gilt.   4 pcs.

WASHINGTON TOKENS AND STORE CARDS.

888 Rebellion Period 1863. All with Washington. Baker, Nos. 466, 469, 471, 473 (perfect and broken dies), 476, 478, 480, 485, 486, 490, 493, 494, 500, 523 (2 metals), 532 (perfect and broken dies), 533 (dent), 535, 537, 543, 552, 554, 558, 562, 566, 567a, 587. Good to unc.   28 pcs.

889 No. 469 Small head, by Wright and Bale r. 399 B'WAY N. Y. 1863. R. I O . U. 1 CENT. Silver. Very rare.

890 No. 473 Head and flags, 1863. R. EXCHANGE. Brass. Unknown to Baker.

891 No. 489 Same obv. as 469. R. UNITED COUNTRY. Silver. Very rare.

892 No. 489 As last. Tin. Unknown to Baker. Very rare.

893 No. 491 Bust r. 13 stars. R. NO COMPROMISE WITH TRAITORS. Copper-nickel. Unknown to Baker.

894 No. 501 Bust r. 13 stars. 1863. R. Shield, flags, cap, stars, etc. Nickel. Unknown to Baker.

895 No. 505 Head of Washington l. 13 stars. 1872. R. CALIFORNIA CHARM In center ½ GOLD. Octagon. Gold. Unc. Rare.

896 No. 506 Abrahams, Mo. Head r. R. WESTON MO. Brass. Unusually fine.

897 No. 507 Abrahams. Same obv. R. INDEPENDENCE MO. Nicks on edge. Brass. Rare.

898 No. 512 Bale & Smith, N. Y. GEN^L GEORGE WASHINGTON The General mounted to r., below B & S N. Y R. Card of Bale & Smith. Copper. Very fine. Extremely rare.

899 No. 517 (2 metals), 520, 521, 522 (4 metals). Brimelow. 8 pcs.

900 No. 524 Same obv. as last. R. Centennial Adv. Co. Copper. Tin. Rare. 2 pcs.

901 No. 526 Chamberlaine. THE FATHER OF OUR COUNTRY Bust l., by Bolen. R. CHAMBERLAINE NORFOLK. Copper. Rare.

902 No. 527 Cogan. No. 530 Dickeson. Copper. Tin. 4 pcs.

903 No. 529 Curtis. Bust l. "THE CINCINNATUS OF AMERICA" etc. R. "SAVE MY COUNTRY HEAVEN" Card of John K. Curtis, N. Y. Copper. Rare.

904 No. 531 Doll. Bust ¾ f. left. Geo. Doll & Co., Phil. Brass.

905 No. 536 Bust as on No. 522. R. J. Henry Gercke, Phila. Copper. Rare.

906 No. 537 Gerdts. Bust r. 1863. Silver. Rare.

907 No. 538 Greaves. Exported solely by W. Greaves & Sons Sheaf Works. Undraped head of Washington r. R. Blank. Copper. Extremely rare.

908 No. 541 Same obv. as 526. R. Apollo Gardens 576 Washington St. Good for 6 cents Hess & Speidel. Copper. Only 10 struck. Extremely rare.

909 No. 542 Hill. Bust l. R. Card of E. Hill, coin dealer. 1860. Copper. Tin. 2 pcs.

910 No. 544 Idler. Obv. copy of Washington ½ dollar. R. Card of Wm. Idler, coin dealer, Phil., 1860. Brass.

911 No. 545 Idler. Bust r. R. Card. Silver. Nickel. Brass. Copper.

912 No. 546 Ivins. Bust r. R. Shield and card. Silver. Nickel. Bronze. Brass. Copper. Tin. Rare set. 6 pcs.

913 No. 556 R. Lovett, Jr. Washington on battlefield. R. Card. Brass. Copper. 2 pcs.

914 No. 557 Magnus. N. Y. Bust r. 100 ENTITLE TO A $2.00 VIEW OF NEW YORK CITY. Brass.

915 No. 559 Mason. Phil. Bust ¾ l. R. Card of Mason & Co., Phil., 1870. Tin. Rare.

916 No. 560   Merriam. Boston. Head r. R. Card of. Brass. Copper. Tin. Scarce.   3 pcs.
917 No. 562   Monk. N. Y. Small head, by Wright & Bale. 1863. Brass. Copper.   2 pcs.
918 No. 568   Robbins, Royce & Hard. N. Y. Bust l. Silver. Copper-nickel. Copper. Tin. Scarce, and the silver one especially so.
                                                                4 pcs.
919 No. 570   Sage & Co. N. Y. Bust right. Tin. Rare.
920 Nos. 571, 572   Sage & Co. N. Y. Bust left. Brass. Copper. Tin. No. 572 copper.   4 pcs.
921 No. 573   Sampson. N. Y. Bust r., border of infantry and cavalry. Silver. Brass. Copper. Tin. Rare set.   4 pcs.
922 No. 76 R. of 574   Stoner & Shroyer. Adamsville, O. Bust l. Same obv. as B, No. 559. Tin. Unknown to Baker.
923 No. 576   Strassburger & Nuhn. New York. Bust l. Plated. Brass.   2 pcs.
924 No. 577   Taylor. Phila. 1862. Bust l. No. 580. Head r. Brass. Copper.   2 pcs.
925 No. 583   Warner. Phila. Bust r. R's. Grant (3), McClellan (6), Seymour (3), Lyle (2), Victoria and Albert (3), Monitor (3) Cedar Mountain (3), Surrender of Lee (2), Washington on clouds (3), Constitution (1). Brass. Copper. Tin. Very rare set of Mules. 18.   35 pcs.
926 No. 590   Wolfe, Spies & Clark. N. Y. Undraped bust of Washington right. R. Bust in octagonal frame of PRESIDENT Jackson. Brass. Very good. Hole near edge broken out, and cracked from this to center. Brass. Very rare.
927 No. 591   Same as last. R. NEW YORK GRAND CANAL OPENED 1(82)3. Holed over head. Brass. Very good. Very rare.
928 No. 594   Wright & Bale. N. Y. Small bust in wreath. R. Card of W. & B. Ex. fine. Very rare.
929 Nos. 596, 597, 598, 600, 601, 603, 605 to 609, 629   Spiel marks. Busts. Brass. Bright.   12 pcs.
930 Nos. 610, 611, 613   State arms of N. Y., Pa., Ill. Washington standing, orderly with horse. Brass. Ex. fine. Rare. 23.   3 pcs.
931 No. 614   New York. Bust, with long neck r. GEORGE WASHINGTON etc. R. Arms of N. Y. Tin. Holed, as usual. Rare. 16.
932 No. 616   Bust r. SECURITY. R. Obverse of the copy of Sommers Island shilling. Hog to l. Copper. Rare. Mule. 20.

933 No. 617 Conn. New Haven Numismatic So. Fac similies of Colonial coins grouped around obverse of 1791 Washington cent. R. NEW HAVEN NUMISMATIC SOCIETY FOUNDED NOV. 25TH 1862. Tin. Very rare. 28.

934 No. 620 Soldier's identification medal. Bust r. UNION R. With CO. REG etc. Another blank, others dif. obv. R. Stamped with soldier's name, reg. and place; latter worn, and lead. 20.
4 pcs.

935 No. 630 St. Patrick's Cathedral. Bust r. R. Edifice. Copper. Tin. 18.   2 pcs.

936 No. 633 Cupid and dolphin. Bust l. PATRIÆ PATER 1732. R. Cupid on a dolphin. 1860. Copper. Brass. Tin. Rare. 18.
3 pcs.

937 Nos. 635, 636 Similar obv. to last. R. Witch on broom WE ALL HAVE OUR HOBBIES. R. NOT TRANSFERABLE 1853. Tin. 18. 2 pcs.

938 No. 639 Parsons family. Bust r. R. EDWARD WILLIS PARSONS OF FLUSHING NEW YORK. Copper. Tin. Rare. 18.   2 pcs.

939 No. 641 Sheldon family. Bust r. 100th Anni. Dec'l of Independence. Bust r. R. Family arms. Bronze. Tin. Rare. 25. 2 pcs.

940 No. 642 McPherson. Bust of Washington l. R. Gen. McPherson on horseback. Brass. Copper, latter unknown to Baker. 13.
2 pcs.

941 No. 647 Bust r. R. Twelve stars. Copper. Rare.

942 No. 649 Undraped bust to r., on edge LANDER. High relief, and of fine work. Copper, oval 11 x 14. Extremely rare.

943 No. 651 Bust r. R. Lord's Prayer. Smallest size it has been struck. Gilt. 8.

WASHINGTON INDIAN PEACE MEDALS.

Unknown to Mr. Baker.

944 Presented to Chief Rabbitfoot of the Choctaw tribe about 1840, and worn by him suspended from his neck. GEORGE WASHINGTON, THE FATHER OF OUR COUNTRY * 1789 * Bust in civilian dress ¾ l. R. FRIEN(D)SHIP at top, at bottom THE PIPE OF PEACE At either side six stars. In central depressed field an olive branch wreath, * at top, tied by ribbon; below clasped hands, 1789, crossed tomahawks. Tin. Holed at top, in which is a brass ring bound with raw hide or buckskin. Edge milled. Fine condition. Very rare. 40.

945 GEO. WASHINGTON. PRES U S. Bust in civilian dress to left. R. PEACE AND FRIENDSHIP Clasped hands, crossed tomahawk and pipe of peace. Cast in lead, bronzed. The obverse unknown to me, while the reverse is probably cast from the Peace Medal issued during Pres. Jefferson's administration. Old, and perfect condition. Probably unique. 31½.

946 GEORGE WASHINGTON PRESIDENT OF THE UNITED STATES 1789 Undraped bust r. R. PEACE AND FRIENDSHIP Crossed pipe of peace and tomahawk; below are clasped hands. Silver. Proof. 48.

947 Same as last. Bronze. Proof. 48.

WASHINGTON MEDALS UNKNOWN TO BAKER.

12. 948 GEORGE WASHINGTON Undraped bust facing right, border of 45 dots. R. LIBERTY The rest of circle composed of 13 stars; in center U. S. shield resting on a prostrate British shield; border of dots. Lead. Holed at top. Very fine. Crude work, and probably made by C. Wyllys Betts. The only example that has ever come under my notice. *Plate. 31.*

7.50 949 WASHINGTON . BORN FEB. 22. 1732 Undraped bust facing r. R. THE DEFENDER OF LIBERTY, olive wreath of two branches tied with a ribbon, enclosing U S A. Border of deep serratures. Lead. Very fine. Crude work, and believed to be unique; the only example I have met with. Probably made by C. W. Betts. *Plate. 22.*

Kraft 2.75 950 Undraped bust to left, enclosed by a wreath. This obverse made by casting, and then soldered perfectly to a ½ cent of 1804. The workmanship appears to be of the period of 1804. Very fine. Unique. *Plate. 15.*

Wilson 4.50 951 LADIES LOYAL LEAGUE Maltese cross, with central boss bearing bust of Washington, draped and surrounded by 13 stars, the legend on three of the arms; shield and flags on other. R. Blank. Silver. Struck loop. Said to have been made in Syracuse. Have never seen another. 15.

5. 952 GEORGE WASHINGTON PRESIDENT OF THE U. S. A. Exquisite undraped bust in high relief to left, below bust C. C. WRIGHT. SC: Trial in lead from the die, and believed to be the only impression taken from the die, which was evidently changed to make the next medal. 36.

953 INSCRIBED TO HIS MEMORY BY CHAS . I. BUSHNELL OF NEW YORK This inscription on a raised ribbon or bands, below 1853. Exquisite undraped bust in high relief to left, below C. C. WRIGHT. S C: R. FILL BLESSED SUN WITH LUSTRE BRIGHT, THE 13 STARS YOU BRO^{T.} TO LIGHT. In center head of Washington on a double star with 13 pointed stars of rays; this enclosed by an endless chain of links, each bearing initials of one of the original 13 States, star in center of each ring. Silver. Probably unique, and dies destroyed. *Plate.* 34.

954 Same. Brass. Probably unique. Dies destroyed. 34.

955 Same. Copper. Excessively rare. Dies destroyed. 34.

956 Same. Tin. Excessively rare. Dies destroyed. 34.

957 GEORGE WASHINGTON FIRST PRESIDENT OF THE UNITED STATES INAUGURATED APRIL 30, 1789. Head by Wright, as on last. R. CENTENNIAL OF THE INAUGURATION OF THE FIRST PRESIDENT OF THE UNITED STATES APRIL 30 1889 Outside stars—one for each State. The central disc is plain, the head of Washington having been removed, otherwise as last. This is the only impression taken from the die when it was being altered from that used to strike the four medals next preceding. Lead. Perfect. 34.

958 Same, but with the head of the sun on central disc. This is from the altered die when completed. Tin. 34.

959 GEORGE WASHINGTON. Undraped bust, similar to last, facing left, by C. C. Wright. Baker, No. 100 obverse. R. SI QUÆRIS MONUMENTUM CIRCUMSPICE surrounded by thirteen links forming an endless chain, each enclosing initials of a State. Struck to order of C. I. Bushnell, and believed to be unique. Silver. 18.

960 Same. Brass. Believed to be unique. 18.

961 Same. Copper. Believed to be unique. 18.

962 Same. Tin. Believed to be unique. 18.

963 WASHINGTON. Bare bust facing l., between two laurel branches. Same head as last, and Baker, No. 152. R. Same. Silver. Believed to be unique. 18.

964 Same. Brass. Believed to be unique. 18.

965 Same. Copper. Believed to be unique. 18.

966 Same. Tin. Believed to be unique. 18.

967 Tomb. R. BORN 1732 DIED 1799. B's 124, 143, the reverse dies combined. Copper. Unique? 17.

968 Head, undraped, facing left, field plain. R. Engraved *Franklin*

Fire Co No 12 1792 to 1872 Jacob Albright Silver. Very fine. Unique. Have never seen another impression of this die. Plate. 29.

969 First in War, etc. Bust l. Same obv. as B 292. R. CENTENNIAL EXHIBITION 1876 MEMORIAL HALL - MAIN EXHIBITION BUILDING AGRICULTURAL HALL. Views of the buildings. Tin. Very fine. The only example I have met with. 32.

970 Bust r., by *Barber.* Same die as used on the Assay Medals of 1876, 1878. R. PAID TO HENRY A. MIDDLETON. CHARLESTON S. C. DEC. 29, 1880 BY WM G. LE DUC. U. S. COMMISSIONER OF AGRICUL-TURE AS CONSIDERATION FOR 20 YEARS LEASE OF U. S. EXPERIMEN-TAL TEA FARM. in 12 lines, the second, seventh, eighth, eleventh and twelfth curved. Lead. I believe this to be unique. Plate. 21½.

971 100TH ANNIVERSARY OF THE DECLARATION ETC 1876. Bust l. B No. 292. R. ATTENTION ETC. PRESENTED TO— Tin. Very rare. 22.

972 SONS OF THE REVOLUTION 1883. Undraped bust r., olive branch before. R. Continental soldier, 1775, in background a cannon and mountains. Tin. Oval. Evidently a trial of the die for the centerpiece of their Order badge. Unique. 10 x 15.

973 ORDER OF WASHINGTON. Undraped bust l., within a pearly border. R. ORDER OF WASHINGTON, semi-wreath of two olive branches. Oval. Bronze proof. Extremely rare, and the only one that I have seen. Plate. 20 x 16.

974 1st Regt. N. G. P. 1884. GEORGE WASHINGTON Undraped bust r. R. Insignia. ORGAN^D APRIL 19. 1861 etc. Bronze. Tin. Another obverse without inscription. Tin. 20.　　3 pcs.

975 Blaine and Logan. Busts l. R. BORN IN (bust of Washington) CO PENNA. Brass, silvered. Nick on edge. 16.

976 National Monument. Laureated bust l. R. View of monument. DEDICATED FEB'Y 21. 1885. Tin. Holed. Rare. 20.

977 Same event. Bust in high relief l. Bust r., in wreath. R. Monument. Tin. 28.　　2 pcs.

978 Same event. Bust r., George Washington. Also same head, enclosed by a dotted band. Tin. 21.　　2 pcs.

979 Centl. of the Constitution. 1887. Very beautiful bust in uniform of Washington facing r. R. View of Independence Hall, above heads of Hamilton and Madison. Bronze. Tin. 22.　　2 pcs.

980 Same event. Bare bust r. R. State House. Tin. Bust r. R.
Bell. R. Brooklyn bridge. Brass. Holed. 24. 16. 3 pcs.

981 Undraped bust r. NATIONAL PRIZE DRILL Washington. 1887. R.
SOUVENIR Wreath and stars. Bronze. Rare. 22.

/´ 982 Same obv. R. Capitol. WASHINGTON . D.C 1887. Tin. 22.

983 GEORGE WASHINGTON FIRST PRESIDENT OF THE UNITED STATES OF
AMERICA. Bust ¾ r. in civilian costume, resting upon two
branches laurel and oak, below in field F. KOCH N. Y. R. GENERAL
GEORGE WASHINGTON BORN FEBRUARY 22. 1732 DIED DECEMBER
14, 1799 *Equestrian figure of Washington to left. Tin. Rare.
40.

984 Centennial of the Inauguration. N. Y. 1789. GEORGE WASHING-
TON. * PATER * PATRIÆ * M.D C.C.LXXXIX * Half length of
Washington left; below which PHILIP.MARTINY.MODELER DESIGN
AND COPYRIGHT BY AVGVSTVS SAINT GAVDENS; around border 13
stars, behind bust fasces. R. TO COMMEMORATE THE INAVGVRA-
TION OF GEORGE WASHINGTON AS FIRST PRESIDENT OF THE UNITED
STATES OF AMERICA AT NEW YORK APRIL XXX MDCCLXXXIX. BY
AVTHORITY OF THE COMMITTEE ON CELEBRATION NEW YORK APRIL
XXX MDCCCLXXXIX. Eagle and arms of N. Y., border of stars.
Bronze. Cast, as all were. Rare. 70.

985 Same event. Angel holds two circular medals, on that to right
UNITED STATES OF AMERICA * IN GOD WE TRUST * Undraped bust
of Washington to left. On the other THE CENTENNIAL OF OUR
NATION * CHICAGO COMMEMORATION. In center 1789 1889 Be-
tween these dates a tablet with APRIL 30; lower part of field
U. S. shield, surmounted by an eagle, behind six flags. R.
TO EDWARD F. CRAGEN FROM HIS FRIENDS AND COLABORERS IN REC-
OGNITION OF HIS VALUABLE SERVICES IN ORIGINATING AND PLAN-
NING THE PATRIOTIC OBSERVANCE AT CHICAGO OF THE CENTENNIAL
OF THE NATION'S BIRTH-DAY. Bronze. Extremely rare. I have
never seen a duplicate. 42.

986 Same event. Beautiful figure of Peace, with medallion of WASH-
INGTON in right, and of MIRABEAU in left; in field at sides and
bottom 1776 1789 1889 R. REPUBLIQUES CENTENAIRES PROGRES
LABEUR In center within a design SALUT. TO ALL MEN, OUR
BRETHREN. A TOUS LES OMMES NOS FRERES 1889. At edge GOR-
HAM CO. MFG. U.S.A. Bronze. Very rare. 28.

987 Same event. GEO. WASHINGTON 1789 BENJ HARRISON 1889. Un-

draped accolated heads facing right. R. DENMAN THOMPSONS PLAY *"Two Sisters"* M^CVICKERS THEATRE CHICAGO APRIL 30TH 1889 CENTENNIAL OF INAUGURATION OF GEO. WASHINGTON AS PRESIDENT OF U. S. A. AT NEW YORK. Bronze. Extremely rare. 24.

988 Same event. Bust l., in frame, oak and laurel branches. R. Washington taking the oath. Tin. 32.

989 Same event. GEORGE WASHINGTON. Bust r. R. Equestrian figure of Washington between arms of State and City. Bronze. Tin. 28.   2 pcs.

990 Same event. Busts accolated r. of Washington and Harrison, 1789-1889. R. Tablet. Bronze. Tin. 24.   2 pcs.

991 Same event. GEORGE WASHINGTON 1789. Bare bust r. R. City arms in wreath. Bronze. 22.

992 Same event. Bust of Washington, undraped, to left in center of a star, 13 stars on edge. FIRST IN WAR etc., the design rounded out by rays. Struck loop at top. Lead, bronzed. Very rare. 34.

993 Same event. Bust on shield within a wreath to l. 1789-1889. etc. R. Arms of State. Lead. Crude. Very rare. 21.

994 Same event. Tin medals, different, all having head of Washington. 13 holed, as issued. 1 bronze. 12-32.   18 pcs.

995 Same event. Bust ¾ face left in sunken field. R. Taking the oath. Bronze, scarce in this metal. 24.

996 Same event. Bust r., undraped. R. NEW YORK APRIL 30, 1889. Bronze. 12.

997 Same event. Medallion bust of Washington, 1789. R. Busts of HARRISON MORTON. 1889. *Copper.* Face of Washington not fully struck. Rare. 24.

998 Evacuation of Valley Forge, 1890. 112th Anni. GEN. GEO. WASHINGTON Bare bust r. R. Headquarters. Bronze. 22.

999 Guns captured at Yorktown, Va., 1781. Bust, undraped, in high relief to l. GEORGE WASHINGTON. R. Two cannon. Bronze. 28.

1000 Same event. Bust, undraped, in wreath. R. As last. Tin. 28.

1001 Washington Monument, Allegheny, Pa., 1891. GENERAL GEORGE WASHINGTON. Undraped bust r. R. Statue. Bronze. Tin. 24.   2 pcs.

1002 G. A. R. 26th Encamp. Washington, 1892. Bust. Bar. Tin. 22.

1003 L. A. W. 13th Annual Meet. Washington, 1892. Bust r. Brass. Holed. 20.

1004 Columbian Exposition, 1893. Medallion heads of Columbus and

Washington vis-a-vis, above eagle E PLURIBUS UNUM Below three arrows and olive branch. G.ORSINI G. N. MILLEFIORI INC ROME. R. COLUMBIAN EXPOSITION CHICAGO MDCCCXCII—III. Columbia standing left welcoming a radiant cross, which casts its rays upon the exhibition. Tin. Rare. One of the largest medals. 58.

1005   Masonic. 1793-1893. Bust ¾ f. l. R. CENTENNIAL ANNIVERSARY OF THE CONSTITUTION OF WASHINGTON LODGE. PHIL^A· etc. Bronze. 22.

1006   Trenton Battle Monument. Undraped bust r. GENERAL WASHINGTON 1776. R. View of monument. Oct. 19, 1893. Bronze. 24.

1007   LAYING THE CORNER STONE OF THE CAPITOL. SEPTEMBER 18. 1783. Medallion bust l., 15 stars above, beneath view of this event. R. CENTENNIAL CEREMONIES AT THE UNITED STATES CAPITAL (sic) SEPT. 18. 1893. View of Capitol, surrounded by 44 stars. Bronze. Tin. 32.   2 pcs.

1008   Same event. GEN. GEO. WASHINGTON and 13 stars on raised band. R. View of Capitol. Bronze. Tin. 22.   2 pcs.

1009   GEORGE WASHINGTON 1796 Head l. Copyrighted shell card. R. Blank. Silver. Gilt. 24.   2 pcs.

1010   Washington Monument, Philadelphia, 1897. View of this magnificent affair. R. Insignia of the Society of the Cincinnati. Copper. Rare. 48.

1011   Same. Tin. 48.

1012   Same event. Bust of Washington in costume and undraped. R. View of this monument. Bronze. 22.   2 pcs.

1013   Same event. Bust undraped r., border of dots. R. Monument. Tin. 20.

1014   Bust in costume r. As Baker No. 463. R. Centennial of his death, 1799. Silvered. Gilt. 10.   2 pcs.

1015   MASONIC CELEBRATION IN COMMEMORATION OF THE CENTENNIAL OF THE DEATH OF WASHINGTON MOUNT VERNON VA. DECEMBER 14. 1899. GEORGE WASHINGTON. Undraped bust r. R. GEORGE WASHINGTON MASTER OF ALEXANDRIA. VA. LODGE N^O· 22. In center G eye, dividers and square. 1788 A. F. A. M. Bronze. Tin. 24.
                                                            2 pcs.

1016   Masonic. Undraped bust with fancy border r. R. Same event. G in compasses and in square. Bronze. Tin. 20.   2 pcs.

1017   STRUCK BY ORDER OF CONGRESS TO COMMEMORATE THE CENTENARY OF WASHINGTONS DEATH. Undraped bust r., in field WASHINGTON

MONUMENT ASSOCIATION ALEXANDRIA. VA. R WASHINGTON SUR-
VEYED ALEXANDRIA 1749 Surveyor's instrument. Silver. Rare.
25.

1018 Same obv. R. WASHINGTON MEMBER OF FRIENDSHIP FIRE COMPANY
1773 Engine. Bronze. 25.

1019 Undraped bust to r., facing high border. R. 1749-1899 SESQUI CEN-
TENNIAL OF ALEXANDRIA. VA OCT 12. Bronze. Tin. 20.   2 pcs.

1020 Same obv. R. STATE CAMP OF PENNA P. O. S. OF A LEBANON PA. AUG
27-31. 1900. Bronze. 20.

1021 Same obv. R. 125th Anniversary of the Battle of Trenton, N. J.
Dec. 26, 1901. Bronze. Tin. 20.

1022 Same obv. R. Sesqui-Centennial and 4th of July Celebration,
Winchester, Va. 1902. Bronze. 20.

1023 Same obv. Also same bust, but stars and GEO. WASHINGTON on
border. Another bust and stars. Size 18. R. WASHINGTON'S
BIRTH DAY FEBY 22. Bronzed. Tin. 20.   3 pcs.

1024 SESQUI-CENTENNIAL OF THE INITIATION OF WASHINGTON INTO FREE-
MASONRY NOV. 4. A. L. 5752. Undraped bust l., FRANK below. R.
PHILA LODGE, Nᴏ· 444, F. & A. M. PHILADELPHIA NOVEMBER 29.
A. D. 1902. Busts accolated l. of Edgar A. Tennis, R. W., Grand
Master, John L. Kinsey, Worshipful Master. Bronze. 32.

1025 GEORGE WASHINGTON 1778 VALLEY FORGE. Bust in uniform, with
cocked hat facing. R. 125th Anniversary, 1778-1903. View of
VALLEY FORGE HEADQUARTERS. Bronze. Scarce. 24.

1026 Undraped bust r. R. INDEPENDENCE HALL. Bronze, holed. Tin.
16.   2 pcs.

1027 GOD OUR COUNTRY AND OUR ORDER P. O. S. OF A. Head of Washington, a star within a shield, etc. R. THE BIBLE AND OUR FLAG OUR
HOPE THE PUBLIC SCHOOL. Tin. 22.

1028 GEORGE WASHINGTON BORN 22 FEBY 1732 DIED 14 DEC 1799. Undraped bust. Stars around border. Same on rev. Edge milled.
Nickel. Vg. Nicked. Very rare. 24.

1029 Bust in wreath r. R. TOKEN OF ESTEEM. Crowned shield with
C N P at sides. Brass. Different dies. Rare. Very fine. 16.
2 pcs.

1030 George Washington, 1792. Obv. as B, No. 209. R. Struck from
cancelled reverse die of the Confederate cent. Copper.
Weakly struck. *Unique.* 12.

1031 Bust on either side, as obverse of Baker, Nos. 137 and 138 combined. Copper. Unique? 18.

1032 Bust on either side, as obverse of Baker, No. 240, combined with obv. of 296. Copper. Tin. Very rare. 18.   2 pcs.

1033 Bust in uniform to left, similar but larger than that used on the funeral medal B 163, by Jacob Perkins; this die, size 9, struck in center of a plain planchet. R. Engraved *A P S* (circa. 1800). Silver. Holed. Unique. 22.

1034 Bust to r., by *Merriam.* NON VI VIRTUTE VICI. R. E * PLURIBUS UNUM EXCELSIOR. Eagle on shield r. Lead. Vg. Rare. 17.

1035 Black, Starr & Frost. N. Y. The Centennial Celebration of Washington's Inauguration, 1789-1889. View of Sub Treasury and Washington Statue. Copper. Rare. Size 32.

1036 Same. Tin. One of the largest store cards.

1037 Carmack. Chicago. Herrmann, 2½c. Bust r. Same obverse. Brass. 20.   2 pcs.

1038 Finck. Undraped bust r., 13 stars, 1776. R. ROCHESTER HOTEL. PROVIDENCE R. I. GEORGE FINCK. Brass. Very fine. Ex. rare. 14.

1039 Shoeneman & Co., Phil. Head r. Diff. revs. Tin. Brass. 2 pcs.

1040 WASHINGTON CENTENNIAL Bust l., by *Childs.* R. ALUMINUM etc. 24.

1041 Schloss & Co. N. Y. Bust r. R. Com. Departure Cont. Army, 1778, etc. Brass. Struck loop. 23.

1042 Shell cards. Bust of Washington l. 5 revs. Paper, dif. colors. 24.   8 pcs.

1043 Undraped head r., below 1863, around 13 stars. Obverse and reverse alike, but one die broken along left edge. Same as B 486. Copper-nickel. Nickel. Ex. rare.   2 pcs.

PLACQUES, MEDALLIONS, TRIALS, ETC.

1044 GENERAL WASHINGTON Very fine uniformed bust, draped around lower portion facing left. Repousse. Brass. Struck loop. Circa. 1800. Very fine production, and the only one I have seen. Valuable. Plate. 36.

1045 WASHINGTON. Bust ¾ face left in civilian dress, line around edge. Oval. Struck on leather. Only one I have seen. Circa. 1800. 41 x 31.

1046 Splendid bust in costume facing left. Copper electrotype. Old. Have never seen a duplicate.

1047 Exquisite head r. *J* on back. Cast in Berlin iron? Probably intended for a ring. Oval. Only one I have seen. Circa. 1800. Plate. 8 x 10.

1048   Undraped head l., within laurel wreath. Silver. Loop attached to edge. Fine work. Only one I have seen. 18.

1049   Bust, aged, draped in Roman style facing r., lined border. Oval. R. Blank. Silver. Old. Size 12 x 15. Only one I have seen.

1050   Undraped bust l. Electrotype shell of a die new to me. Oval. 8 x 11.

1051   Undraped bust l. Trial of a die on a piece of lead. Never saw another impression from this die. 7.

1052   Heads of Washington. Trials in lead cut to shape.   3 pcs.

1053   Bust l. in costume. Trial on a piece of lead. Possibly Bolen's work. Octagonal 9 x 10. Only one I have met with.

1054   Bust in costume l. Trial on piece of lead of a minute die. I never saw another impression.

1055   Star with head of Washington, in center UNION—a letter in each angle. Trial of a die of which this is the only impression I have seen. Lead. 13.

1056   Trial of Paquet's die in lead. Electrotype of another.   2 pcs.

1057   GEORGES WASHINGTON Head l. R. Blank. Brass. Nick on cheek. 10½.

1058   Undraped bust r., on base LOVETT and in field below RA. Trial on octagonal planchet with fancy border stamped in. R. Blank. Copper. Unique. Plate. 15 x 17.

1059   Same, but without the maker's name. Copper. 13½ x 15½.

1060   Bust ¾ face to left in civilian dress. Struck on an octagonal planchet, edge stamped in. High relief and fine work. R. Blank. Similar to B 201. Copper. Unique. Plate. 9 x 12.

1061   Same die, trial on a square piece of copper. Unique. 22.

1062   Same die, trial on a round piece of copper, which is broken off below bust. Unique. 10.

1063   Undraped bust l. 1862, as on Taylor card. Border stampel in. Brass. Octagonal 17 x 18.

1064   Head as Taylor card, B 580. R. Bust as B 363. Another with obverse as first. R. Blank. Copper. 16.   2 pcs.

1065   Half length in civilian dress, with sword resting in right arm, facing r. This appears to me to be made by the graver out of copper, and then soldered to a copper planchet with beaded, raised edge. A very fine piece of work and old, possibly circa. 1850. Unique. Plate. 22.

1066 Undraped bust l. within beaded circle. Struck on a U. S. cent of 1900? New die to me.

1067 Trials of die of Wright & Bale's card. Equestrian fig. r. Copper. Tin.   2 pcs.

1068 STAND BY THE STARS AND STRIPES Another "1868" Daguerreotype in metal frame. Diff. Very fine. 12, 15.   2 pcs.

1069 G W Plow and eagle within ornamental border. Feuchtwanger metal. Very rare. 11.

1070 KTS. ST. JONOTHAN. OUR COUNTRY FEB. 22 1832. Eagle with U. S. shield. Trial of star on piece of copper. 19 x 21.

1071 Bust in civilian costume in high relief l. A very fine production, cast in Berlin iron. 68.

1072 GEN. WASHINGTON 1789.-1889. Head to left. Cast in lead, bronzed. 70.

1073 Martha Washington. Bust ¾ f. r. 1876. R. IN MEMORY OF WOMEN OF THE 1776 REVOLUTION. Ring at top. Silver. Gilt. Very rare. 12.

1074 Martha Washington. Bust l. 1876. R. 21st Anni—Jersey City S S, 1876. Silver. 17.

1075 Martha Washington. Bust l., in cap MARTHA WASHINGTON BALTO. FEB. 22 1875. R. PEGGY STEWART ANNAPOLIS OCTOBER 19 1774. Sloop to r. DORMAN below. Brass. Very rare. 15.

COINS OF THE UNITED STATES
SINCE THE ESTABLISHMENT OF THE MINT.

GOLD COINAGE.

1076 1864 Gold proof set. $20, $10, $5, $3, $2½, $1. Brilliant proofs. In case. Excessively rare. Sold as a set. The market value of gold in 1864 was some two and a half times that of paper, so that it is quite likely but very few gold sets were bought.

1077 1876 Gold proof set. $20, $10, $5, $3, $2½, $1. Excessively rare. Sold as a set.

1078 1908 Gold proof set. $20, $10, $5, $2½. Dull, sand-blasted surface. Very rare, as but few sets were struck. Sold as a set.

1079 1850 $20. 1st year of regular issue. Very fine. Desirable.

1080 1864 $20. Brilliant proof. Excessively rare. Gold value in 1864 was about $50, so it is very probable but only a few were preserved.

1081   1869 $20. Brilliant proof. Excessively rare.

1082   1795 $10. Very fine. Very rare, and the first gold coined at the Mint.

1083   1797 $10. 4 stars before bust, 12 behind it. R. Eagle standing on a palm branch with olive wreath in his beak, as on 1795. Extremely fine. Minute dent on edge. Excessively rare.

1084   1798 $10. Over 1797. 4 stars before bust, 9 behind it. R. Heraldic eagle with shield on breast. Very fine. Excessively rare.

1085   1799 $10. Small stars. Extremely fine. Mint lustre.

1086   1804 $10. Very fine. Profile, while a trifle weak is much stronger than the usual specimen. Very rare.

1087   1860 $10. New Orleans Mint. Extremely fine. Very rare in such high preservation.

1088   1798 $5. Large date. Large eagle. Very fine. Scarce.

1089   1800 $5. Extremely fine, only miscroscopic hairlines. Sharp impression, and a beautiful piece.

1090   1804 $5. Small 8. Same superb condition as the last. Sharp, even impression. Scarce.

1091   1812 $5. Extremely fine. Sharp, even impression.

1092   1813 $5. Superb example, only the slightest cabinet friction. Mint lustre.

1093   1804 $2½. Extremely fine; only the merest sign of friction. Sharp, beautiful example. Very rare.

1094   1825 $2½. Extremely fine; only the slightest cabinet friction.

1095   1898 $2½. Brilliant proof, slightest abrasion.

THREE DOLLARS.

1096   1854   First year of coinage. Extremely fine. Mint lustre.

1097   1854   New Orleans Mint. Only year coined at this Mint. Very fine.

1098   1855   Extremely fine. Mint lustre.

1099   1856   Extremely fine.

1100   1856   San Francisco Mint. Very fine.

1101   1857   Extremely fine.

1102   1857   San Francisco Mint. Very good. Scarce.

1103   1858   Very fine. Pin point nick in field. Rare.

1104   1859   Uncirculated. Brilliant and mint lustre.

1105   1860   Extremely fine. Mint lustre. Scarce.

1106 1860 San Francisco Mint. Very good. Rare.
1107 1861 Brilliant proof. Excessively rare. I think about eight
            known in this condition.
1108 1863 Uncirculated. Brilliant mint lustre. Very rare.
1109 1864 Brilliant proof. Slight spot of tarnish. Excessively rare,
            as gold was at such a great premium but few bought them, and
            probably about eight would cover all that are known to-day.
1110 1866 Uncirculated. Mint lustre. Scarce so fine.
1111 1867 Brilliant proof. Excessively rare.
1112 1868 Semi-proof. Slightest abrasion.
1113 1869 Extremely fine. Rare.
1114 1870 Extremely fine. Rare.
1115 1871 Uncirculated. Brilliant mint lustre. Rare.
1116 1872 Brilliant proof. Extremely rare.
1117 1873 Brilliant proof. So remarkably boldly struck on obverse
            that center of reverse shows a trifle weakness in center, as they
            nearly always do. A magnificent example. Extremely rare.
1118 1874 Very fine.
1119 1878 Uncirculated. Slight proof surface on obv.
1120 1879 Uncirculated. Brilliant mint lustre.
1121 1880 Uncirculated. Brilliant mint lustre.
1122 1881 Dull proof. Rare.
1123 1882 Extremely fine. Rare.
1124 1883 Brilliant proof. Very rare. Only 940 coined.
1125 1885 Extremely fine. Very rare. Only 950 coined.
1126 1886 Uncirculated. Mint lustre. Only 1,121 coined.
1127 1887 Extremely fine.
1128 1888 Extremely fine.
1129 1889 Uncirculated. Mint lustre.

GOLD DOLLARS.

1130 1849 Wide open top to wreath, 12 berries. Extremely fine.
1131 1849 Charlotte Mint. Very good. Rare.
1132 1849 Dahlonega Mint. Very fine. Rare.
1133 1849 New Orleans Mint. Fine.
1134 1850 Fine. Scarce.
1135 1850 New Orleans Mint, rarest O. Mint. Very fine.
1136 1851 Extremely fine.
1137 1851 Charlotte Mint. Very good.

6

2 25 1138   1852   Extremely fine.

4. 1139   1852   Charlotte Mint.   Extremely fine.   Faint pin scratch on obv.   Rare.

2.--1140   1853   Dahlonega Mint.   Very good.   Faint scratch, slight nick on edge.   Rare.

2.25 1141   1853   New Orleans Mint.   Very good.

16.-- 1142   1854   San Francisco Mint.   Small size.   Extremely fine.   Very rare.

.3--1143   1854   Large type.   Head of Indian Queen.   1st year of issue.   Uncirculated.   Mint lustre.

2.52 1144   1855   Charlotte Mint.   Very good.   Rare.

2.25 1145   1855   New Orleans Mint.   Very fine.   Strong imp.

5.5 1146   1856   Slanting 5.   Uncirculated.   Brilliant mint lustre.

2.25 1147   1856   San Francisco Mint.   Fine.   Pin point dent.   Rare.

2.25 1148   1857   Brilliant proof.   Excessively rare.

2.25 1149   1857   Charlotte Mint.   Very good.   Rare.

3.50 1150   1858   Uncirculated.   Brilliant mint lustre.   Rare in this condition.

2.30 1151   1858   San Francisco Mint.   Fine.   Rare.

2.50 1152   1859   Uncirculated.   Mint lustre.

.3.90 1153   1859   Dahlonega Mint.   Entire obverse die recut.   Fine.   Very rare.

3.90 1154   1859   San Francisco Mint.   Extremely fine.   Rare.

8.25 1155   1860   Brilliant proof.   Very rare.

2.50 1156   1861   Uncirculated.   Brilliant mint lustre.

8.25 1157   1862   Brilliant proof.   Very rare.

31. 1158   1863   Uncirculated.   Brilliant mint lustre.   Extremely rare. (27.sans)

27. 1159   1864   Uncirculated.   Brilliant mint lustre.   Extremely rare. (vf.16.)

35. 1160   1865   Uncirculated.   Brilliant mint lustre.   Extremely rare. (30.0)

7. 1161   1866   Uncirculated.   Slight proof surface.   Very rare. (7. fragt)

36. 1162   1867   Brilliant proof.   Extremely rare. (6. me. 14.sans)

5. 1163   1868   Uncirculated.   Brilliant mint lustre. (5.Pru'[polisher])

10. 1164   1869   Uncirculated.   Brilliant mint lustre.   Very rare. (2.11.Elder)

6 1165   1870   Uncirculated.   Brilliant mint lustre.   Rare.

6.-- 1166   1871   Uncirculated.   Brilliant mint lustre.   Rare. (m.....l dust m.6.3.Slms)

10. 1167   1872   Proof.   Brilliant mint lustre.   Very rare. (nw.9. e)

2.25 1168   1873   Proof obverse.   R. Uncirculated.   Brilliant lustre.

2. 1169   1874   Uncirculated.   Mint lustre.

85. 1170   1875   Brilliant proof.   Excessively rare. (56.C)

1171 1876 Brilliant proof. Rare.
1172 1877 Uncirculated. Brilliant mint lustre. Rare.
1173 1878 Extremely fine. Very scarce.
1174 1879 Uncirculated. Brilliant mint lustre. Scarce.
1175 1880 Brilliant proof. Very rare.
1176 1881 Brilliant proof. Scarce.
1177 1882 Brilliant proof. Scarce.
1178 1883 Proof. Scarce.
1179 1884 Proof. Scarce.
1180 1885 Brilliant proof.
1181 1886 Proof.
1182 1887 Uncirculated. Brilliant mint lustre.
1183 1888 Brilliant proof.
1184 1889 Proof. Last year of regular coinage.
1185 1893 Jefferson. Bust l. Uncirculated.
1186 1893 McKinley. Bust l. Uncirculated.

PRIVATE ISSUES OF GOLD COINS.

1187 (1834-1842) Carolina. $5. CAROLINA GOLD 134.G. * 21 CARATS. R. C. BECHTLER AT RUTHERF: * 5 DOLLARS. Very fine. Rare.

1188 (1834-1842) Carolina. $1. * CAROLINA DOLLAR ONE (sic) in center. R. BECHTLER RUTHERF. 28.G. Very fine. Scarce.

1189 (1834-1842) Carolina. $1. CAROLINA GOLD. 27.G 21.C. R. A BECHTLER 1 DOL. Very fine. Has been bent across to test quality of the gold.

1190 (1834-1842) Carolina. $1. * CAROLINA DOLLAR In center ONE. R. BECHTLER RUTHERF * In center 28C No periods as on regular issue. Georgia $5. GEORGIA GOLD. 22 CARATS. In center 12.8.G.* R. C. BECHTLER, AT RUTHERF: * In center 5 DOLLARS. Brass. Fine. From counterfeit dies, which tradition says were made by a son of Bechtler and intended to pass on the reputation of his father's gold coins, as they show slight traces of having been gold plated. Extremely rare.   2 pcs.

1191 1850 California. Moffat & Co. $5. Head of Liberty. MOFFAT & CO on diadem. R. S.M.V. CALIFORNIA GOLD FIVE DOL. Eagle. Very good.

1192 1854 California. Kellogg & Co. $20. Head of Liberty, with KELLOGG & CO in small letters on diadem. R. SAN FRANCISCO CALIFORNIA TWENTY D. Eagle and shield. Very fine.

1193   1854? California. Kellogg & Co. $20. Type as last. Very good. Light nicks.

1194   1853 California. U. S. Assay Office. $20. Eagle and shield. R. Engine turned. Very fine. Slight dent on edge.

1195   1850? California. Pattern for a $20? MINES D' OR DE BURNS CREEK Beautiful figure of an Indian Queen seated on a rock scattering coins from her right hand, while her left supports a cornucopiæ; the sea and ship in background, in ex'g. CALIFORNIE. R. Blank. Trial in lead from a die made in France. Perfect. Only one I have seen; unpublished.

1196   (1854) California. $1. Octagon. Head of Liberty. R. Eagle with scroll. Fine. Plugged over head.

1197   1853 California. $½. Octagon. Head of Liberty, F.D. 13 stars, 1853. R. CALIFORNIA GOLD 50. CENTS. Eagle, with rays behind head; arrow in talons. Die broken on edge. Extremely fine. Very rare.

1198   1853 California. $½. Round. Small head Liberty, 13 stars. R. HALF DOL. CALIFORNIA GOLD In center 1853. Unc., but filed on edge.

1199   1871 California. $½. Oct. Head of Liberty, 13 stars, G C one above the other between head and 1871. R. HALF DOLLAR CAL. Proof. Rare variety.

1200   1881 California. $½. Round. Indian head. 13 stars, 1881. R. ½ CAL. GOLD. Proof.

1201   1881 California. $½. Round. Indian head. 13 stars, 1881. R. ½ DOLLAR. Proof.

1202   (1852?) California. $¼. Round. No date. Head of Liberty. 11 stars. R. ¼ DOLLAR Ex. fine. Slightly bent.

1203   1854 California. $¼. Oct. Head of Liberty. 5 stars. R. ¼ DOLLAR 1854 in circle of dots. Weak die on head. Very fine. Rare.

1204   1869 California. $¼. Round. Head of Liberty, G below; 13 stars. R. ¼ DOLLAR 1869. Fine.

1205   1870 California. $¼. Oct. Head of Liberty. 13 stars, G 1870 R. ¼ DOLLAR CAL. Proof.

1206   1870 California. $¼. Oct. R. ¼ in shield. Fine. Holed at top.

1207   1876 California. $¼. Oct. Indian head. Proof.

1208   1876 California. $¼. Round. Indian head. Uncirculated.

1209 1849 California. Eagle and stars. R. CALIFORNIA 1849 In wreath MODEL HALF EAGLE. Milled edge. Brass. Unc. Rare.

1210 1849 California. Eagle, stars, 1849. R. CALIFORNIA MODEL DOLLAR in wreath l. Brass. Very fine. Very rare.

1211 1847-9 California. Tokens of $5 and $10 size. 3 types. 2 holed. Brass. Good.   12 pcs.

1212 1860 Colorado. Clark Gruber & Co. $10. PIKES PEAK GOLD TEN D. *View of Pike's Peak* below DENVER. R. CLARK GRUBER & CO 1860 Eagle. Extremely fine. Very rare.

1213 1861 Colorado. Clark Gruber & Co. $20. Head of Liberty. PIKES PEAK on diadem, 13 stars, 1861. R. CLARK GRUBER & CO DENVER TWENTY D. Eagle, etc. *Copper.* Good. Rare.

1214 1861 Colorado. Clark Gruber & Co. $10. Type as last. Gold. Good. Rare.

1215 1861 Colorado. Clark Gruber & Co. $2½. Type as last. Gold. Very good. Rare.

UNITED STATES PROOF SETS.

Each set consisting of the silver, copper and nickel coins of the year. All fine proofs. Sold so much a set.

1216 1857 $1, $½, $¼, $1/10, $1/20, 3c., 1c. large copper, 1c. nickel, ½ cent. Brilliant proofs. Beautiful set. The copper cent and half cent dull red. Very rare.   9 pcs. as 1 set.

1217 1858 $1, $½, $¼, $1/10, $1/20, 3c., 1c. (small letters). Beautiful proof set. Very rare.   7 pcs. as 1 set.

1218 1859 $1, $½, $¼, $1/10, $1/20, 3c., 1c. Dollar brilliant proof, rest uncirculated.   7 pcs. as 1 set.

1219 1860 $1, $½, $¼, $1/10, $1/20, 3c., 1c. Scarce.   7 pcs. as 1 set.

1220 1861 $1, $½, $¼, $1/10, $1/20, 3c., 1c. Rare.   7 pcs. as 1 set.

1221 1862 $1, $½, $¼, $1/10, $1/20, 3c., 1c.   7 pcs. as 1 set.

1222 1863 $1, $½, $¼, $1/10, $1/20, 3c., 1c. Rare.   7 pcs. as 1 set.

1223 1864 $1, $½, $¼, $1/10, $1/20, 3c., 2c., 1c. nickel, 1c. copper. Very rare.   9 pcs. as 1 set.

1224 1865 $1, $½, $¼, $1/10, $1/20, 3c. silver, 3c. nickel, 2c., 1c. Rare.   9 pcs. as 1 set.

1225 1866 $1, $½, $¼, $1/10, $1/20, 3c. silver, 5c. and 3c. nickel, 2c., 1c.   10 pcs. as 1 set.

1226	1867	$1, $½, $¼, $1/10, $1/20, 3c. silver, 5c. (no rays) and 3c. nickel, 2c., 1c.	10 pcs. as 1 set.
1227	1868	$1, $½, $¼, $1/10, $1/20, 3c. silver, 5c. and 3c. nickel, 2c., 1c.	10 pcs. as 1 set.
1228	1869	$1, $½, $¼, $1/10, $1/20, 3c. silver, 5c. and 3c. nickel, 2c. 1c.	10 pcs. as 1 set.
1229	1870	$1, $½, $¼, $1/10, $1/20, 3c. silver, 5c. and 3c. nickel, 2c. 1c.	10 pcs. as 1 set.
1230	1871	$1, $½, $¼, $1/10, $1/20, 3c. silver, 5c. and 3c. nickel, 2c. 1c.	10 pcs. as 1 set.
1231	1872	$1, $½, $¼, $1/10, $1/20, 3c. silver, 5c. and 3c. nickel, 2c. 1c.	10 pcs. as 1 set.
1232	1873	$1, $½, $¼, $1/10, $1/20, 3c. silver, 5c. and 3c. nickel, 2c. 1c. Rare.	10 pcs. as 1 set.
1233	1873	Trade dollar, $½, $¼, $1/10, these three with arrow heads at date; 5c., 3c., 1c. Rare.	7 pcs. as 1 set.
1234	1874	$1, $½, $¼, $1/10, 5c., 3c., 1c.	7 pcs. as 1 set.
1235	1875	$1, $½, $¼, $1/5, $1/10, 5c., 3c., 1c. Scarce.	8 pcs. as 1 set.
1236	1876	$1, $½, $¼, $1/5, $1/10, 5c., 3c., 1c. Scarce.	8 pcs. as 1 set.
1237	1877	$1, $½, $¼, $1/5, $1/10, 5c., 3c., 1c. Very rare.	8 pcs. as 1 set.
1238	1878	$1 2 types, $½, $¼, $1/5, $1/10, 5c., 3c., 1c. Very rare.	9 pcs. as 1 set.
1239	1879	$1 2 types, $½, $¼, $1/10, 5c., 3c., 1c.	8 pcs. as 1 set.
1240	1880	$1 2 types, $½, $¼, $1/10, 5c., 3c., 1c.	8 pcs. as 1 set.
1241	1881	$1 2 types, $½, $¼, $1/10, 5c., 3c., 1c.	8 pcs. as 1 set.
1242	1882	$1 2 types, $½, $¼, $1/10, 5c., 3c., 1c.	8 pcs. as 1 set.
1243	1883	$1 2 types, $½, $¼, $1/10, 5c., 3c., 1c.	8 pcs. as 1 set.
1244	1884	$1, $½, $¼, $1/10, 5c., 3c., 1c.	7 pcs. as 1 set.
1245	1885	$1, $½, $¼, $1/10, 5c., 3c., 1c.	7 pcs. as 1 set.
1246	1886	$1, $½, $¼, $1/10, 5c., 3c., 1c.	7 pcs. as 1 set.
1247	1887	$1, $½, $¼, $1/10, 5c., 3c., 1c.	7 pcs. as 1 set.
1248	1888	$1, $½, $¼, $1/10, 5c., 3c., 1c.	7 pcs. as 1 set.
1249	1889	$1, $½, $¼, $1/10, 5c., 3c., 1c.	7 pcs. as 1 set.
1250	1890	$1, $½, $¼, $1/10, 5c., 1c.	6 pcs. as 1 set.
1251	1891	$1, $½, $¼, $1/10, 5c., 1c.	6 pcs. as 1 set.
1252	1892	$1, $½, $¼, $1/10, 5c., 1c.	6 pcs. as 1 set.
1253	1893	$1, $½, $¼, $1/10, 5c., 1c.	6 pcs. as 1 set.
1254	1894	$1, $½, $¼, $1/10, 5c., 1c.	6 pcs. as 1 set.

c *?* 1255 1895 $1, $½, $¼, $1/10, 5c., 1c. Very rare.   6 pcs. as 1 set.
c *?.57* 1256 1896 $1, $½, $¼, $1/10, 5c., 1c.   6 pcs. as 1 set.
c 1257 1897 $1, $½, $¼, $1/10, 5c., 1c.   6 pcs. as 1 set.
c 1258 1898 $1, $½, $¼, $1/10, 5c., 1c. Scarce.   6 pcs. as 1 set.
1259 1899 $1, $½, $¼, $1/10, 5c., 1c. Scarce.   6 pcs. as 1 set.
2 1260 1900 $1, $½, $¼, $1/10, 5c., 1c.   6 pcs. as 1 set.
1261 1901 $1, $½, $¼, $1/10, 5c., 1c.   6 pcs. as 1 set.
1262 1902 $1, $½, $¼, $1/10, 5c., 1c.   6 pcs. as 1 set.
1263 1903 $1, $½, $¼, $1/10, 5c., 1c.   6 pcs. as 1 set.
1264 1904 $1, $½, $¼, $1/10, 5c., 1c. Scarce. Last year of dol.
                                                                  6 pcs. as 1 set.
1265 1905 $½, $¼, $1/10, 5c., 1c.   5 pcs. as 1 set.
1266 1906 $½, $¼, $1/10, 5c., 1c.   5 pcs. as 1 set.

UNITED STATES PROOF SETS.

Presented to a former Sheriff of Philadelphia. All in the fine presentation cases with the inscriptions on, except first two, 1867, 1868, have silver plates on cover. Sold so much a set, cases included.

1267 1862 $1, $½, $¼, $1/10, $1/20, 3c., 1c.   7 pcs. as 1 set.
1268 1863 $1, $½, $¼, $1/10, $1/20, 3c., 1c.   7 pcs. as 1 set.
1269 1864 $1, $½, $¼, $1/10, $1/20, 3c., 1c. nickel. Very rare.
                                                                  7 pcs. as 1 set.
1270 1865 $1, $½, $¼, $1/10, $1/20, 3c. silver, 3c. nickel, 2c., 1c. (copper, dull). Rare.   9 pcs. as 1 set.
1271 1866 $1, $½, $¼, $1/10, $1/20, 3c. silver, 3c. nickel, 2c., 1c. (no 5c. nickel).   9 pcs. as 1 set.
1272 1867 $1, $½, $¼, $1/10, $1/20, 3c. silver, 3c. and 5c. nickel, both types with rays (very rare) and without rays, 2c., 1c. Rare set.
                                                                  11 pcs. as 1 set.
1273 1868 $1, $½, $¼, $1/10, $1/20, 3c. silver, 3c. and 5c. nickel, 2c., 1c.
                                                                  10 pcs. as 1 set.
1274 1869 $1, $½, $¼, $1/10, $1/20, 3c. silver, 3c. and 5c. nickel, 2c., 1c.
                                                                  10 pcs. as 1 set.
1275 1870 $1, $½, $¼, $1/10, $1/20, 3c. silver, 3c. and 5c. nickel, 2c., 1c.
                                                                  10 pcs. as 1 set.
1276 1856 $½, $¼, $1/10, $1/20, 3c., 1c. 2 varieties, ½c. Uncirculated.
                                                                  8 pcs. as 1 set.

Real

1.50 1277 1857 $½, $¼, $1/10, $1/20, 3c., 1c. large and small, ½c. Uncirculated.   8 pcs. as 1 set.

1.25 1278 1858 $½, $¼, $1/10, $1/20, 3c., 1c. both sizes of letters. Uncirculated.   7 pcs. as 1 set.

S.C.S PM.

Hunter col 2-2 PM   **SILVER DOLLARS.**

1279 1795 Bust of Liberty, undraped, the hair flowing loose. The variety with short bar (in die) in field behind head. Lower curl
far from stars. Every star sharp, broad milling. R. Three leaves
under each wing. Uncirculated, brilliant mint lustre. Shows
a few microscopic nicks or the slightest abrasion. A superb example. Plate. *Plated 45°*

1280 1795 Same type. Head far from LIBERTY, lower curl almost
touches first star. Sharp stars. R. As last. Very fine.

S A C   3.75 1281 1795 Same type. Large head, lower curl touches point of first
star. R. Two leaves under each wing. Fine. Small dents on
neck.

C   7. 1282 1795 Same type. Tall, narrow head, resembling somewhat that
on the 1794. Star on each side of date well below the bust.
Curl nearly touches two points of first star. R. Two leaves under each wing. Scratch across eagle's legs where another coin
had fallen on it. Very fine. Rare variety. Plate.

A .C   5.25 1283 1795 Same type. Small, low head far from LIBERTY Lower curl
joins two points of first star. R. Two leaves. Fine, and the
obverse really very fine for this rare variety, which always has
a curious frosting of the surface about the head. Plate.

C   17. — 1284 1795 Bust of Liberty, draped, and the hair tied at the back by a
fillet terminating in a large bow of ribbon. The variety with
bust in left of obverse field. R. Small eagle standing on clouds
to left. Extremely fine, practically uncirculated, only showing
the slightest abrasion. Very rare when in this superb condition.
Plate.

Callen   3.05 1285 1795 Type as last. Bust in center of field. Fine. Scarce.
C
Kraft   4.75 1286 1796 Large date. R. Small letters. Die broken between I c Four
stars not sharp. Fine. Scarce.

1287 1796 Small date. R. Small letters. Fine. Scarce.

J A C   17. — 1288 1797 6 stars before bust, 10 behind it. R. Large letters. Extremely fine. Mint lustre. Rare in this beautiful condition.
Plate. *small uncirculated*

1289 1797 7 stars before bust, 9 behind it. R. large letters. Good.

1290 1797 Obv. as last. R. Small letters. Good. Dent on edge. Rare.

1291 1798 15 stars. R. Small eagle on clouds. Good. Rare.

1292 1798 13 stars. R. Small eagle on clouds. Very good. Rare.

1293 1798 13 stars, type as last. Date even and wide. R. Displayed eagle, stars about head. Very sharp impression.

1294 1798 Erratic uneven date, with fine crack up from edge through 9 and along edge to first star. R. Stars over eagle are weak. Very fine.

1295 1798 Wide, uneven date, the 8 touches bust. Nick on edge below 9. Very fine.

1296 1799 5 stars before bust; 8 behind. Die cracked across bust. Slight dent on milling. Very fine. Rare, and seldom seen in this condition. Plate.

1297 1799 6 stars before bust, 9 behind it. Small stars. Very fine.

1298 1799 As last, last star close to bust. Very fine.

1299 1799 No berries on laurel. Very fine. Scarce.

1300 1800 Die broken around date, and crack extending up the field. Extremely fine. Sharp imp. Mint lustre. Plate.

1301 1800 Small bust, lower lock almost touches curl. Very fine.

1302 1800 Bust close to LIBERTY, last curl on top large. Very fine. Broad, even milling on obverse and reverse.

1303 1801 Extremely fine. Sharp, beautiful impression. Plate.

1304 1802 Over 1801. Very fine. Scarce.

1305 1802 Perfect date. Uncirculated. Sharp, even impression. Mint lustre. Slight microscopic abrasion on neck. A beautiful dollar. Plate.

1306 1803 Large 3. Uncirculated, the slightest microscopic abrasion on neck. Magnificent dollar. Sharp, even impression with lustre. Broad milling on both sides. Extremely rare in such condition. Plate. *Placid 21*

1307 1803 Small or italic 3. Very fine. Sharp, even impression. Scarce. Plate.

1308 1836 Proof. Minute nick in field. Beautiful specimen, and rare.

1309 1839 Extremely fine, was a proof, hairmarked. Sharp impression. Very rare.

1310 1840 Very good. Scarce.

1311 1841 Uncirculated. Slight nicks on rev. Mint lustre. Scarce in this condition.

		No.	Year	Description
Brown	1.00	1312	1842	Very fine. Slight nick on reverse.
Seam	1.30	1313	1843	Very fine.
	1	1314	1844	Extremely fine.
		1315	1845	Fine.
	1.60	1316	1846	Uncirculated. Mint lustre. A beauty.
Brown	1.20	1317	1847	Extremely fine. Mint lustre.
C	1.30	1318	1848	Very fine. Scarce.
C	1.30	1319	1849	Extremely fine.
C	6.50	1320	1850	Brilliant proof, very slight hairmarks. Rare.
C	2.30	1321	1850	New Orleans Mint. Extremely fine. Mint lustre. Rare so fine.
	2.00	1322	1853	Uncirculated. Mint lustre.
	16.50	1323	1854	Brilliant proof. Very rare.
C	5.	1324	1855	Fine. Rare.
Rea	2.25	1325	1856	Very fine. Scarce.
S.H.C	8.50	1326	1857	Proof, slightest hairmarks. Sharp stars. Rare thus.
Elder	2.30	1327	1857	Proof surface. Weak stars. Slightly hairmarked.
C	1.25	1328	1859	New Orleans Mint. Uncirculated. Minute nick in field. Beautiful example.
Ryde	7.75	1329	1859	San Francisco Mint. Extremely fine. One of the finest known. Very rare in this condition.
Sears	1.70	1330	1859	San Francisco Mint. Good. Rare.
C	1.10	1331	1860	New Orleans Mint. Very fine.
C	1.25	1332	1860	Dull proof, slightly hairmarked.
Mark	2.80	1333	1861	Uncirculated. Much more rare than its present price would indicate.
C	1.25	1334	1862	Proof.
C	1.35	1335	1863	Proof, hairmarked. Scarce.
C	1.35	1336	1864	Proof, hairmarked. Scarce.
	1.10	1337	1865	Proof, hairmarked. Scarce.
Brown	1.10	1338	1867	Extremely fine. Slight abrasion. Proof surface.
Earl	1.65	1339	1868	Brilliant proof.
C	1.30	1340	1869	Brilliant proof.
C	1.30	1341	1870	Brilliant proof.
C	1.30	1342	1871	Brilliant proof.
Mark	1.50	1343	1871	Uncirculated. Mint lustre.
Stew	8.50	1344	1871	Carson City Mint. Good. Extremely rare.
Earl	1.30	1345	1872	Brilliant proof.
Hess	2.00	1346	1872	Carson City Mint. Good. Rare.

1347   1872   San Francisco Mint. Very good. Rare.

1348   1873   Brilliant proof. Last year of issue of this type.

1349   1873   Carson City Mint. Uncirculated. Slightly hairmarked.
                   Mint lustre. Probably the first known. Excessively rare and
                   valuable.

1350   1878   Carson City Mint. Very good. Scarce.

1351   1878   San Francisco Mint. Extremely fine. 7 feathers. Scarce.

1352   1879 to 1887 inclusive. Beautiful proofs.   9 pcs.

1353   1882   San Francisco Mint. Extremely fine. Scarce.

1354   1883   Oddity. Half of edge milled, other half plain. Very good.
                   Rare.

1355   1887   Oddity. Half of edge milled, other half plain. Very good.
                   Rare.

1356   1890   Carson City Mint. Fine. Scarce.

1357   1891   New Orleans Mint. Uncirculated. Mint lustre.

1358   1895   Brilliant proof. Only 860 dollars coined this year at Phila-
                   delphia Mint. Very rare.

1359   1895   New Orleans Mint. Uncirculated. Mint lustre.

1360   1895   San Francisco Mint. Uncirculated. Slightly chafed.

1361   1897   New Orleans Mint. Uncirculated. Mint lustre.

1362   1897   San Francisco Mint. Uncirculated. Mint lustre.

1363   1808   San Francisco Mint. Uncirculated. Mint lustre.

1364   1899   New Orleans Mint. Uncirculated. Mint lustre.

1365   1900   Washington-Lafayette. Bust r. R. Statue at Paris to
                   Lafayette. Uncirculated.

1366   1900   New Orleans Mint. Uncirculated. Mint lustre.

1367   1900   San Francisco Mint. Uncirculated. Mint lustre.

1368   1902   Brilliant proof.

1369   1902   New Orleans Mint. Uncirculated. Mint lustre.

1370   1903   San Francisco Mint. Uncirculated. Mint lustre.

1371   1904   Brilliant proof. Last year of the dollar. Rare.

TRADE DOLLARS.

Becoming very scarce, as they are being constantly melted.

1372   1873   Proof. First year of issue. Scarce.

1373   1873   Extremely fine. Mint lustre.

1374   1873   Carson City Mint. - Good. Scarce.

1375   1874   Proof. Scarce.

1376   1874   Uncirculated. Slightest chafing. Mint lustre.

1377 1874 San Francisco Mint. Very good. Once sold for $65 at auction.
1378 1875 Good. Slightly hairmarked.
1379 1875 Carson City Mint. Extremely fine. Scarce.
1380 1875 San Francisco Mint. Uncirculated. Mint lustre.
1381 1876 Has been a proof, now extremely fine.
1382 1876 Carson City Mint. Good.
1383 1876 San Francisco Mint. Large S. Extremely fine.
1384 1876 San Francisco Mint. Minute S. Very fine. Rare.
1385 1877 Extremely fine. Mint lustre.
1386 1877 San Francisco Mint. Large S. Uncirculated.
1387 1877 San Francisco Mint. Minute S. Very fine. Rare.
1388 1878 Brilliant proof.
1389 1878 Carson City Mint. Very good. Scarce.
1390 1878 San Francisco Mint. Uncirculated. Mint lustre.
1391 1879 Brilliant proof.
1392 1880 Brilliant proof.
1393 1881 Brilliant proof. Scarce.
1394 1882 Brilliant proof. Scarce.
1395 1883 Brilliant proof. Scarce.

HALF DOLLARS.

1396 1794 Lower curl touches *second* star; last star at point of bust
      points above the bust. Very good. Rare. Plate.
1397 1794 Lower curl passes through point on *first* star; last star under bust points well below point of bust. Very good. Rare
1398 1795 Curl passes through first star; last star points above point
      of bust. R. 8 berries on left branch, last two on either side of
      stem; 9 berries on right branch. Die on head perfect. Uncirculated. Stars behind head weak. R. Eagle shows the small
      feathers on bust. Edge not struck up quite full. Rare. Plate.
1399 1795 Same obverse, die cracked across ear. R. 7 berries on left
      branch, 10 berries on right branch. Leaf touches D Very fine.
      Plate.
1400 1795 Same obv. R. 7 berries on left, 9 on right branch. Very
      good. Slight nick on edge.
1401 1795 Curl touches top of first star; last star points to level of
      front of bust. R. 9 berries on left and 8 on right branch. Very
      fine, light planchet scratches on head; reverse shows small
      feathers on eagle. Rare so fine.

2.50 1402—1795 Curl cuts through first star; last star points above bust, slight break in die under this star. R. 9 berries on each branch; die cracked from tip of right wing to E. Fine.

2.75 1403 1795 Curl cuts through first star; last star points well above bust. R. 7 berries on left and 8 on right branch. Fine. Slight edge dents. Edge not struck up well.

2.10 1404 1795 Curl cuts through first star; last star points well above bust; die broken between 5 and star. R. 9 berries on each branch. Very good.

4. 1405—1795 Curl high between first and second star; last star above point of bust. R. 9 berries on left and 8 on right branch. Very fine, with broad milling.

1406 1795 Same obv. as last. R. 10 berries on left, 7 on right branch. Fine.

1407 1795 Curl touches two points of first star; arm of last star touches bust. Same as last. Very good. Nick on cheek.

4. 1408 1795 Curl cuts into two points of first star; last star close to bust, points above it. R. As last. Very fine.

1409 1795 Curl spans two points of first star, but does not touch it; last star points well above bust, slight break in die below it. R. 10 berries on left, 7 on right branch; center dot on right wing. Very good.

1410 1795 Date twice engraved, first time lower than last. Curl high and terminates even with point of star. R. 9 berries on left, 8 on right branch. Slight scratch behind head. Very fine, bold impression. Its great rarity is probably accounted for by the fact of the obverse die being cracked across. Plate.

2.00 1411 1795 Curl appears to be cut off and terminates above center of star, but a glass shows it to have a fine line passing on through top of star. R. 9 berries on left, 8 on right branch. Fine.

4.75 1412 1795 Small head with short locks terminating high above star; last star above point of bust. R. 9 berries on left and 7 on right branch. Very good. Very rare.

1412a 1795 Small head with short locks; last lock cuts through point of first star; last star points just level with bust. R. 9 berries on each branch. Good. Very rare.

70. 1413 1796 15 stars. –Fine. Bold, even impression. Very slight nick in field and on reverse edge. Excessively rare. Plate.

35. 1414 1797 Very good. Well struck in every part. Extremely rare. Plate.

Norris 2.50 1415 1801 Very good. Rare.

Hth 1.50 1416 1802 Extremely fine. Very rare, and seldom seen in this high state of preservation. Plate.

Mer 2.80 1417 1803 Small or italic 3. Very fine. Scarce.

Kuah 1.10 1418 1803 Large 3. Fine.

1419 1805 Over 1804. The very rare die with the 4 showing distinctly; die cracked from nose. Good.

1420 1805 Over 1804. The 4 shows but not so prominently as last. Very good. Rare.

1421 1805 Triangular break in die below chin and crack over date. R. 5 berries. Die broken on edge. Fine.

1422 1805 4 berries on laurel branch. Weak on center, otherwise fine.

Raff ... 1423 1806 Blunt 6 over 1805. Very good. Rare.

Sciar .90 1424 1806 Pointed 6 over inverted 6. Good. Rare.

Thompson 2.25 1425 1806 Die broken across reverse, so badly that one half is slightly sunken. Good. Only example I have seen.

1.75 1426 1806 Close date; pointed 6. Extremely fine. Beautiful specimen. Plate.

Brown 1.10 1427 1806 Wide date; pointed 6. Die cracked along lower edge. Extremely fine.

C 1.70 1428 1807 Bust facing r. Semi-proof—a most beautiful specimen. Blister in field back of head. Sharp impression. Plate.

Rossy 1.10 1429 1807 Suction marks of edge of clouds over date. Extremely fine. Sharp.

Brown 1.30 1430 1807 Bust of Liberty with liberty cap facing left. R. Small eagle to r.; E PLURIBUS UNUM on band above head. 50c over 20c. Extremely fine.

1.30 1431 1807 Obverse as last. R. Perfect 50c. Extremely fine. Rare.

Fobc .78 1432 1808 Over 1807. Die cracked. Good. Scarce.

1433 1808 Die cracked up side of o in date. Uncirculated. Mint lustre.

1.25 1434 1809 Uncirculated. Sharp, even impression. Mint lustre.

Krefha .80 1435 1809 Broken bottoms to 50. Very fine.

C 2.10 1436 1810 Perfect dies. Close 50c. Beautiful specimen. Uncirculated. *Plate 325*

C 2.50 1437 1810 Perfect die. Wide 50c. Every star struck up sharp and even. A remarkable specimen of this coin, and I believe the finest I have seen. Rare. Plate. *Plate 2.5*

Hoff .70 1438 1810 Die cracked under bust. Extremely fine. Sharp, even impression.

1439 1811 Small date, with period between 8.1 Very fine. Rare.

1440 1811 Small date. Uncirculated. Beautiful example. Mint lustre.

1441 1811 Large 8 in date. Uncirculated. Sharp stars. Mint lustre. Rare.

1442 1812 Over 1811. Stars flat before face. Extremely fine. Mint lustre.

1443 1812 Perfect date. Uncirculated. Mint lustre.

1444 1812 Die shattered, cracks through various parts of the obv. and across rev.; slight corrosion spot. Uncirculated. Beautiful mint lustre.

1445 1813 Uncirculated. Every star sharp; even, full milling. Remarkable impression for this year, and rare so. Close date.

1446 1813 Wide date. Slight suction lines on both sides. Every star sharp and centered. Bold impression. Mint lustre. Rare in this condition.

1447 1814 Uncirculated. Sharp hair and every star up. Mint lustre.

1448 1814 Suction marks of motto above date. R. Die broken from wing to scroll. Extremely fine.

1449 1815 Fine. Date bold. Stars sharp. Rare.

1450 1817 Over 1813. Uncirculated. Every star sharp. Superb specimen. Mint lustre. Very rare in this condition. Plate.

1451 1817 7 high. Extremely fine. Sharp, even imp. Scarce.

1452 1817 81 close and 1 and 7 far from them. Break in die from top of cap has given some persons the idea of calling this the "crested" variety. Extremely fine. Sharp imp. Rare.

1453 1817 Wide, small date. Very fine. Not sharp on hair.

1454 1817 Separated date—the space between 1817 wide. Ex. fine. Sharp imp.

1455 1818 Over 1817. Very wide date. Small 8. The last 8 with top filled and tops of 7 above like horns. Extremely fine. Sharp, even imp. Scarce.

1456 1818 Over 1817. Very wide date. Large 8. Top of last 8 clear, only tops of 7 show above 8. Sharp, brilliant impression with mint lustre. Slight rub in field. Very rare in this condition. Plate.

1457 1818 Uncirculated. Sharp, perfect imp. Mint lustre.

1458 1819 Over 1818. Uncirculated. Sharp imp. Mint lustre. Pin head speck before the throat. Scarce.

Nassau 65 1459 1819 Extremely fine, practically uncirculated. Sharp impression.

71 1460 1820 Over 1819. 19 very plain under 20. Extremely fine. Sharp stars. Rare.

.90 1461 1820 Over 1819. Last 0 shows the 9 more like an 8. Extremely fine. Sharp imp. Rare.

65 1462 1820 Small 0, curled 2. Very fine. Sharp stars.

Knut 90 1463 1820 Large 0, the 2 with knob and square base. Obverse die cracked. Extremely fine. Sharp stars. Rare.

. 90 1464 1820 Large date, the 2 with curled top and square base. Sharp stars. Splendid specimen.

175 1465 1821 Proof, Sharp, beautiful example. Pink-purple color. Very rare.

.15 1466 1822 Proof surface obverse and reverse; slightly hairmarked. Sharp impression.

70 1467 1823 Poorly formed 3. Uncirculated. Minute nick on edge. Mint lustre. Sharp stars, beautiful example.

71 1468 1823 Wide 3. Proof surface both obverse and reverse, but worn in field. Sharp stars. Die cracked across top.

170 1469 1823 Narrow 3, the most perfectly formed of any of this year. Uncirculated, only tips of hair rubbed.

25 1470 1824 Over 1820, etc. Very fine. Rare in this condition.

.80 1471 1824 Over 1821. Shows the 1 both sides of top of the 4. Date wide. Uncirculated. Mint lustre. Scarce so fine.

X0 1472 1824 Over 1821. Shows 1 to left of 4, the 2 and 4 almost touch. Uncirculated. Mint lustre.

1473 1824 2 and 4 almost touch. Die broken across neck. Uncirculated. Sharp stars. Mint lustre.

65 1474 1824 Wide, evenly spaced date. R. Die cracked from beak to wing of eagle. Ex. fine.

75 1475 1824 Nose double cut. Extremely fine. Sharp stars. Mint lustre.

.60 1476 1824 Whole profile double cut—very marked. Very good.

1477 1825 Double cut profile from end of nose to chest. Very fine. Pin head dent on rev.

1478 1825 Double cut profile—very marked. Very fine.

1479 1825 Edge FIFTY CENTS OR ALF A DOLLAR. Very fine. Nick in field.

85 1480 1825 Die has fine ribbing at point of bust. Uncirculated. Sharp stars. Brilliant example.

1481 1825 Perfect die. Uncirculated. Sharp imp. Mint lustre. A superb example.

2 --1482 1826 Close date. Brilliant proof obverse; reverse uncirculated. 5 stars before face not centered, otherwise a beautiful piece.

...丁1483 1826 Large, low 8. Die cracked from beak to wing. Very fine.

1484 1826 Profile double. Very fine.

1485 1827 Over 1826, flat 2. Uncirculated. Slight defect on edge (like a chip cut off) in planchet, but hardly shows. Mint lustre. The finest example I have seen of this rare variety.

1486 1827 Curled-bottomed 2. Very fine. Rare.

1487 1827 Flat based 2. Uncirculated.

) 1488 1828 Large curled 2, large 8's. Uncirculated. Mint lustre. A gem. Scarce so fine.

6.c 1489 1828 Large curled 2 with knob, large 8's. Very fine.

4. 1490 1828 Large, flat-bottomed 2, *large* 8's. Uncirculated. Rare.

7/ 1491 1828 Small 8, small, flat 2. Uncirculated. Mint lustre.

/ /. 1492 1829 Recut date, under the 29 are figures like *1 1*. Uncirculated.

1493 1829 Uncirculated. Sharp stars. Mint lustre.

1494 1830 Small 0 in date. Proof. Sharp, beautiful piece. Very rare.

3'·1495 1830 Large 0 in date. Uncirculated. Mint lustre. Sharp. Rare.

1496 1830 Large and small date. Ex. fine. Lustre.   2 pcs.

1497 1831 Uncirculated. Sharp, even impression. Mint lustre.

1498 1832 Large letters on rev. Die broken at right wing. Fine. Rare.

1499 1832 Small letters on rev. Uncirculated. Sharp. Mint lustre.

1500 1833 Uncirculated. Sharp, even imp. Mint lustre.

1501 1834 Double profile from nose to chin. Large date. R. Large letters. Large 50c. Ex. fine.

1502 1834 Large, poorly formed 4. Protruding lips. R. Small letters. Small 50c. Proof surface.

1503 1834 Large date, 3 and 4 recut. R. Large letters. 50c. close. Uncirculated.

1504 1834 Small date; large bust; prominent lips. R. Small letters. Uncirculated. Mint lustre. Sharp.

1505 1834 Small date; small bust, like 1835. Uncirculated.

1506 1835 Same as last. Uncirculated.

1507 1836 Uncirculated. Sharp stars.

1508 1836 Gobrecht design. R. 50 CENTS. *Edge milled.* Semi-proof. Slight abrasion. Very rare.

1509 1836 Milled edge, as last. Fine. Rare.

7

1510	1837	Same as last. Uncirculated. Sharp. Mint lustre.
1511	1838	Uncirculated. Stars sharp. Mint lustre.
1512	1839	As last. Uncirculated. Mint lustre.
1513	1839	Liberty seated, no drapery from point of elbow. Uncirculated. Mint lustre. Rare.
1514	1839	Liberty seated, drapery from elbow. Extremely fine. Scarce.
1515	1839	As last. Very fine. Scarce.
1516	1839	New Orleans Mint. o over date. Extremely fine. Sharp.
1517	1840	New Orleans Mint. Large o. R. Die cracked. Very fine.
1518	1840	New Orleans Mint. Minute o Good. A pinscratched in field. Rare.
1519	1840	Small letters on rev. Uncirculated. Scarce so fine.
1520	1841	Extremely fine, the slightest abrasion. Sharp. Mint lustre. Rare in this beautiful condition.
1521	1841	New Orleans Mint. Very good. Scarce.
1522	1842	Small date. Die broken on rev. edge. Extremely fine, slightest abrasion. Mint lustre. Rare in this condition.
1523	1842	Large date. Very fine.
1524	1843	Extremely fine.
1525	1843	New Orleans Mint. Extremely fine. Beautiful specimen.
1526	1844	Uncirculated. Sharp. Beautiful specimen. Rare so.
1527	1844	8 recut. Fine.
1528	1844	N. O. Mint, o over space between F D. Extremely fine. Mint lustre. Beautiful example.
1529	1844	N. O. Mint, o over F. Very fine.
1530	1845	Fine.
1531	1845	N. O. Mint, o low over F Uncirculated. Mint lustre. Rare in such condition.
1532	1845	N. O. Mint, o high over left side of F Extremely fine. Mint lustre.
1533	1846	6 cut over a prostrate 6 thus ∽. Extremely fine. Very rare.
1534	1846	6 over 5? Fine. Rare.
1535	1846	Medium tall 6. Very fine.
1536	1847	Extremely fine. Die cracked around star.
1537	1847	New Orleans Mint. Extremely fine.
1538	1848	Very fine. Scarce.
1539	1848	New Orleans Mint. Extremely fine. Scarce.
1540	1849	Low date. Extremely fine. Scarce in this condition.

	1541	1849	High date. Extremely fine. Scarce in this condition.
	1542	1849	New Orleans Mint. Low date. Very fine.
	1543	1849	New Orleans Mint. High date. Extremely fine.
	1544	1850	New Orleans Mint, o high, almost touches stem. Uncirculated, but slightly abraded. Mint lustre. Rare.
	1545	1850	New Orleans Mint, o slightly lower. Extremely fine. Rare.
	1546	1850	Very good. Scarce.
	1547	1851	N. O. Mint. Uncirculated. Slightly hairmarked. Brilliant mint lustre. A beauty. Rare.
	1548	1852	Uncirculated. Mint lustre. Rare.
	1549	1852	New Orleans Mint. Very fine. Rare.
	1550	1853	Arrow heads at date. R. Rays around eagle. Ex. fine. Only year of this type.
	1551	1853	N. O. Mint. Extremely fine. Mint lustre. Very rare in this condition.
	1552	1854	Proof. Very rare. From a set.
	1553	1854	N. O. Mint. 854 recut. Uncirculated. Mint lustre.
	1554	1855	N. O. Mint. Uncirculated. Mint lustre.
	1555	1855	Very fine.
	1556	1856	N. O. Mint. Double cut 6. Ex. fine.
	1557	1858	Brilliant proof. Rare.
	1558	1858	N. O. Mint. Proof, fully so and as much as if it was a Phila. Mint. Never saw another so fine. Extremely rare.
	1559	1860	N. O. Mint. Proof surface. Remarkable for this mint, and the finest I have seen.
	1560	1866	No motto. s Mint. Good.
	1561	1866	Motto IN GOD WE TRUST 1st year of issue. Proof, hairmarked.
	1562	1871	San Francisco Mint. Uncirculated. Sharp, even imp. Brilliant mint lustre. Probably the finest known, and in such superb condition it is very rare.
	1563	1872	San Francisco Mint. Low s. Fine. Rare.
	1564	1872	S. Mint. Different positions of the s. Good. 3 pcs.
	1565	1873	S. Mint. Arrow-heads at date. R. The s high, almost touches end of arrow. Extremely fine. Mint lustre. Very rare.
	1566	1874, 1875, 1876, 1877. s Mint. Very fine. 4 pcs.
	1567	1877	S. Mint. High and low s Uncirculated. 2 pcs.
	1568	1879	Uncirculated. Mint lustre. Scarce.

QUARTER DOLLARS.

1569 1796 Extremely fine, only the slightest abrasion visible with a glass. Proof surface. Broad milling. First four stars not struck up, and across them and the milling are planchet scratches made when planchet was sawn out. A beautiful specimen. Very rare. Plate.

1570 1796 Extremely fine. Broad milling which is not struck up before point of bust, and corresponding spot on reverse under OF. Very rare. Plate.

1571 1796 Extremely fine. Sharp, even impression in every part, which is very unusual with this coin. Very light scratch from throat to star. Very rare. Plate.

1572 1804 Very good; better than usual. Rare.

1573 1806 Over 1805. Very fine. Stars behind head not up; otherwise a bold impression. Rare so fine. Plate.

1574 1807 Small date. Uncirculated. Milling not struck up over LIBERTY. Mint lustre. One of the finest known. Extremely rare. Plate.

1575 1807 Large date. Fine. Scarce.

1576 1815 Very fine. Sharp impression. Scarce.

1577 1818 Wide date. Uncirculated. Sharp imp. Mint lustre.

1578 1819 Small date. Extremely fine. Sharp impression.

1579 1819 Large date. Fine. Scarce.

1580 1820 Large date. Fine.

1581 1820 Small date. Fine.

1582 1821, 1822 Very good.   2 pcs.

1583 1824 Over 1822. Very good. Rare.

1584 1825 Uncirculated. L lightly stamped above head.

1585 1828 Very fine. Sharp impression.

1586 1831 Proof. Small letters on reverse. Rare in this beautiful condition. *plain*

1587 1832 Uncirculated. Slight black mark on both sides

1588 1833 Obverse struck from a rusted die! Very good.

1589 1834, '5, '6, '7, '8 Extremely fine. Nice set.   5 pcs.

1590 1838 Liberty seated. Uncirculated. From Winsor Coll.

1591 1838 Liberty seated, '39, '40 drapery, '1, '3, '4, '5, '6, '7, '8. Vg.
                                                              10 pcs.

1592 1840 to '44, '7, '50, '1, '4, '6, '7, '60 O. Mint. 2 var. of 1840. Vg.
                                                              14 pcs.

hol hampt. .*7*	1593	1840	O. Mint. Two positions of o. No drapery. Vg. Fine. 2 pcs.
f.t.dec. .*47.*	1594	1840	O. Mint. Drapery from elbow. Very fine. Rare.
Aean *1.5*	1595	1847	O. Mint. Extremely fine. Rare.
Iqdr. *2.*.*1596*	1596	1848	Uncirculated. Sharp imp. Mint lustre. Very rare. *!* *1.50*
h.?	1597	1849	Very fine.
sta *hr*	1598	1850	Extremely fine.
teje.f .*?b*	1599	1850	O. Mint. Extremely fine. Mint lustre. Rare.
. *...* *.?1*	1600	1850 to '56, '8 Very good to fine.	8 pes.
Hines *13.*	1601	1853	No arrow-heads at date. No rays around eagle. Uncirculated. Sharp impression. Mint lustre. Very rare. Plate.
$ gay .*.3v*	1602	1853	With arrow-heads and rays. Only year of this type. Ex. fine.
c.dr. *1.75*	1603	1854	Brilliant proof. Very rare.
-fC *2.80*	1604	1855	Brilliant proof. Very rare. *Placed 3.50*
Jarus *.50*	1605	1855	Uncirculated. Mint lustre. Scarce.
.~ *1.90*	1606	1856	Brilliant proof. Rare.
2.ren., *120*	1607	1857	Brilliant proof. Scarce.
Aitean .*3b*	1608	1857, 1858 Uncirculated.	2 pcs.
Ean *1.—*	1609	1858	Brilliant proof. Scarce.
*.*Ivln* *340*	1610	1859, 1860, '61, '2, '3 Brilliant proofs. Scarce.	5 pcs.
90	1611	1864	Brilliant proof. Scarce.
32.	1612	1865, '67, '68, '71, '72, '73 no arrows. Brilliant proofs.	6 pes.
32.	1613	1875 to 1888. Brilliant proofs. Nice lot.	14 pes.
t.in. *2.50*	1614	1893	Isabella. Beautiful *proof.* Rare in this condition.

TWENTY CENTS.

. c *6.*	1615	1875	Proof. Scarce.
.. *.15*	1616	1875	Uncirculated. Mint lustre.
flxu *55*	1617	1875	Carson City Mint. Uncirculated. Mint lustre. Scarce.
h *40*	1618	1875	San Francisco. Uncirculated. Mint lustre.
firang *1.—*	1619	1876	Proof. Scarce.
Rulatf .*55*	1620	1876	Uncirculated. Mint lustre. Scarce.

DIMES.

C. *2.50*	1621	1796	Perfect die. Fine. Light scratch on obv. R. Scratch across eagle.
dcin *2.75*	1622	1796	Die broken at first star. Very fine. Plate.
He *840*	1623	1797	13 stars. Fine. Very rare. Plate.

C..	20.	1624	1797 16 stars. Die cracked over date. Slight scratch above ERT Very fine. Very rare. Plate.
		1625	1798 Perfect date. Very fine. Has been mounted. Slight solder mark at top and bottom on edge. Two pin nicks in field and one on edge. Very rare. Plate.
	6.-	1626	1800 Very fine. Sharp impression. Very rare. Plate.
	32.	1627	1801 Very fine. Very rare and seldom obtainable. Plate.
	.3.	1628	1802 Good. Rare.
C.	9.-	1629	1803 Extremely fine. Obverse die perfect; reverse die cracked. Extremely rare in such superior condition. Plate.
H	6.50	1630	1804 Very fine. Bold impression. Hole over head cutting out E Could easily be filled. Extremely rare. Plate.
	17.-	1631	1804 Very good. Extremely rare. Plate.
	1.	1632	1805 4 berries on branch. Fine.
	4.	1633	1807 Uncirculated. Four stars sharp, others flat; half of edge not struck up. Mint lustre. While weak, as usual, it is a beautiful specimen. Plate.
	5.	1634	1809 Fine. Bold impression. Rare. Plate.
	.90	1635	1811 Over 1809. Very good.
C. -	2.10	1636	1814 Large date. Extremely fine.
C.	2.10	1637	1820 Uncirculated. R. Scroll ends at D. Sharp imp. Plate.
	1.00	1638	1820 Uncirculated. R. Scroll ends under E. Sharp.
	16.	1639	1821 Small date. Very fine.
	.45	1640	1821 Large date. Very fine.
	39.	1641	1822 Uncirculated. Sharp, bold, even impression. Mint lustre. Very rare and seldom obtainable in this condition. Plate.
		1642	1823 Over 1822. Extremely fine. Sharp imp. Plate.
	14	1643	1824 Over 1822. Slight proof surface. Uncirculated. Sharp, even imp. One of the finest known. Very rare. Plate.
	2.50	1644	1825 Proof. Splendid sharp impression. Rare in such magnificent condition. Plate.
	1.30	1645	1827 Proof. Scarce in this beautiful condition. Plate.
	100	1646	1828 Large date. Very good. Scarce.
	1	1647	1828 Small date. Very fine. Minute nicks.
	.80	1648	1829 Small 10c. Uncirculated. Mint lustre. Scarce so fine.
		1649	1829 Large 10c. Very good. Rare.
C	2.	1650	1830 Proof surface obv. R. Uncirculated. Sharp. Mint lustre. Beauty.
	55	1651	1830 Uncirculated. Sharp. Mint lustre.

1652	1831	Slight proof surface. Sharp. Scarce so fine.
1653	1832	Uncirculated. Sharp. Mint lustre.
1654	1833	Uncirculated. Sharp. Slightest abrasion.
1655	1834	Uncirculated. Large 4. Mint lustre.
1656	1835	Uncirculated. Mint lustre. Sharp.
1657	1836	Uncirculated. Mint lustre. Die cracked across obv.
1658	1837	Bust of Liberty. Die cracked across. Uncirculated. Mint lustre. Scarce.
1659	1838	No stars. O. Mint. Uncirculated. Mint lustre. Rare.
1660	1838	Small stars. Extremely fine. Very rare.
1661	1838	Large stars. Uncirculated. Mint lustre.
1662	1839	Uncirculated. Mint lustre.
1663	1839	O. Mint. Extremely fine. Scarce in this condition.
1664	1840	Without drapery from elbow. Extremely fine.
1665	1841	Uncirculated. Mint lustre.
1666	1841	O. Mint. Uncirculated. Mint lustre. Scarce so fine.
1667	1842	Uncirculated. Mint lustre. Rare in this condition.
1668	1842	O. Mint. Very good.
1669	1843	Very good.
1670	1844	Extremely fine. Rare in this condition.
1671	1845	Uncirculated. Brilliant mint lustre.
1672	1846, 1847 Good. Scarce. 2 pcs.
1673	1848	Fine. Scarce.
1674	1849	Extremely fine.
1675	1849 and 1850 2 sizes of 0; '51, '2, '4, '6, '7, '9. O. Mint. 1850's poor, others good to very fine. 8 pcs.
1676	1850	Extremely fine.
1677	1851	Uncirculated. Mint lustre. Rare.
1678	1852	Uncirculated. Slightest abrasion.
1679	1853	No arrow-heads. Vg. Arrows. Unc. 2 pcs.
1680	1854	~~Brilliant~~ proof. Very rare.
1681	1855	Very fine.
1682	1856	Small date. Brilliant proof. Rare.
1683	1857	Brilliant proof. Rare.
1684	1858	Brilliant proof. Scarce.
1685	1859	Brilliant proof.
1686	1860, 1861, 1862 Brilliant proofs. 3 pcs.
1687	1860	S. Mint. Stars on obverse. R. UNITED STATES OF AMERICA ONE DIME. Very good. Scarce.

1688   1860   O. Mint.   UNITED STATES OF AMERICA 1860   R. ONE DIME.
Extremely fine. Believed to be the finest known, and as the
others are poor to good, it is at once apparent what a wonderful
example this is. Plate.

1689   1864   Brilliant proof. Scarce.

1690   1866, '68, '69, '70, '71, '73 both types, '74 to '88 incl., '89. Proofs.
                                                                        23 pcs.

1691   1875, '76, '77 Carson City Mint. Uncirculated.   3 pcs.

HALF DIMES.

1692   1792   Half disme. Bust of Liberty, or, as some suppose, Martha
Washington, l., LIB.PAR.OF.SCIENCE & INDUSTRY. Beneath bust
1792. R. Eagle flying left, UNI STATES OF AMERICA HALF DISME*.
Extremely fine. Slight planchet scratches across cheek. Sharp,
even impression. Extremely rare and very desirable, as it is the
first coin struck after the establishment of the mint, and Washington supplied some silver plate to provide the metal from
which to make them. Plate.

1693   1794   Die cracked across obverse, 4 of date recut, first curl free of
star and curls. R. 7 berries on left and 5 on right branch. Extremely fine. Small nick before mouth. Light scratches on rev.
Sharp, evenly centered. A gem. Very rare. Plate.

1694   1794   Curl joins first star. R. Six berries on each branch. Very
fine. Deep, even milling. Beautiful specimen. Rare. Plate.

1695   1795   Die broken over TY* Uncirculated. Sharp impression.
Mint lustre. A gem. Plate.

1696   1796   Very fine. Rare. Plate.

1697   1797   15 stars. Very fine. Rare. Plate.

1698   1797   16 stars. Very good. Rare.

1699   1800   LIBERTY Extremely fine. Sharp, even impression.

1700   1801   Good. Rare.

1701   1803   Good. Almost invisible scratch on neck. Rare.

1702   1805   Fair. Very rare.

1703   1829 to 1837 Large and small date of 1835. Complete set of the
bust type. Uncirculated. Choice set.   10 pcs.

1704   1837   Liberty seated, no stars. Curved and straight dates. Unc.
                                                                        2 pcs.

1705   1838   No stars. O. Mint. Very good. Rare.

1706 1838 With stars. Uncirculated. Mint lustre.
1707 1839 Uncirculated. Mint lustre.
1708 1839 O. Mint. Extremely fine. Scarce.
1709 1840 Uncirculated. Sharp imp. Mint lustre.
1710 1840 O. Mint. No sleeve. Large and small o. Poor. Rare. 2 pcs.
1711 1841 Uncirculated. Mint lustre. Beauty.
1712 1841 large o, 1844, '48 large and small o, '49 bent, '50 l. o, '52, '3
      arrows, '4, '5, '6, '7, '8, '9, '60. All o Mint. Early ones poor,
      others good. Some rare.   15 pcs.
1713 1842 Uncirculated. Mint lustre. Scarce.
1714 1843 Uncirculated. Mint lustre. Scarce so beautiful.
1715 1844 Double cut date. Very fine. Rare.
1716 1844 Perfect date. Uncirculated. Mint lustre. Scarce.
1717 1845 Uncirculated.
1718 1846 Very good. Rare. In my experience of some 38 years I
      believe I never met with an 1846 ½ dime in the thousands of
      half dimes examined in the various lots.
1719 1846 Good. Rare.
1720 1847 Uncirculated. Mint lustre. Scarce so fine.
1721 1848 Brilliant proof. Excessively rare. Small date. R. Upside
      down.
1722 1848 Small date. R. Regular. Uncirculated. Mint lustre.
      Scarce.
1723 1849 Brilliant proof. Excessively rare. Double cut 9.
1724 1849 Regular date. Uncirculated. Mint lustre.
1725 1850, '1 (o ex. fine), '2, '3 arrows, '4, '7, '8, '9 o, '60 o. Uncir.
      Choice lot.   9 pcs.
1726 1854 Brilliant proof. Very rare.
1727 1855 Brilliant proof. Very rare.
1728 1856 Brilliant proof. Very rare.
1729 1858 Brilliant proof. Scarce.
1730 1859 to '63, '67 to '73 inclusive. Brilliant proofs.   12 pcs.
1731 1860 Stars on obverse. R. HALF DIME in wreath. No mention of
      the United States. Uncirculated. Sharp imp. Mint lustre.
      Very rare, and rapidly advancing in price.
1732 1863 S. Mint. Uncirculated. Mint lustre. Rare so fine.
1733 1864 Brilliant proof. Very rare.
1734 1866 S. Mint. Uncirculated. Mint lustre. Rare so fine.

1735 1868 S. Mint. Uncirculated. Mint lustre. Rare so fine.
1736 1872 S. Mint. Very fine.
1737 1873 S. Mint. Uncirculated. Mint lustre. Scarce.

THREE CENTS SILVER.

1738 1851, '1 o only year, '2, '3. Unc. Choice lot.   4 pcs.
1739 1854 Proof, slightly hairmarked. Very rare.
1740 1855 Uncirculated. Mint lustre. Rare.
1741 1856 Uncirculated. Brilliant mint lustre.
1742 1857 Proof. Scarce.
1743 1858 Proof. Scarce.
1744 1859 to 1862 inclusive. Brilliant proofs.   5 pcs.
1745 1863 Brilliant proof. Scarce.
1746 1864 Brilliant proof. Very rare.
1747 1865 Brilliant proof. Rare.
1748 1866 Brilliant proof. Scarce.
1749 1867, 1868 Brilliant proofs.   2 pcs.
1750 1869 Proof, slightly hairmarked. Rare.
1751 1870, 1871 Brilliant proofs.   2 pcs.
1752 1873 Proof, slightly hairmarked. Rare.

CENTS.

1753 1787 Franklin cent. FUGIO 1787 Sun dial, sun above; below
MIND YOUR BUSINESS. R. 13 links, enclosing STATES * UNITED *
WE ARE ONE. Very fine. Very rare this variety with STATES
UNITED divided twice with a star. Crosby, plate VII, 5.

1754 1787 Franklin cent. Type as last, but cinquefoil of five dots instead of stars; the rims enclosing STATES UNITED are raised.
Slight chip off of edge. Extremely fine. Brown color. Very
rare.

1755 1787 Franklin cent. No rim to edge of band on reverse. Uncirculated. Bright red.

1756 1787 Franklin cent. Shows slight suction marks on obv. Unc.

1757 1787 Franklin cent. As last, but on a very heavy planchet,
weighing 218½ grains! while the one just preceding weighed
162 grains, about the usual weight. Good, but date very weak,
just discernible.

x#c. 3 – 1758 1787 Franklin cent. Club rays. Type as above, but some nine rays prominent, causing it to be known as the Club rays variety. R. UNITED STATES Otherwise as last. Very fine. Sharp imp. Rare.

2.. /.3₀ 1759 1787 Franklin cent. Type as above. R. UNITED STATES. Slight depression on edge. Uncirculated. Bright red. Rare.

~ /.,₋ 1760 1787 Franklin cent. Type as above, but showing suction marks around date. STATES UNITED. Uncirculated. Bright, original color. Struck slightly off center.

Thau /.' 1761 1787 Franklin cent. Waterbury restrike. Type of last, but strange to say no contemporary impression is known to exist. Bronze. Uncirculated.

Re.#r; 2.0 1762 1787 Franklin cent. As last. Obverse die cracked. Copper. Uncirculated. Red. Accompanying this piece is a printed note as follows, and as it decides a point in the history of these restrikes, I reprint it in full so as to record it. The original accompanies this coin:

"First United States cent, known as the Ring or Franklin cent. July 6th, 1787, the United States Government ordered the mint-int of its first coin. Messrs. Groome & Platt, of New Haven, Conn., did some part of the coinage. About the year 1860 the undersigned found (and still retains) the original dies among their effects in New Haven. The dies were taken to Waterbury, Conn., and a few coins struck for cabinet specimens, the enclosed being one of the restrikes. Horatio N. Rust, Chicago, 1875."

It is interesting to note that Horatio N. Rust is No. 8 of Sage's Numismatic Gallery tokens.

S+#.C. 9. _1763 1787 Franklin cent. *Original Die,* obverse only. Similar to last coin, but the *1 of date close to rays. Steel. Unique, valuable and highly interesting object.

C. .3₀ _ 1764 1793 Chain. AMERICA. Head of Liberty with short hair. Very fine. Steel color. Surface very finely eroded, but so minute that to the naked eye it does not show. Even impression. Extremely rare. Plate. Crosby 1-C.

C 2/. 1765 1793 Wreath. Head of Liberty with massive locks, LIBERTY and 1793 small, leaves large. Very fine. Right half of obverse surface eroded very lightly. Brown color. Very rare. Plate. C. 7-F. *~* *Lymanhale*

Brown   *37.50*   1766   1793 Wreath. Head of Liberty with flowing hair. Extremely fine. Surface shows very light erosion. Sharp, even impression. Brown color. Very rare. Plate. C. 9-H.

2.6   1767   1793 Wreath. Sprig with straight-up leaf. Fair. Very rare variety. C. 10-I.

Trace   *35.25* 1768   1793 Lettered edge. Extremely fine. Beading all around obverse, though not quite even, runs to edge at lower side. ~~Bold impression.~~ Light olive. Very rare. Plate. C. 11-J. *Hair much worn*

1769 1794 Hays Nos. 2, 3, 5. Very poor.   3 pcs.

1770 1794 Hays No. 10. Good. Rare.

1771 1794 Hays Nos. 13, 14. Good. Light dents on edge.   2 pcs.

1772 1794 Hays No. 15. Good.

1773 1794 Hays Nos. 16, 37, 45, 51, 52 dented. Poor.   5 pcs.

1774 1794 Hays No. 17. Very fine. Surface pitted by fine erosion. Brown color. Even impression.

Trace   *3.*   1775 1794 Hays No. 19. Good. Slight oxidation.

1776 1794 Hays No. 20. Very good. Steel color. Very rare.

1777 1794 Hays No. 21. Good.

1778 1794 Hays No. 22. Good.

Eagry   *2.50* 1779 1794 Hays No. 23. Very good. Reddish light olive.

Cosmir K   *.7* 1780 1794 Hays No. 25. Good. Extremely rare. Fair, in Guy sale brought $28.

Serson   *375* 1781 1794 Hays No. 26. Good. RTY weakly struck. Rare.

5. 1782 1794 Hays No. 31. Good. Apparently has been in a fire, color rubbed. Very rare.

Gilbert   *9.25* 1783 1794 Hays No. 33. Presents a very fine appearance, but hair has been delicately touched up with a graver, and field slightly burnished. Brown color.

1.00 1784 1794 Hays No. 39. Very good. Broad planchet. Steel color.

10. 1785 1794 Hays No. 43. Extremely fine. Surface very lightly eroded. Sharp, even impression. Brown color. A beautiful cent. Plate.

Rare   *505* 1786 1794 Hays No. 46. Good. Surface lightly eroded. Rare.

Scott   *165* 1787 1794 Hays No. 47. Poor. Deep dents on both sides.

3 1788 1794 Hays No. 48. Die shattered. Good. Slight dent on reverse edge. Rare.

K   *3.50* 1789 1794 Hays No. 49. Die broken on edge. Good. Very rare.

K   *70* 1790 1794 Hays No. 54. Good. Slight nicks.

1791 1794 Hays No. 56. Good. Slight dents on edge.

1792 1793 Lettered edge. Top of 5 touches bust. Very good. Even milling. Brown color. Scarce.

1793 1795 Plain edge. ONE CENT high in wreath. Uncirculated. Beautiful, sharp impression, with even milling. Considerable original red around outlines, turning to a pale steel color. Very rare. Plate.

1794 1795 As last. Extremely fine. Sharp, even impression. Beautiful light olive color. Rare. Plate.

1795 1795 ONE CENT in center of reverse. Extremely fine. Beautiful light olive, and a splendid match for last lot. Rare. Plate.

1796 1796 Liberty cap. High 6. Fine. CENT weak. Steel color. Rare. Gilbert A and far superior to piece he illustrates.

1797 1796 Bust of Liberty, draped, and hair tied with a ribbon. Uncirculated. Date rather weak, and die cracked below it. Deep, even milling. Rich brown color. Very rare. Plate. Gilbert 15.

1798 1797 Close date. R. Slender wreath. Very fine. Deep, even milling. Light brown color. Rare. Plate.

1799 1797 Wide date. R. Heavy small wreath. Very good. Milling around both sides.

1800 1798 Over 1797. Large date. Fair. Rare.

1801 1798 Large date. R. Slender wreath, 4 berries on left, 5 on right stem. Good. Rare.

1802 1798 Close, small date. Die broken over U. Uncirculated. Beautiful light olive. Very rare in such condition. Plate.

1803 1798 Wide, small date. R. Small, slender wreath, 5 berries on each stem. Very fine. Fine, even milling around both edges. Steel color. Pin scratch from chin.

1804 1799 Perfect date. Very good. Strong, even impression. Date wonderfully strong and bold, and LIBERTY also good. R. Three pin-head spots of corrosion on reverse. Brown color. Very rare. Plate.

1805 1800 Over 1798. Very fine. Slight nicks. Brown color. Rare.

1806 1800 79 under 80. Extremely fine. Sharp, even impression. Steel color. Very rare in such beautiful condition. Plate.

1807 1800 Break in die partly fills center of o and makes a tail to it as well, so that it looks like a Q Similar break between IB of LIBERTY. Uncirculated. Steel color, with traces of original color on reverse. Extremely rare. Plate.

1808 1800 Die broken below date; also under L. Fine. Broad planchet with milling. Two pin-point nicks at ER and pin-head dent in field. Color rubbed on cheek. Brown.

1809   1801   Wavy lines down field before face. Extremely fine. Steel color. Very rare in such splendid condition. Plate.

1810   1801   Perfect die. Extremely fine. Steel color. Bold impression. Rare so fine. Plate.

1811   1801 $\frac{1}{100}$. Very good. Four dents on edge. Brown color.

1812   1802   Obverse die perfect; reverse die broken over ST. Extremely fine. Brown color. Sharp, even impression. Plate.

1813   1802   Die broken over RTY. Uncirculated. Weak on point of the bust and OF on reverse. Beautiful light olive color. Plate.

1814   1803   Uncirculated. Superb impression. Beautiful pale light olive color, with traces of original color. Die cracked at point of bust. R. Small $\frac{1}{100}$.

1815   1803   The top of the 3 rests on the bust. R. Small $\frac{1}{100}$ wide 100. Suction marks before throat. Four small defects on obverse. Brown color. Extremely fine.

1816   1803   Large $\frac{1}{100}$. Perfect dies. Uncirculated. Superb, sharp, even impression. Mostly original color. A gem. Plate. *Placed 's.*

1817   1803   Large $\frac{1}{100}$. Die cracked in a semicircle from 1 to edge through hair. Beautiful light olive. Uncirculated. Plate.

1818   1804   Dies broken on edge, minute nick in field. Fine. Steel color. Very rare. Plate.

1819   1804   So-called restrike. Die cracked. R. Set upside down. Planchet of nearly double thickness. Uncirculated. Bright red.

1820   1805   Blunt 1 in date. Uncirculated. Sharp, even impression. Three slight dents on edge. Brown color. A beautiful cent. Very rare. Plate.

1821   1805   Blunt 1 in date. Extremely fine. Minute nick on cheek. Splendid, even impression. Steel color. Plate. -

1822   1806   Extremely fine. Light olive. Very rare so fine. Plate.

1823   1807   Over 1806. Large 7. Extremely fine. A few microscopic nicks. Splendid, bold impression, which is very unusual for this date. Rare. Plate.

1824   1807   Large $\frac{1}{100}$. Slight suction marks under chin. Extremely fine. Splendid, bold impression, which is very unusual for this date. Rare. Plate. A perfect match for last lot.

1825   1808   Very fine. While stars are not sharp, yet it is evenly struck and head and date strong. Brown steel color.

1826 1809 Over 1808. Very fine. Bold impression. Very light, almost invisible, hair line scratches in field before face. Brown color. Plate.

1827 1810 Over 1809. Extremely fine. Sharp impression. Brown steel color. Rare in this preservation. Plate.

1828 1810 Perfect date. Fine. Bold, even imp. Brown color.

1829 1811 Over 1810. Obverse slightly off center. Fine. Black.

1830 1811 Perfect date. Very fine. Stars behind head not centered; milling off on right side. Steel color. Rare.

1831 1812 Small and large dates. Fine. Steel color.   2 pcs.

1832 1813 Extremely fine. Stars weak. Chip cut off edge behind head. Red, changing to steel color, possibly cleaned long since.

1833 1814 Plain 4. Extremely fine, practically uncirculated, only the tips of the hair and wreath show friction. Sharp, even impression. Light brown color. Plate.

1834 1814 Crossed 4. Extremely fine. Sharp impression. Dark brown color.

1835 1816 Perfect die. Uncirculated. Unusually bold, even impression. Beautiful light olive, and slight rub on cheek.

1836 1816 Die broken on obverse edge. Uncirculated. Bright red.

1837 1817 13 stars, as are following six lots. 1 before point of bust, stars far from each side of date. Close date. Uncirculated. Sharp imp. Beautiful light olive. Plate.

1838 1817 1 before point of bust. Large, open, uneven date. Ex. fine. Brown color.

1839 1817 Date under bust, all so following. Wide, even date, star at each side close to date; 6th star points at peak of diadem. Extremely fine. Sharp imp. Steel color.

1840 1817 Close, uneven date. Extremely fine. Steel color. Two very slight dents on edge of rev.

1841 1817 Open date, wide space between 18 17 Two stars blunt, otherwise sharp, but not quite even. Extremely fine. Brown color.

1842 1817 Large, open date. Extremely fine, only tips of hair touched. Sharp imp. Not quite even. Light olive.

1843 1817 Connected date by crack in die. Very good.

1844 1817 15 stars. Very fine. Steel color. Rare.

1845 1818 Cracked die around stars. Unc. Bright red. Slight spotting.

.L-(i)ic,   2. - 1846   1819 Over 1818. Large date. Uncirculated. Beautiful light olive, traces of red. Scarce.

Sears   1,10 1847   1819 Small, close date. Uncirculated. Minute nick. Steel color.

C   1. - 1848   1819 Small, wide date. Uncirculated. Sharp. Light olive and red. Beauty.

K   .65 1849   1820 Large 0 in date. Die cracked around stars. Unc. Brilliant red. Exceptionally fine.

Hines   50. 1850   1821 Wide date. Uncirculated. Sharp, even impression. Mostly original bright red color, changing to light olive. A few microscopic nicks on obverse. A superb cent. Plate.

Ic.   3. 1851   1822 Wide date, with inner line between stars and serratures for three-quarters of the distance. Extremely fine. Bold impression. Plum color. Rare so fine.

7. 1852   1822 Wide date, without inner line. Uncirculated. Stars bold, but not centered. Deep, even milling. Beautiful light olive color. Rare so fine. Plate.

src   7. 1853   1823 Over 1822. Fine. Bronzed? long since, now presents a nice appearance. Rare. Plate.

Hines   36. 1854   1824 Close date. Uncirculated. Stars all sharp. Beautiful light olive color, with some original red color. A splendid cent and very rare, more so than those who have not sought to get this year in this state of preservation know. Plate.

Ic.   25. 1855   1824 Wide date. Uncirculated. Stars not centered, otherwise an even impression. Obverse considerable original red color. R. Light olive. Very rare. Plate.

Hall.   2. 1856   1825 Wide date. Very fine. Bold impression. Small dent on reverse edge. Rich brown color. Scarce.

1 50 1857   1825 Close date. Very fine. Slight edge dent. Brown color. Scarce.

3.- 1858   1826 Close date. Uncirculated. Sharp, even impression. Light steel color, with considerable original red color.

3 - 1859   1827 Extremely fine, one slight rubbing on cheek and tips of the hair. Sharp, with deep, even milling. Dark brown, with traces of red. Plate.

Sears   4. 1860   1828 Large date. 8 between 82. Extremely fine. Light olive. Rare. Plate.

1861   1828 Large date. 82 touch at top; crack connects 28 at bottom. Extremely fine. Sharp. Nick on edge and at 1. Steel color.

1862   1828 Large date, each figure separate. Extremely fine. Sharp. Steel color.

1863   1828   Small date.   Fine.   Bold, even imp.   Dark brown color.
Rare.

1864   1829   Small head.   Sixth star points at point of diadem.   R.
Large letters.   Very fine.   Steel color.

1865   1829   Large head.   Sixth star points below point of diadem.
First four stars weak.   R. Large letters.   Bold impression.
Plum color.   Extremely fine.

n.25 1866   1829   First four stars connected by a crack, sixth star points
above diadem.   R. Large letters.   Extremely fine.   Sharp imp.
Light steel color.   Plate.

1867   1830   Inner line; also stars connected by crack in die.   Uncirculated.   Minute nick on chin.   Very strong impression for this
year.   Brown color. '

Trace   5. 1868   1831   Small letters on reverse.   Uncirculated.   Stars not cen-
tered, otherwise sharp.   Original color.   Few trifling specks.
Extremely rare in this condition with small letters on rev.
Plate.

/ 1869   1831   Die cracked around stars.   R. Large letters.   Extremely
fine, only slightest touch of friction on cheek.   Sharp, even impression.   Beautiful light olive color.   Plate.

Uluc   1.80 1870   1831   Same as last, same condition.   Steel color.

Arner   4.25 1871   1832   Large letters on rev.   Uncirculated.   Steel color and traces
of original red, obverse trifle mottled.   Rare.   Plate.

Hrner   4— 1872   1832   Double profile.   Large letters.   Extremely fine.   Beautiful
light olive color.   Rare.

Stong   3.25 1873   1832   Small letters on rev.   Uncirculated.   Olive steel color.

—   c 3. 1874   1833   Sixth star points above diadem.   Uncirculated.   Sharp, even
imp.   Faint scratch in field behind head.   Beautiful light olive,
traces of red.   Plate.

Jhma   1.5 1875   1833   Sixth star points below point of diadem.   Ex. fine.   Light
steel color.

SmM   8.00 1876   1833   Die has a fine crack around connecting stars.   Bold, even
impression.   Bright red original color.

deuny   10 1877   1834   Small, wide date.   Crack connects stars, which are not all
centered.   Beautiful light olive, with traces of red.   Plate.

ilder   2.70 1878   1834   Slightly double profile.   Uncirculated.   Most beautiful
light olive color.   Plate.

Sigr 3. 1879   1834   Small, close date.   Faint crack connects stars.   Uncirculated.   Minute nick in field.   Beautiful light olive obverse, reverse darker shade.

8

Call   5.50 1880 1834 Large 8, small stars, small serratures inside high rim. Extremely fine. Steel color. Rare so fine.

K   7.50 1881 1834 Large date and stars, which are connected by a crack in the die. Very fine. Steel color. Scarce.

Jfries   2.50 1882 1835 Small date. Uncirculated. Stars not centered, but bold. Obverse bright red. R. Beautiful steel color. A gem. Plate.

     1883 1835 Diadem heavier on point, stars large. Profile double at mouth and chin. Very fine. Brown color.

Seay   1.50 1884 1835 Blunt diadem, similar to 1834. Small stars. Very fine. Light olive.

Gilbert   .80 1885 1835 Large date, large stars. Deep milling. Fine. Reddish brown.

     2— 1886 1836 Perfect die. Uncirculated. Dull original color, two specks.

Brown   2.25 1887 1836 Die broken at 6th star. Uncirculated. Beautiful, sharp, even impression. Steel, and traces of original red. Plate. *Placed 2*

Hines   .5.75 1888 1837 Plain hair cord. Short bust. Uncirculated. Brilliant bright red on both sides. A gem. Plate.

Brown   1.00 1889 1837 Plain hair cord, larger bust. Uncirculated. Sharp, even imp. Beautiful light golden color.

Elder   1.50 1890 1837 Beaded hair cord. Not struck sharp on border. Uncirculated. Beautiful light olive, traces of red.

Seay   .80 1891 1838 Uncirculated. Beautiful specimen. Steel and red color.

Gilbert   2.25 1892 1839 Over 1836. Die just shows crack from nose to edge. Good. Very rare.

     1893 1839 Head as 1838. Uncirculated. Not struck up sharp on border. Pale steel color and red. Scarce.

     1894 1839 Booby head. Weak on stars. Uncirculated. Pale steel color and red.

     1895 1839 Silly head. Bar below CENT Die cracked across obv. Not struck up on border. Very fine. Brown color.

Seay   3.40 1896 1839 Head as on 1840. Uncirculated. Beautiful light olive. Rare so fine.

Hy   3.50 1897 1840 Small date. Uncirculated. Sharp, even imp. Dull red. Plate.

     1898 1840 Large date. Very fine. Sharp. Steel color.

     3.50 1899 1841 Uncirculated. Beautiful specimen of rich, dull red color. Rare thus. Plate.

     1900 1842 Large date. Extremely fine. Slight nick on edge. Light olive.

Started   5.83 *Jly* *a/3 lots*
       2.25

1901 1843 Type as 1842. Extremely fine. Sharp. Brown color.

1902 1843 Type as 1844. Very fine. Nick on obv. and edge. L. o.

1.30 1903 1844 Uncirculated. Sharp. Light brown. Scarce.

3.0 1904 1844 First 4 double cut. Uncirculated. Bright red. Rare. *Place 1.20*

3.25 1905 1845 Date far from bust. Uncirculated. Brilliant bright red, pin-head speck on obv. Rare in such a high state of preservation.

5.25 1906 1846 Low 6. Dull *proof*. Sharp. Purple and red color. Extremely rare in this high condition. Plate. *Place 1*

1907 1846 As last. Uncirculated. Light olive. Sharp.

1908 1847 Date far from bust, curl over right side of 8. Small stars. Uncirculated. Sharp. Mostly bright red. Scarce variety.

1909 1847 1 before and touches bust, curl rests on 4, date high. Uncirculated. Considerable red. Scarce variety.

1.75 1910 1847 18 twice engraved. Uncirculated. Sharp. Steel and red color. Rare.

*— *1911 1848 1 before bust, curl points between 84. Uncirculated. Sharp. Beautiful color.

.60 1912 1848 Date below bust, curl points to 8. Extremely fine.

1913 1849 Date close to bust. Uncirculated. Sharp. Mostly red.

1. 1914 1849 Date from bust. Broad margin. Ex. fine. Steel color.

.75 1915 1849 1 before bust, curl between 84. Uncirculated.

1916 1850 Uncirculated. Bright red.

.70 1917 1851 Uncirculated. Brilliant bright red.

1.65 1918 1851 So-called over 1881. Remarkably clear. Very fine. Light olive.

2.75 1919 1852 Uncirculated. Brilliant bright red. Slight proof surface. Broad margin. A beauty.

1920 1853 1 double cut on bottom of base; also invades point of the bust. Uncirculated. Bright red.

1921 1853 1 double cut above base of 1. Uncirculated.

1922 1853 Curl touches 8 and 5. Uncirculated. Dull red.

1923 1853 3 double cut. Very fine.

1924 1854 Uncirculated. Bright red. Scarce.

1925 1855 Slanting 55. Proof. Red. Rare so.

1926 1855 Slanting 55. So-called 12 stars variety, one very weak. Unc.

1927 1855 Slanting 55. Knob over ear—break in die. Very fine.

1928 1855 Upright 55. Uncirculated. Partly red.

1929 1856 Upright 5. Uncirculated. Partly red.

1930   1856   Slanting 5. Uncirculated. Bright red.
1931   1857   Large date. Uncirculated. Obverse red. R. Light olive.
1932   1857   Small date. Uncirculated. Dull red.

HALF CENTS.

1933   1793   Crosby 1-A. Very fine. Even impression. Very slight dent on edge. Light olive. Very rare. Plate.

1934   1793   Crosby 1-B. Good. Rare.

1935   1793   Crosby 2A. Double profile. Very large planchet, size 13½, while the regular is 12½. Perfectly centered, with 1/16 inch margin on obverse and reverse outside the beading. Light olive. Plate. I have never met with another example like this.

1936   1793   Crosby 2-C. Fine. Rare.

1937   1794   Large, low bust. R. Bow far from leaves. Six berries on each branch. Extremely fine. Milling not up before bust. The obverse has numerous pits, owing to the planchet being defective. Light olive. Very rare so fine. Plate.

1938   1794   Similar, but L farther from cap. R. 5 berries on left and 4 on right stem, bow under leaf to right. Very fine. Steel color. Rare.

1939   1794   Small bust. R. Die crack from edge through E to stem. High bow. 6 berries on each stem. Very fine. Light brown color. Rare.

1940   1794   Same obv. R. As next preceding. Fine. Lightly eroded surface. Dark olive.

1941   1795   Lettered edge. Pole to cap. Very good. Deep, even milling.

1942   1795   Thick planchet, plain edge. No pole to cap. R. Die sunken across center. Extremely fine. Broad, even milling on both sides. Remarkably fine for this variety, as it shows the words HALF CENT while it is usual for these not to be visible. Brown color. Plate.

1943   1795   Same obverse die, thin planchet, plain edge. R. Different die, fraction line short. Extremely fine. Even imp. A few microscopic specks of corrosion on obv. Brown color. Plate.

1944   1795   Pole to cap. Date with period 1.795. Fair. HALF CENT so weak as to be invisible.

1945   1796   No pole to cap. Die broken across obv. R. Everything shows. Good. Excessively rare. Plate.

1946 1796 With pole to cap. Obverse fair. R. Poor, though nearly everything shows. Excessively rare. Plate for obverse.

1947 1797 1 over 1 of date. Very fine. Stronger impression than usual, and even. Brown color. Rare. Plate.

1948 1797 Low head, almost touching date. Good. Nick on cheek. Rare.

1949 1800 Uncirculated. Light olive and original red. Very rare in this condition. R. Slender wreath.

1950 1802 Over 1800. Very good. Rare.

1951 1803 Uncirculated. Dull original red, turning to pale steel color. The 3 double cut on bottom. R. $\frac{1}{100}$ close. One of the finest specimens known, and any collector who has sought this date in the condition which this one is in knows of its great rarity. Plate.

1952 1803 Wide $\frac{1}{100}$. Extremely fine. Bold imp. Dark olive.

1953 1804 Crossed, large 4. R. No ends to stems below bow. Uncirculated. Light olive.

1954 1804 Crossed, large 4. R. Ends to stems. Uncirculated. Beautiful light olive, traces of red. Not common in such a high state of preservation.

1955 1804 As last, but die broken, making it appear as if Liberty had her tongue out, and a spike from chin. Extremely fine. Light olive.

1956 1804 Same obverse. R. Die broken from near A of AMERICA round to I in UNITED Fine. Scarce.

1957 1804 Small, uncrossed 4. R. No ends to stems. Very fine.

1958 1804 Small, uncrossed 4. R. Ends to stems below bow. Corroded surface. Fair. Very rare.

1959 1805 No ends to stems. Very fine. Light olive.

1960 1805 Ends to stems. Very good. Scarce.

1961 1806 Small 6. R. No ends to stems. Uncirculated. Beautiful light olive. Rare in this condition.

1962 1806 Large 6. R. Ends to stems. Uncirculated. Partly red. Strong imp.

1963 1807 Very fine. Dark olive.

1964 1808 Over 1807. Fine. Light olive. Rare.

1965 1808 Extremely fine. Bold imp. Plum color. Rare so fine.

1966 1809 Perfect date. Uncirculated. Sharp impression. Beautiful light olive color, not common in this condition.

1967   1809   0 in date double cut. Good. Very rare.

1968   1809   So-called over 1808. Very good.

1969   1810   Uncirculated. Most beautiful light olive, and one of the finest I have seen. Rare. Plate.

1970   1811   Perfect die. Very good. Bold impression. Rare.

1971   1825   Uncirculated. Slight nick on edge. Red and l. o.

1972   1826   Uncirculated. Pale pink color. Scarce so beautiful.

1973   1828   12 stars. Uncirculated. Sharp imp. Plum color.

1974   1828   13 stars. Uncirculated. Brilliant bright red. Slight discoloration on rev.

1975   1829   Uncirculated. Sharp. Beautiful light olive.

1976   1832   Uncirculated. Traces of red.

1977   1833   Proof. Steel and red color. Rare in proof.

1978   1834   Uncirculated. Partly red.

1979   1835   Uncirculated. Bright red. Slight dark spot on obv.

1980   1836   *Original.* Proof. Sharp, even impression. Red and steel color. Extremely rare. Plate.

1981   1841   Original. Die cracked around stars before face. Sharp, even impression. Very rare.

1982   1843   Original. Good. Has been in circulation for a considerable period, and probably the only known specimen that has. Extremely rare. Plate.

1983   1846   Restrike. Proof. Sharp, even impression. Steel color. Excessively rare, only 18 struck. Plate.

1984   1847   Original. Extremely fine. Sharp impression. Steel color. Excessively rare. Plate.

1985   1847   Restrike. Proof. Sharp, even impression. Steel and red color. Extremely rare. Only 18 struck. Plate.

1986   1848   Restrike. Proof. Two leaves weak. Red, changing to steel color. Excessively rare, only 18 struck. Plate.

1987   1849   Small date. Restrike. Proof. Bright red. Excessively rare, only 18 struck. Plate.

1988   1849   Large date. Uncirculated.

1989   1850   Proof. Bright red.

1990   1851   Uncirculated. Light olive and red.

1991   1852   Restrike. Proof. Bright red. Extremely rare, 18 made. Plate.

1992   1853   Uncirculated. Light olive.

1993   1854   Uncirculated. Bright red, a few specks.

1994 1855 Proof. Bright red.
1995 1855 Uncirculated. Bright red.
1996 1856 Uncirculated, trace of proof surface. Bright red.
1997 1857 Slight proof surface. Half obverse dark, otherwise red.
1998 1857 Uncirculated. Dull red.

HARD TIMES TOKENS, 1834-1841.

Numbered by L. H. Low's book on this series, 1900 edition.

1999 Low No. 4. Jackson. Bust r. Uncirculated. Brass. Very rare.
2000 No. 5. Jackson. Bust in uniform ¾ l. in wreath. R. Eagle. Very fine. Brass. Very rare.
2001 No. 8. Bust of Jackson. R. Boar running. Uncirculated.
2002 No. 9. As last. Brass, with original white surface. Extremely fine. Rare.
2003 No. 10. Bust of Jackson, with broad shoulders. Very good. Rare.
2004 No. 12. Jackson standing with sword defending money bags. Ex. fine. Light olive. Sharp imp.
2005 No. 16. Verplanck. Bust l. R. Eagle. Brass. Uncirculated. Bright. The finest I have ever seen. Very rare.
2006 Nos. 18, 19, 20. Jackass running. Vf., and bright red.   3 pcs.
2007 Nos. 21, 22, 23, 28, 29 (poor, weak rev.). Head of Liberty. First and last have NOT erased. Good. Rare.   5 pcs.
2008 No. 30. Liberty, 55 stamped on it. Vg. Rare.
2009 Nos. 31, 32, 33, 34, 36, 37, 38, 39, 40. Head of Liberty. Fine.   9 pcs.
2010 No. 33. Uncirculated. Dull red. Rarely seen so fine.
2011 No. 38. LBENTONIAN Uncirculated. Traces of red. Scarce.
2012 No. 44. Jackson in safe. R. Wrecked ship. Uncirculated. Dull red, very slight stain in two places. Rare in this condition.
2013 No. 45. Phoenix. Extremely fine.
2014 Nos. 46, 48. Phoenix. Fine. Slight nicks.   2 pcs.
2015 No. 47. Phoenix. Uncirculated. Dull red. Rare in such exceptional condition.
2016 No. 49. Half cent. Extremely fine.
2017 No. 51. Jackson in chest, all spaces on end filled. Unc. Part red. Scarce.
2018 No. 51. As last. Part of end of chest filled with bars. Unc. Light olive.

2019   No. 51. As last. Only bottom line of squares filled. Unc. L. o.

Sect   ,3ɔ 2020   No. 52. As last. *Brass.* Good. Rare.

2021   No. 53. As last. Bigheaded Jackson, etc. Fine.

Scan   .35 2022   No. 54. Slave. Uncirculated. Unusually choice specimen.

"   .25 2023   No. 55. LOCO FOCO. Very fine.

2024   No. 56. Bust of Van Buren. Fine. Copper. Holed, as always.

2025   No. 58. Ship. Uncirculated. Brown color.

2026   No. 59. Ship. Very fine.

2027   No. 60. Ships. Extremely fine.

2028   No. 62. Ships. Uncirculated. Bright red. Rare state of preservation.

2029   No. 64. Ships. Extremely fine. Light olive.

mc   1,70 2030   No. 65. Head of Liberty. R. Ship. Very fine. Dents on edge. Rare.

Ite.   3— 2031   No. 66. Steer r. A FRIEND TO THE CONSTITUTION. R. Ship. Fine. Rare.

2032   Nos. 67, 68. 1841. Head of Liberty. Very fine.   2 pcs.

C   .40 2033   No. 69. 1841. Head of Liberty. Uncirculated. Traces of red.

Eldw   ,10 2034   No. 73. Cheapside. New Bedford, 1833. Badly dented on edge.

2035   No. 74. City Coal Yard, Providence. Uncirculated.

.11 2036   Nos. 75, 76. Very Good.   2 pcs.

.45 2037   No. 76. Robinson. Uncirculated. Traces of original red.

.50 2038   No. 78. Handy. Eagle Fine.

,30 2039   No. 80. Haskins. Very fine.

act   3.— 2040   No. 81. HOWELL WORKS GARDEN R. SIGNUM 1834. Good. Rare.

Eldw   .85 2041   No. 83. Richards. Lafayette standing. Uncirculated. Partly red. Rare condition.

Mather   .50 2042   No. 84. Schenck. Planing machine. Uncirculated. Scarce.

.40 2043   No. 86. Wilkins. Lafayette standing. Vg. Edge dents.

e/cc   .25 2044   No. 88. Head of Liberty r. Very poor. No. 145 badly dented on edge. Rare.   2 pcs.

Course (c) 2045   No. 92. Bucklin. 1835. Good.

Scan ,10 2046   No. 94. Clark & Anthony. Lafayette standing. Extremely fine. Scarce so fine.

.25 2047   No. 95. Old Merchants' Exg. R. NOT ONE CENT. Uncirculated.

.15 2048   No. 97. Old Merchants' Exg. Uncirculated. Partly red.

Erst .20 2049   No. 98. New Merchants' Exg. Uncirculated. Sharp. Light olive.

2.—70 2050   No. 99. Walsh. LANSINGBURG. N. Y., 1835. Ex. fine.

2051 No. 100. Walsh. Lafayette standing. Fine.
2052 No. 101. Walsh. LANSINBURG. Lafayette standing. Very fine.
          Scarce.
2053 No. 103. Robinson. Very fine.
2054 No. 104. Robinson. Uncirculated, traces of red.
2055 No. 105. Robinson. With *hyphen* between NEW-YORK. Good.
          Very rare.
2056 No. 107. Anderson. Boot. Uncirculated.
2057 No. 110. Center Market. Uncirculated. Bright red. Rare state
          of preservation.
2058 No. 111. Center Market. Very fine.
2059 Nos. 112, 113. Crossman. Very fine.   2 pcs.
2060 No. 114. Obverse fair. R. Very poor.
2061 No. 115. Deveau. Very good. Scarce.
2062 No. 120. Feuchtwanger cent. Eagle. Uncirculated.
2063 No. 122. Jarvis. Fine.
2064 No. 123. Jarvis. Extremely fine. Scarce.
2065 No. 124. March-Simes. Fine.
2066 No. 125. Maycock. Very good.
2067 No. 126. Maycock. Eagle. Extremely fine.
2068 No. 129. ROXBURY COACHES. R. NEW LINE 1837. Feuchtwanger
          metal. Fine. Rare.
2069 No. 132. Sise & Co. Fine.
2070 Nos. 133, 136 (holed). Smith. Very good.   2 pcs.
2071 No. 143. BERGEN IRON WORKS STORE. Eagle; die cracked behind.
          Extremely fine. Sharp and even. Rare.
2072 No. 145. Bucklin, West Troy. Good. Very rare.
2073 No. 148. Duseaman. R. Bouquet. Bas-Canada. Very fine.
2074 No. 151. Steer. R. W. GIBBS AGRICU (LTU) REIST (sic.) N. YORK.
          Very good. Holed and bruised on edge for half an inch. Very
          rare.
2075 No. 153. Riker. N. Y. Very fine.
2076 No. 162. M. VAN BUREN. Stars; bust of the Pres. r., below a
          wreath. R. INDEPENDENT TREASURY JULY. 4. 1840 Eagle. Holed.
          Good. Very rare.
2077 No. 164. Richards. Very good.
2077a Unknown origin. 1811. Snake and 15 stars. R. Eight separate
          triple leaves, enclosing OIE DIOE, outside .1.0.8 * O.I D S Feucht-
          wanger metal. Size of a dime. Good. Have never met with

another—though bearing date of 1811, I take it to be of 1835-1840 work.

HISTORICAL MEDALS OF AMERICA.

Arranged and numbered according to the book, "Colonial History, Illustrated by Contemporary Medals," by C. Wyllys Betts, N. Y., 1894. Closing number refers to the size in 16th of an inch.

2078   No. 21. 1602. Holland Covets Spanish America. POSSVNT QVÆ POSSE VIDENTUR 16 MARTY. 1602 (They are able to do what seems to be possible; March 16, 1602). Spanish galleon St. Jago between two Dutch ships, alluding to a naval combat when the Dutch drove the Spanish galleon ashore, at St. Helena, at the close of 1601. R. NON SVFFICIT ORBIS (One world does not suffice). Horse leaping from a globe (the device and motto of Philip II of Spain indicating his American possessions), on right lion of Zeeland leaping out of the sea. QVO SALTAS INSEQVAR (Whither thou leapest I will follow). Silver. Extremely fine. Very rare. 32.

2079   No. 39. Dampville. Beautiful bust r. R. Arms. Restrike. Copper. Very fine. Leroux 303. 32.

2080   No. 42. St. Christopher. Bust of Louis XIV r., long hair by MAVGER. Bronze. Restrike. Proof. 26.

2081   No. 42a. St. Christopher. Different bust, the hair drawn forward, covering the neck. R. As last. Bronze. Very early impression—possibly an original, as it *has not* BRONZE or CUIVRE on edge. Not given by Betts. Very rare. 26.

2082   No. 52. Victory at Tobago. Head of Louis XIV r. R. Victory and galley. Bronze. Very fine. 26.

2083   No. 57. Same event. Head L. XIV. R. As last. Copper. Fine. 16.

2084   No. 59. Same event. Head of Louis XIV. R. Tobago attacked. Bronze. Restrike. 26.

2085   No. 68. Quebec attacked. Head as last. R. France on rocks. *Silver*. Proof. Restrike. 26. Leroux 306a.

2086   No. 68. Quebec attacked. As last. Bronze. Perfect. Restrike. 26. Leroux 306a.

2087   No. 110. American aloe blooming at Nuremberg, 1726. Tin, with copper plug. Extremely fine. Rare. Unknown to Betts in this metal. 31.

Yhlen *1.50* 2088 No. 113. Company of the Indies. Arms with Indian with bow at either side; exg. COMPAGNIE DES INDES 1723. R. SPEM AUGET OPESQUE PARAT (It increases hope and prepares wealth). A ship under full sail to left. Silver. Very fine. Very rare. Zay 272. Plate.

" *3* – 2089 No. 143. Louisburg Founded 1720. Bust of Louis XV r. R. View of the fort of Louisburg, large church and houses. Silver. Perfect. Restrike. 26. Leroux 308.

2089a No. 143. Same as last. Bronze. Restrike. 26. Leroux 308.

2090 No. 169. Jernegan Cistern, 1736. Pallas. R. Caroline watering palm trees. Silver. Ex. fine. 24.

Old *.15* 2091 No. 180. Vernon. Half length l. ADMIRAL VERN(ON) (T)OOK PORTO BELLO. R. Porto Bello. Piece broken out of edge. Poor. Very rare. 24.

C *.40* 2092 No. 192. Vernon. Half length l. R. Porto Bello. Brass. Extremely fine. Very rare. Small, only size 16.

C *.40* 2093 No. 198. Vernon. Very fine. 23.

Cdel *.85* 2094 No. 222. Vernon. Admiral standing, with cannon and ship in field. Brass. Very good. 25.

Rno *.90* 2095 No. 226. Vernon standing to r., anchor behind him, cannon before. R. Harbor of Porto Bello, 1739. Brass. Cracked. Slight straight edge in planchet under cannon. Very fine. Very rare. Size 17.

Flac *.10* 2096 No. 246 Vernon and Brown standing, ship and crown between. R. The Devil with rope around neck of Sir Robert Walpole, whom he is leading into the jaws of a dragon. Very fine. 21.

Re *10.40* 2097 No. 314 and three others, 1 holed. Poor.   4 pcs.

40 2098 No. 323. THE PRIDE OF SPAIN HUMBLED BY A^D. VERNON. Vernon, Don Blass and Ogle. R. THEY TOOK CARTHAGENA APRIL 1741. Very good. 24.

2099 No. 324. Vernon and Ogle standing WE LOOK FOR DON BLASS. R. Similar to last. Very good.

C *.25* 2100 No. 325. Vernon and Don Blass. R. VERNON CONQUERD CARTAGENA APRIL 1741. Harbor and forts. Dented. Corroded. Very rare. 24.

C *-.20* 2101 No. 331. Vernon, cannon and anchor. Good.

.41 2102 No. 334. ADMIRAL : VERNON : VEIWING (sic) : THE : TOWN : OF : CARTHAGANA (sic) Ex'g 1740:1. Vernon and town. R. Carthagena. THE FORTS OF CARTHAGENA DESTROYED BY AD^M. VERNON Fine. 23.

1 berry   *10 2 5* 2103 Unpublished Vernon. IN . PORTO . BELLO . THERS . NOT . HIS . FEL-
LOW. This ins. on a ribbon. In center, full length of Vernon
standing on a grill, facing right, sword in right and baton in left,
which is extended. Behind him a ship sailing right, before him
cannon; above with line separating it from field is ADMIRAL
VERNON. R. TOOK PORTO BELLO WITH SIX SHIPS ONLY.. enclosed
by a line. Space before TOOK may have contained HE while it
is not visible, there is a slight suggestion of it. View of town,
with a fort at either side. Six ships to right, and at top two
small boats. Exergue NOV. 22 1739 Very good. Brass. Unknown to Betts, and I know of only one duplicate, that owned
by H. R. H., Prince Louis of Battenberg. Plate.

. 80 2104 No. 400. Kittanning destroyed, 1756. Arms of Phil. R. View
of the destruction of the Indian village. Pewter. Very good.
Slight edge dents. Original. Very rare. 28.

1 — 2105 No. 400. Same dies. When so shattered that it is remarkable this
medal could be made—it is interesting to exhibit what a condition the die came to. Bronze. 28.

Pedlow *. 80* 2106 No. 400. The mint reproduction of the above, the original dies
destroyed. Bronze. Proof. 31.

14 2107 No. 401. Indian peace Medal, 1757. GEORGIVS . II . DEI . GRATIA.
Bust of Geo. II l. R. LET US LOOK TO THE MOST HIGH WHO
BLESSED OUR FATHERS WITH PEACE 1757. Quaker and Indian
seated before a fire smoking a pipe of peace; above the sun.
Pewter. Extremely fine. *Original.* Extremely rare. 28.
NOTE.—This and lots Nos. 2104, 2105 were the first two medal
dies made in America.

— 2108 No. 401. As last. Restrike in bronze after the dies cracked.
Since destroyed, and this will be rare in time. 28.

.5 2109 No. 515. Pitt. Bust l. R. THE MAN. Copper. Original. Fine.
26.

2110 No. 517. Pitt. Similar to last. I. W. under bust. Original. Copper. Good. 26.

*2111 No. 531. Penn. Bust r. R. BY DEEDS OF PEACE PENSYLVANIA
SETLED 1681. William Penn shaking an Indian by the hand.
Bronze. Perfect. Rare. 26.

2 2112 No. 533. Coffin, of Nantucket, Mass. TRISTRAM COFFIN THE FIRST
OF THE RACE THAT SETTLED IN AMERICA Full length, standing on
a pedestal, inscribed 1642. R. DO HONOR TO HIS NAME. BE UNITED.

Four hands united. Bronze. Fine, but nicked and edge dented. Very rare, and seldom obtainable. 34.

2113 No. 545. Franklin. BEN^{M.} FRANKLIN . L. L. D. Fine bust in wig, and coat to l. R. Blank. Bronze. Extremely fine. Excessively rare, and probably the earliest medal of Franklin (1762?). 24.

2114 No. 546. Franklin. LIGHTNING AVERTED TYRANNY REPELL'D Bust of Franklin draped r. R. Oak tree, beaver gnawing it, 1776. Bronze. Perfect. 26.

2115 No. 547. Franklin. B. FRANKLIN OF PHILADELPHIA L.L.D. F. R. S. Young bust ¾ left, wearing loose cap and shirt. R. NON IRRITA FULMINA CURAT (He cares not for the ineffectual thunderbolt.) In ex'g 1777+. A tree struck by lightning. Bronze. Proof; perfect, beautiful specimen of this extremely rare medal. Plate. 29.

2116 No. 553. Cook. Fine bust l. R. Fortune standing, leans on a column, rudder, globe, etc. Bronze. Perfect. 28.

REVOLUTIONARY WAR.

2117 No. 557. Burgoyne's surrender at Saratoga. Bust of Gen. Gates l., by *Gatteaux*. HORATIO GATES DUCI STRENUO Ex'g COMITIA AMERICANA (The American Congress to Horatio Gates, the valiant Commander). R. SALUS REGIONUM SEPTENTRIONAL. Ex'g HOSTE AD SARATOGAM IN DEDITION ACCEPTO DIE XVII. OCT. MDCCLXXVII (The safety of the Northern Regions secured by the surrender of the enemy received at Saratoga, Oct. 17, 1777). View of Gen. Gates receiving the sword of Gen. Burgoyne; the victorious and vanquished troops in the background. Silver. *Original.* One of the few presented to officers. A few light nicks on obv., but the medal is in very fine condition and of extreme rarity. 36.

2118 No. 557. As last. Tin. Original. Two dents on obv. Proof. Extremely rare. 36.

2119 No. 557. As last. Bronze. Original. Holed at top, and evidently has seen much service as a decoration. 36.

2120 No. 557. As last. A perfect impression from the original dies, but not of the time. Bronze. 36.

2121 No. 566. Storming of Stony Point, N. Y., 1779. VIRTUTIS ET AUDACIÆ MONUM . ET PRÆMIUM ex'g, D. (sic) DIE FLEURY EQUITI

GALLO PRIMO SUPER MUROS RESP. AMERIC, D.D. (A monument and reward of valor and bravery; to M. de Fleury, a French officer, the first to mount the walls, the American Republic presented this gift). De Fleury, in ancient armor, standing amid the ruins of a fort, short sword drawn in right hand; his left holding a standard, on which he places his foot; AGGERES FALUDES IIOSTES VICTI, ex'g STONY-PT. EXPUGN. XV. JUL. MDCCLXXIX (Fortifications, marshes and enemies overcome). Bird's-eye view of the fort; and river. Bronze. Perfect. Excessively rare. Plate. 29.

No. 568. John Paul Jones. For capture of Serapis. Very fine bust r., by *Dupre.* R. View of the engagement. Bronze. Proof, from the perfect original dies. 36.

No. 568. The mint reproduction after the original dies broke. Bronze. Proof. 36.

No. 571. Treaty of Neutrality, 1780. Very fine bust of Catherine II of Russia. R. MARE LIBERVM (A free ocean) MDCCLXXX. Neptune, Mercury, sailors. Silver. Extremely fine. Rare. 31½.

No. 572. Treaty of Neutrality, 1780. GEWAP ENDE NE UTRALI TEIT. (Armed Neutrality.) A mailed arm, holding a sword and four shields united by a chain. R. JEHOVAH etc. Silver. Proof. 20.

No. 573. Treaty of Neutrality, 1781. Sailor standing, ships, etc. R. Long ins. Silver; unknown to Betts in this metal. Perfect. Very rare. 20.

No. 575. Maj. Henry Lee, for Paulus Hook, 1779. Bust to r., by *J. Wright.* R. Ins. in wreath. The obverse from the original die. R. Modern. Bronze. Perfect. 29.

No. 583. Action off Cadiz, 1781. Sea fight between the Netherlands and Great Britain. VIS VI FORTITER REPULSA (Violence bravely repelled by force), ex'g PROPE GADES XXX MAY MDCCLXXXI. (Near Cadiz, May 30, 1781). The four frigates after the action. R. ATIQUA VIRTV TE DVVM VIRI (By the old time valor of two men). Trident of Neptune standing erect in the ocean, etc. Silver. Extremely fine. Very rare. 28. See article on this medal by Mr. Parsons in the Am. Jo. of Numismatics.

No. 583. Battle of Doggersbank, 1781. PAX QVAERITVR BELLO. (Peace is sought by war). In field V . AVG . MDCCLXXXI. Exquisite figure of Victory standing on the prow on an antique galley -DOGGERSBANK- R. MVNIFICENTIA PRINCIPIS AVRIACI (By this liberality of the Prince of Orange), in center within wreath EXIMIAE VIRTVTIS PRAEMIVM (The reward of distinguished valor). Silver. Oval, ring on edge for suspension. Extremely fine. Very rare. *Plate.* 24 x 18.

2130   No. 587.   Honor of Rear Admiral Bentinck, mortally wounded in the above action. Funeral urn, etc. Long ins. R. Monument. Silver. Ex. fine. 28.

2131   No. 589.   Battle of the Doggersbank. INJVRIIS COACTA (Compelled by injuries), ex'g IN VADO ASELL . V. AVG. MDCCLXXXI. (On the Doggersbank, August 5, 1781.) Holland—a female—lion, etc. R. Seven wreaths, enclosing names. Silver. Ex. fine. 29.

2132   No. 590.   Battle of the Doggersbank. Lion of Batavia at altar. R. Laudatory ins. of the success of the Dutch fleet. Silver, not known to Betts in this metal. Ex. fine. 17.

2133   No. 593.   Battle of the Cowpens, 1781. Daniel Morgan. Medal presented in gold by Congress. America, as an Indian queen, placing wreath on the General's head. R. View of the engagement. Bronze. An original, and as such extremely rare. Ex. fine. 36.

2134   No. 593.   Same medal, more modern impression from the same dies. Bronze. Perfect. 36.

2135   No. 594.   Same event. William Washington. Medal presented in gold by Congress. The Col. leading a charge. Bronze. Original impression. Ex. fine. 29.

2136   No. 595.   Same event. John Egar Howard. Medal presented by Congress in gold. The Col. mounted to right, accompanied by Victory, chasing a color bearer. Bronze. Original impression. Ex. fine. 29.

2137   No. 597.   Battle of Eutaw Springs. Nathaniel Greene. Medal presented in gold to him. NATHANIELI GREEN EGREGIO DVCI COMITIA AMERICANA (The American Congress to Nathaniel Greene, the distinguished leader). Bust in uniform l. R. SALUS REGIONUM AUSTRALIUM (The safety of the Southern territories). Victory to left, alighting on a trophy of arms, ex'g HOSTIBUS AD EUTAW DEBELLATIS DIE VIII SEPT . MDCCLXXXI (The enemy vanquished at Eutaw, Sept. 8, 1781). Bronze. Very fine. Excessively rare. 31.

2138   No. 600. British Indian Chief's Medal (1777-8?). Presented to the Indian allies who aided the British fight the Americans. GEORGIUS III DEI GRATIA. Young bust in armor r. R. The Royal arms. Silver. Extremely fine. Small hole at top where a swivel or loop has been. Very rare. Plate. 50. Leroux 832.

THE INDEPENDENCE OF UNITED STATES RECOGNIZED.

2139   No. 602. Recognition by Frisia, Holland, 1782. Frisian standing, clasping hand of America, Cupid above with liberty cap; behind him female—Great Britain—offers olive branch. Silver. Proof. 28.

2140   No. 603. Holland receives John Adams as Envoy, 1782. LIBERA SOROR SOLEMNI DECR. AGN. 19 APR. MDCCLXXXII (A Free Sister, acknowledged by solemn decree April 19, 1782). Two beautiful females—Holland, America. R. TYRANNIS VIRTUTE REPULSA Ex'g SUB GALLIÆ AUSPICIIS (Tyranny repelled by valor under the auspices of France). Unicorn (Great Britain) has broken his horn against a rock (America). Silver. Field slightly abraded. Extremely fine. Rare. 28½.

2141   No. 604. Treaty of Commerce between Holland and the U. S., 1782. FAVTISSIMO FOEDERE JUNTÆ DIE VII OCTOB. MDCCLXXXII. (United by a most auspicious treaty, Oct. 7, 1782.) Fame on clouds. R. Monument, Mercury, etc. Silver. Proof. 29.

2142   No. 606. Same event. EN DEXTRA FIDESQUE (Behold, here is my right hand, and the pledge of my good faith). America, with U. S. flag, advancing to seated female—Holland. R. Ins. trs. (Hail to you, American, who have fought out your freedom: All Netherlands accepts your friendship. God's grace unite two free lands, to mutual good, through solid ties). Silver. Very rare. Perfect. 20¼.

2143   No. 608. Peace of Versailles. LIBERTAS AMERICANA. Louis XVI enthroned, pointing to a shield with 13 bars which a female has just hung to a Liberty column. R. COMMVNI CONSENSV (By Common Consent). Pallas standing with shields of France, England, Spain and Holland. Silver. Very fine. Rare. 29.

2144   No. 608. As last. Tin, with copper plug (inserted before striking). Extremely fine.

2145   No. 610. The treaty of Paris, 1783. SIC HOSTES CONCORDIA IVNGIT AMICOS (Thus Concord unites enemies as friends). Peace and

America standing, below view of Paris. R. Peace standing victorious over War, and long ins., and too many accessories to be described here. Silver. Extremely fine. Excessively rare in this metal. 27½. Plate.

2146 No. 610. As last. Pewter, with copper plug. Good.

2147 No. 611. The treaty of Paris, 1783. Bust of Louis XVI in rich attire r. R. PAX FRANCIAM INTER ET ANGLIAM VERSALIIS MDCCLXXXIII (Peace between France and England, at Versailles, 1783). Peace standing. Silver. Proof. Old restrike. 27.

2148 No. 612. Same event. Bust in plain drapery r., by Du Vivier. R. Same as last. Silver. Original. Very fine. Extremely rare. Unknown to Betts in this metal. 27.

2149 No. 615. LIBERTAS AMERICANA (American Liberty), in ex'g 4 JUIL. 1776 (July 4, 1776). Beautiful undraped head of Liberty to l., hair flowing, cap and staff behind. R. NON SINE DIIS ANIMOSUS INFANS (The infant is not bold without divine aid). Ex'g ⊹ OCT ⊹⊹⊹ DUPRE F. Infant Hercules on a shield, strangling two serpents (the armies of Burgoyne at Saratoga and Cornwallis at Yorktown). Minerva (France) protecting him from an attack by the British lion. Silver. Extremely fine. Very rare. 30. See Mr. Parson's article on this medal, A. J. N., XXIII, 31. A most interesting medal, designed by Benj. Franklin and struck in 1782.

2150 No. 615. As last. Bronze. Proof. Exceptional condition and seldom seen.

2151 No. 615. As last. Bronze. Very fine; slight nicks, as usual.

2152 LIBERTE FRANCOISE L'AN I DE LA R.F. Exquisite bust of Liberty with flowing hair to left, liberty staff with cap behind. R. A LA CONVENTION NATIONALE PAR LES ARTISTES REUNIS DE LYON. PUR METAL DE CLOCHE FRAPPE EN MDCCXLII. Bronze. Ex. fine. Rare. 23. It is an open question whether it was from the last or this medal that the head on the cent of 1793 was copied.

2153 No. 619. Franklin. Splendid bust l., by Dupre. R. ERIPUIT etc. (He snatched the thunderbolt from heaven and the sceptre from tyrants.) Beautiful figure of Truth standing. Bronze. Original. Extremely fine. 29.

2154 No. 619. Franklin. As last. Silver. Proof. Restrike. 29.

2155 No. 619. Franklin As last. Bronze. Proof. Restrike. 29.

9

AMERICAN MEDALS NOT IN BETTS' BOOK.

2156 American Prosperity. AMERICANA PROSPERITAS Family group—
the mother seated suckling a baby, while another child stands at
her right and a third asleep at her knee; behind this group
stands a cow, over the back of which the father leans, observing
the happy group before him; to right stands Mercury, and in
distance masts of a ship; legend above. Contemporaneous cast
in lead from the artist's model, which was probably intended for
a medal. While no name of the artist appears, it is probably a
work of about 1790 period. A charming composition and unique.
Has been cracked across and successfully repaired. Plate. 38.

2157 Diplomatic medal, 1776. TO PEACE AND COMMERCE IV. JUL.
MDCCLXXVI America seated with bales of goods, Mercury before
her. R. Arms of U. S. The mint copy from the original.
Bronze. Perfect. 43.

2158 Peace of Ghent, 1814. PEACE SPREADS HER INFLUENCE O'ER THE
ATLANTIC SHORES. Exquisite figure of Peace sailing on the sea
in a shell; below G. MILLS INVEN. ET. SCULP R. CONCORD BETWEEN
GREAT BRITAIN AND AMERICA. Dove of peace, etc. Bronze. Ex.
fine. Extremely rare. 28½. Sold for $8 at Mickley and $7.50
Bushnell sale.

2159 Peace of Ghent, 1814. Peace standing on part of the globe. R.
TREATY OF PEACE & AMITY BETWEEN GREAT BRITAIN AND THE
UNITED STATES ETC Wm., silvered. Rare. 29. Leroux 875.

2160 Fox, Chas. Jas. Bust r., by *James*. RT. HE. C. J. FOX. R. American
Indian with bow and tomahawk walking r. IF RENTS I ONCE CON-
SENT TO PAY MY LIBERTY IS PAST AWAY. Edge, SPENCE DEALER IN
COINS LONDON. ½ penny token. Perfect. Very rare.

2161 Fox, Chas. Jas. Friend of America during the Rev. Bust ¾ r.
GLORY BE THINE INTREPID FOX, FIRM AS OLD ALBIONS BATTERED
ROCKS. R. RESISTLESS SPEAKER etc. Edge, MANUFACTURED BY W.
LUTWYCHE BIRMINGHAM. Penny token. Perfect. Brass.
Rare. 22.

2162 BROUGHAM AND GREEVEY. R. PEACE WITH AMERICA AND A FREE TRADE
TO INDIA. Tin. Holed for suspension. I have never seen a duplicate. This came from the Bushnell Coll. 26.

2163 Rush, Benj., Dr. Signer of the Declaration of Indep. Bust l.
BENJAMIN RUSH M : D : OF PHILADELPHIA. R. Country view, with

Schuylkill river, name of his estate, SYDENHAM. Open book. Rock inscribed READ THINK OBSERVE ex'g A. MDCCCVIII. Bronze. Slightly worn. Fine. Very rare. 27.

Miln. .76 2164   New York. DE WITT CLINTON.MAYOR. Bust r. R. View of NEW YORK CITY HALL FOUNDED MAY 26 1803 OCCUPIED MAY 4 1812. Hole at top. Tin. Vg. Extremely rare. 22.

225 2165   Fulton, Robert. View of his steamboat the "Clearmont." R. SACRED TO THE MEMORY OF ROBERT FULTON. ONE OF THE MOST ILLUSTRIOUS BENEFACTORS OF MANKIND. Tin. Very fine. Slight nicks. Very rare. 33.

6x 2166   Florida. DUCE MAC GREGARIO LIBERTAS FLORIDARUM Cross in wreath. R. AMALIA VENI VIDI VICI In wreath 27 JUNII 1817. Bronze. Very fine. Excessively rare. 21.

/- 2167   Commercial treaty between France and America, 1822. Bust of Louis XVIII. R. Statue of Mercury, at sides of which stand France and America personified by two beautiful females. Bronze. Proof. Original. 32.

/. 2168   West, Benj. Celebrated painter, and though an American Friend was President of the Royal Academy of England. Bust l. R. Names of men who in 1815 subscribed to the fund to purchase and present to the Nation his great picture of Christ in the Temple! Bronze. Proof. Very rare. 26.

/—2169   Latrobe. Monument. U. S. MILITARY ACADEMY WEST POINT. R. Eagle with scroll, DETUR DIGNIORI. Below, FROM THE CORPS OF CADETS TO J. H. B. LATROBE ESQ 1825. Bronze. Proof. Excessively rare. 17.

Cullen .75 2170   Pinckney, Chas. Cotesworth. Bust r., by *Wright*. R. A PATRIOT AND OFFICER OF THE REVOLUTION BORN FEB. 25TH. 1746 DIED AUG 16TH. 1825 AGED 79 YEARS. Artist's trial cast in lead in the dies; no struck impression known of the two dies. Excessively rare. 29.

/—2171   Pinckney. Same obverse as last. R. Blank. A struck impression on a lead planchet. Ex. fine. Probably unique. 29.

Mild 5.7r 2172   Holland. William I. Bust of King r. R. AB ANGLIS ET AMERICANIS SEPTEMTRIONAL. DE TERMINO MOTO ARBITER VOCATUS 1829. Silver. Proof. 27. Rare and interesting, as it was struck to commemorate his having acted as arbiter in the dispute over the North-Eastern Boundary between U. S. and Canada. Leroux 830.

2173   Witherspoon, John. Patriot and signer of Decl. of Independence, etc. Full length. Struck by the Centennial Com. of the Pres. Church in U. S., 1876. Copper. Proof. Scarce. 32.

2174 Generals in the Revolutionary War. Com. medal of events. Maj. Gen. Anthony Wayne, Gen. Moses Cleveland, Gen. Nath. Massie, Maj. John Andre. Bust. Bronze. Proof. 22-24.   4 pcs.

2175 Warren. View of battle of BUNKER HILL 17 JUNE 1775. R. BATTLE OF BUNKER HILL DEATH OF GENERAL WARREN 17. JUNE 1775 BOSTON MOURNS HER GALLANT SON. Wm. Proof. I have never met with a duplicate of this medal! 29.

2176 Erie Canal, 1825, opening. Arms of N. Y., etc. R. Pan and Neptune seated. Tin. Proof. A few slight nicks on edge. Very rare. 52.

2177 Erie Canal. Same event. Presented by the City of N. Y. In box (broken) made from wood of first boat to pass through. *Silver.* Proof. Very rare. 28.

2178 National Jubilee 50th Anni. of Decl. of Independence, 1826. Eagle, shield, flags, arms, etc., above 13 stars; below NATIONAL JUBILEE 1826. R. DECLARATION OF INDEPENDENCE SIGNED JULY 4: 1776. FOR THE SUPPORT OF THIS WE PLEDGE TO EACH OTHER OUR LIVES OUR FORTUNES & OUR SACRED HONOUR. Silver. Proof. Holed at top for ring. Excessively rare in this metal, and I believe the only example that I have seen. 35. From Bushnell Col.

2179 Same. Struck on two brass planchets and then joined. Have never seen another in this metal.

2180 Same. Copper. Holed at top. Fine, but edge dented. Rare.

2181 Same. Tin. Holed at top. Very fine. Rare.

2182 New Haven, Conn. Bi Centennial, 1638-1838. Roger Williams preaching to the colonists and Indians. QUINNIPIACK 1638. R. NEW HAVEN 1838. View of city. Silver. Proof. Very rare, and seldom obtainable in this metal. 36.

2183 Clay, Henry. Bust l., by *Wright.* R. Wreath, enclosing history of his life. Obv. slight dents. Bronze. Extremely rare. Published at $30. 56.

2184 Clay, Henry. Same bust as last. R. Scroll AMERICAN SYSTEM on the rock CONSTITUTION, arm and hand before it; THE ELOQUENT DEFENDER OF NATIONAL RIGHTS etc. Splendid medal. Bronze. 48.

2185 Webster, Daniel. Great statesman. Bust r., by Wright. R. Column surmounted by a globe I STILL LIVE. Silver. Original case with publication circular. "Dies cost $1,200." Proof. Excessively rare, as but two struck in this metal. 48. NOTE.— From Hoffman and Bushnell Collections.

2186 Webster. As last. Bronze. Proof. 48.

2187 Japan Embassy, 1860. Bust r. of MILLARD FILLMORE PRESIDENT OF THE UNITED STATES 1850. R. IN COMMEMORATION OF THE FIRST EMBASSY FROM JAPAN TO THE UNITED STATES 1860. Bronze. Ex. fine. Slight spot on obv. 48. Remarkable and unique mule, as the obverse should have been Jas. Buchanan, as the next medal—as this is it makes two dates, 1850 and 1860, and under the wrong President. How such a blunder was made by the mint is extraordinary.

2188 Japan Embassy, 1860. Bust r. of JAMES BUCHANAN, PRESIDENT OF THE UNITED STATES. R. As last. Bronze. Proof. 48.

2189 San Francisco. Wreck of S. S., 1853. The rare medal presented by Congress to those who rescued the passengers, officers and men. Columbia wreathing a sailor. R. Man and woman on a raft. Slightly spotted. 50.

2190 Shipwreck. U. S. Gov. award medal for saving life. Arms of U. S. R. Man with victim in his arms. Bronze. 40.

2191 Life Saving. U. S. Gov. award. Second class. Angel directing man in the water. R. Wreath. ACT OF CONGRESS JUNE 20TH. 1874. etc. Dull tin. In case. 40.

2192 Life Saving. Congress to—FOR COURAGE AND HUMANITY IN THE SAVING OF LIFE—S. S. METIS 1872. View of. Bronze. Scarce. 40.

2193 Mechlenburg. Declaration of Independence, 20 May, 1775. Beehive and liberty cap on a branch, 1775-1875, clasped hands below, rays behind all of it. Silver. Ex. fine. Rare. 19½. More importance should be given to this Mechlenburg event, for it was really the first Declaration of Independence from Great Britain.

2194 Great Seal of U. S. Centl. Cel., 1782-1882. Views of seals. Br. Proof. 40.

2195 Columbian Exp. Chicago, 1893. Bust of Columbus on disc in center, Indians and Columbia at sides, globe above, eagle beneath. R. Progress, attended by cherubs, Indians in foreground. Beautiful medal of Columbus. Bronze. 36.

2196 Francis. THE UNITED STATES OF AMERICA BY ACT OF CONGRESS 27 AUGUST 1888 TO JOSEPH FRANCIS INVENTOR AND FRAMER OF THE MEANS FOR THE LIFE SAVING SERVICE OF THE COUNTRY, border of stars. Bust left. R. Sea coast, with life saving apparatus in action. Copper. 64. One of the largest medals ever struck by the Government, and seldom offered.

*3—*2197 Field. HONOR AND FAME ARE THE REWARD. INDOMITABLE PERSE-VERANCE AND ENDURING FAITH ACHIEVED THE SUCCESS. Head of Field on clouds, being crowned from above; below ships laying cable; at sides globes—EUROPE and AMERICA joined by chain. R. BY RESOLUTION OF THE CONGRESS OF THE UNITED STATES MARCH 2, 1867 TO CYRUS W. FIELD OF NEW YORK FOR HIS FORESIGHT, FAITH AND PERSISTENCY, IN ESTABLISHING TELEGRAPHIC COMMUNICATION BY MEANS OF THE ATLANTIC TELEGRAPH CONNECTING THE OLD WITH THE NEW WORLD. Copper. 64. One of the largest medals ever struck by the U. S. Commemorates a great step in the World's Progress!

2— 2198 Brown, John. Bust ¾ f. r., by *Warden.* R. A LA MEMOIRE DE JOHN BROWN ASSASSINE JURIDIQUEMENT A CHARLESTOWN LE 2 DECEMBRE 1859 etc. Impression in bronze from same dies that struck the one in gold which Frenchmen presented to his widow. Dies destroyed. Proof. Very rare. 36.

NATIONAL MEDALS.
PRESIDENTS OF THE UNITED STATES.

Impressions of the medals given in silver to the Indians by the Presidents. Obverse, bust of the President, with birth, date and name. R. PEACE AND FRIENDSHIP. Clasped hands of an Indian and U. S. A. officer, crossed tomahawk and pipe of peace. Where other device is used it is noted.

All are in bronze, perfect condition (exceptions noted), and nearly all (first excepted) early impressions, with proof surface, and not as now made with sand-blasted surface. Closing number refers to size in 16ths of an inch.

2.40 2199 1789 Washington, George. Bust r. R. Clasped hands. 48.

2.50 2200 1797 Adams, John. Large bust in plain coat and queue r., by *Leonard.* R. As last. Cast in lead. Only example I have ever seen from this die, and probably unique. 38.

2201 1801 Jefferson, Thomas. Bust l. Extremely rare of this great size 64! One of the largest medals made by U. S., and has not been struck for many years.

2202 1801 Jefferson. As last. 48.

2203 1801 Jefferson. As last. Proof in tin, toned, and from its appearance probably contemporaneous impression. Never heard of a duplicate in this metal. Proof. 32.

2204 1801 Jefferson. As last. Bronze. Rare of this size, 32.

2205 1809 Madison, James. Bust to left. 48.

2206 1809 Madison. Obverse die rusted. 40.

2207 1809 Madison. Rare of this size, 32.

2208 1817 Monroe, James. Bust to right. Size 48.

2209 1817 Monroë, James. Rare of this size, 32.

2210 1825 Adams, John Quincy. Bust r. 48.

2211 1825 Adams. Rare of this size, 32.

2212 1825 Adams. JOHN QUINCY ADAMS PRESIDENT OF THE UNITED STATES MARCH 4. 1825. Draped bust r. R. SCIENCE GIVES PEACE AND AMERICA PLENTY. Pallas as Peace hands olive branch to Indian—America—seated on a cornucopiæ. Tin. Very fine. Very rare. 32.

2213 1829 Jackson, Andrew. Bust r. R. Clasped hands. 48.

2214 1829 Jackson. Scarce. Size 40.

2215 1837 Van Buren, Martin. Bust r. 48.

2216 1837 Van Buren. Scarce. Size 40.

2217 1837 Van Buren. Slightly chafed. Rare. Size 32.

2218 1837 Van Buren. Bust r R. INAUGURATED MARCH 4TH A.D. 1838. Rare. 40.

2219 1841 Tyler, John. Bust left. 48.

2220 1841 Tyler. Slightly chafed. Rare of size 32.

2221 1841 Harrison, Wm. Henry. Bust ¾ l. R. INAUGURATED PRESIDENT OF THE UNITED STATES MARCH 4. 1841 DIED APRIL 4. 1841. 48.

2222 1845 Polk, Jas. K. Bust l. R. Clasped hands. 48.

2223 1845 Polk. Chafed. Rare of size 32.

2224 1849 Taylor, Zachary. Bust l. Rare of size 32.

2225 1850 Taylor. Splendid bust r. R. History of his life. Very fine. Rare. 36.

2226 1850 Fillmore, Millard. Head r. R. Settler and Indian before U. S. flag, etc. 48.

2227 1857 Buchanan, James. Bust r. R. As last. 48.

2228 1860 Buchanan. Same obv., except no date. R. IN COMMEMORATION OF THE FIRST EMBASSY FROM JAPAN TO THE UNITED STATES 1860. Slight nicks. 48.

2229   Buchanan. Same obverse as last. R. TO Dᴿ· FREDERICK ROSE, ASSISTANT SURGEON ROYAL NAVY, G. B. FOR KINDNESS AND HUMANITY TO OFFICERS AND CREW OF THE U. S. STEAMER SUSQUEHANNA. Æsculapius, etc. 48.

2230   1862 Lincoln, Abraham. Bust r. R. Civilized Indians, surrounded by an Indian scalping another Indian. Quiver, bow, peace pipe, etc. Nicked. 48.

2231   1865 Lincoln. Head r. R. INAUGURATED PRESIDENT—ASSASSINATED APRIL 14.1865. 48.

2232   1865 Johnson, Andrew. Bust r. R. Pedestal with PEACE, above bust of Washington; before it Indian clasping hand of Columbia. 48.

2233   1865 Johnson. As last. Rare size of 40.

2234   1867 Johnson. Bust r. R. WITH COURAGE AND FIDELITY HE DEFENDED THE CONSTITUTION AND BY JUSTICE AND MAGNANIMITY RESTORED ALIENATED STATES. Rare. 48.

2235   1869 Grant, U. S. Head r. R. INAUGURATED FIRST TERM MARCH 4, 1869. SECOND TERM MARCH 4, 1873. 48.

2236   1871 Grant. Indian Peace Medal. Bust r., Peace pipe and olive branch below. R. Globe, Bible, implements of Peace. 40.

2237   1877 Hayes, R. B. Head l. R. INAUGURATED MARCH 5.1877. 48.

2238   1881 Garfield, J. A. Bust l. R. INAUGURATED MARCH 4. 1881. 48.

2239   1881 Garfield. Bust l. R. Settler showing his homestead to an Indian, PEACE. Indian Peace Medal. Oval. 38 x 48.

2240   1881 Arthur, C. A. Bust r. R. INAUGURATED SEPTEMBER 20 1881. 48.

2241   1885 Cleveland, G. Bust r. R. INAUGURATED, etc. Copper. 48.

2242   1889 Harrison, Benj. Bust l. R. INAUGURATED etc. 48.

2243   1893 Cleveland. Bust r. R. SECOND TERM etc. 48.

2244   1897 McKinley, W. Bust l. R. INAUGURATED etc. 48.

MEDALS AWARDED NAVAL OFFICERS BY THE CONGRESS OF THE UNITED STATES.

DIFFICULTY WITH FRANCE.

2245   Truxtun, Capt. Thos. Bust l. R. Engagement bet. *Constellation* and *La Vengeance*, Feb. 2nd, 1800. Bronze. Proof. 36.

WAR WITH TRIPOLI.

2246 Preble, Com. Ed. Bust l. R. View of bombardment of Tripoli, 1804. Original. Struck before dies broke. Obverse bronzing slightly mildewed. Very rare. 41.

MEDALS AWARDED NAVAL OFFICERS BY THE CONGRESS OF THE UNITED STATES.

WAR OF 1812 WITH GREAT BRITAIN.

All in bronze, perfect and size 40.

2247 Hull, Capt. Isaac. Bust l. R. Engagement bet. *Constitution* and *Guerriere*, Aug. 19, 1812.

2248 Jones, Capt. Jacob. Bust r. R. Engagement bet. *Wasp* and *Frolic*, Oct. 18, 1812.

2249 Decatur, Capt. Stephen. Bust r. R. Engagement bet. *United States* and *Macedonian*, Oct. 25, 1812.

2250 Bainbridge, Capt. Wm. Bust r. R. Engagement bet. *Constitution* and *Java*, Dec. 29, 1812.

2251 Lawrence, Capt. Jac. Bust r. R. Engagement bet. *Hornet* and *Peacock*, Feby. 24, 1813.

2252 Burrows, Lieut. W. Tomb, he was killed in the action. R. Engagement bet. *Enterprise* and *Boxer*, Sept. 4, 1813.

2253 McCall, Lieut. E. R. Bust r. R. As last.

2254 Perry, Capt. O. H. Bust r. Presented by State of Pa. R. *Battle of Lake Erie*. Sept. 10, 1813. Reverse die cracked, and cannot longer be used. 38.

2255 Perry. Same obv. R. Wreath TO—. Pres. by State of Pa. for patriotism and bravery in battle of Lake Erie.

2256 Perry. View of action. "WE HAVE MET THE ENEMY AND THEY ARE OURS" R. Wreath TO—, BY RESOLUTION OF THE KENTUCKY LEGISLATURE FEB. 11. 1860. Brass. Rare. 27.

2257 Perry. Same as last. Bronze. Tin. 2 pcs.

2258 Perry. Bust r. U. S. Gov. award medal. Bust r. R. Battle of Lake Erie, Sept. 10, 1813.

2259 Elliott, Capt. J. D. Bust r. R. Same as last. Small spot on obverse.

2260 Warrington, Capt. L. Bust r. R. Engagement bet. *Peacock* and *Epervier*, March 29, 1814.

2261 Blakeley, Capt. J. Bust r. R. Engagement bet. *Wasp* and *Reindeer*, June 28, 1814.

.55 2262 Macdonough, Capt. T. Bust r. R. *Battle of Lake Champlain,* 11 Sept. 1814.

.5 2263 Henley, Capt. R. Bust r. R. Same as last.

.50 2264 Cassin, Lieut. S. Bust r. R. Same as last.

.55 2265 Stewart, Capt. C. Bust r. R. Engagement bet. *Constitution* and *Cyane* and *Levant,* Feb. 20, 1815.

.55 2266 Biddle, Capt. J. Bust r. R. Engagement bet. *Hornet* and *Penguin,* Mch. 23, 1815.

MEDALS AWARDED ARMY OFFICERS BY THE CONGRESS OF THE UNITED STATES.

WAR OF 1812 WITH GREAT BRITAIN.

All in bronze, perfect condition, and size 40.

.50 2267 Croghan, Col. Geo. Bust r. R. Battle of Sandusky, 2 Aug. 1813.

.80 2268 Shelby, Gov. Isaac. Bust r. R. Minute view of the battle of The Thames, Oct. 5, 1813.

.55 2269 Harrison, Maj. Gen. W. H. Bust r. R. Columbia wreathing trophy of arms. Battle of the Thames.

.50 2270 Miller, Brig. Gen. Jas. Bust r. R. View of battle. BATTLES OF CHIPPEWA JULY 5. 1814. NIAGARA JULY 25 1814. ERIE SEP. 17. 1814.

2. 2271 Miller. Obverse as last. R. Same as used on the Jacob Brown medal No. 2273. A column with flags, shields with NIAGARA. ERIE. CHIPPEWA. Eagle standing on British flag. Exergue names of battles as last. Very slight abrasion in field. A mule, and the only example I have ever heard of. *It is most unusual for any error in the employment of the dies to occur at the U. S. Mint.* This is an old impression. 40.

.52 2271a Porter, Maj. Gen. P. B. Bust r. R. Victory alighting with flags bearing names of Chippewa, Niagara, Erie. For same battles as last.

.62 2272 Scott, Maj. Gen. W. S. Bust r. R. Names as last.

.50 2273 Brown, Maj. Gen. J. Bust r. R. Trophy. Same battles as last.

.50 2274 Ripley, Brig. Gen. E. W. Bust r. R. Fame attaching a shield with names of same battles as last to a palm tree.

.50 2275 Gaines, Maj. Gen. E. P. Bust r. R. Victory wreathing a cannon, etc. Battle of Erie, Aug. 15, 1814.

.60 2276 Macomb, Maj. Gen. A. Bust r. R. View of the battle of PLATTSBURG, SEPT 11. 1814.

2277 Jackson, Maj. Gen. Bust r. R. Peace staying the hand of the Recording Angel (the war was over before this battle was fought). Battle of New Orleans, January 8, 1815.

WAR OF 1812 BETWEEN THE UNITED STATES AND GREAT BRITAIN.

MEDAL PRESENTED BY THE GOV. OF GREAT BRITAIN FOR BATTLE OF FORT DETROIT.

2278 VICTORIA REGINA 1848 Head l. R. TO THE BRITISH ARMY 1793-1814. The Queen wreaths Wellington, who kneels before her. Edge, J. COAKLEY, 41ST FOOT. Bar FORT DETROIT Slight nicks. Fine. Ribbon. Excessively rare . 23.

NOTE.—See lot No. 2371 for the CHATEAUGUAY medal.

MEXICAN WAR, 1846-1848.

2279 Bliss, Lt. Col. Presented by State of N. Y. Bust r. R. Arms of State of N. Y., names of battles in Mexico. Very rare. 40.

2280 Duncan. Brevt. Col. Jas., U. S. A. Bust r., by Wright. Around names of six battles in Mexico. R. Names of six more battles. PRESENTED BY THE CITIZENS OF N. YORK .. DEC 28TH. 1848. Bronze. Ex. fine. Obverse die cracked across, rendering the striking of more medals rather doubtful. Very rare. 34.

2281 Duncan. As last. Tin. Ex. fine. Very rare.

2282 New York City. PRESENTED BY THE CITY OF NEW YORK TO THE N. Y. REGIMENT OF VOLUNTEERS IN MEXICO. Arms of the City. R. Columbia hurling thunderbolt, Mexican ports in distance; names of battles around. Bronze. Perfect. Very rare. 32.

2283 Same. Tin. Slight dents on edge. Ex. fine. Very rare. 32.

2284 Scott, Maj. Gen. W. S. Res. by Congress, 1848. Bust l. R. Minute views of seven battles. Splendid medal. Two small spots on obv. 56.

2285 Scott. From Va., 1847. Bust above tablet. R. Column and Mexican views. Splendid medal. 56.

2286 South Carolina. Charleston. PRESENTED BY THE CITY OF CHARLESTON TO THE CHARLESTON COMPANY OF VOLUNTEERS IN MEXICO. Female, ship, view of city, etc., by C. C. Wright. R. Officer with flag, standing in opening in a fort; names of battles around; Recipient's name engraved below, Fredr. Hillerhilagher. Swivel broken off edge. Silver. Fine. Excessively rare. Holland's (1878) brought $42, Bushnell's (1882) $34. 36.

Cully   5,25 2287   South Carolina. Presented by SOUTH CAROLINA TO THE PALMETTO REGIMENT. Palmetto with shields, 1846-1847. Eagle above, also in field Dickinson, Butler, Gladen, motto around. Below tablet with recipient's name engraved, *J. Friedeberg.* R. View of troops with flag of S. C. landing from boats; names of battles around. Silver. Extremely fine. Excessively rare. 31.

2_ 2288   Shield-shaped badge. Man of war, crossed arms, cannon, 29 stars; in center in wreath MEXICO cactus, fortress, 1846. Along border names of battles Uniface. Bronze. Extremely rare. 34 x 36.

Culley   4-600 2289   So. Carolina. Washington Light Infantry. VIRTUE AND VALOR W.L.I. Fame to left blowing her trumpet, from which is a cloud inscribed WASHINGTON. Below R. L PHILA (Robert Lovett die sinker). R. Arms of State, W. L. I. CAP^T SIMONTON 144 MEN 4TH JULY 1860 Scroll with names of men around. Bronze. Perfect. Extremely rare 24.

MEXICAN WAR, 1845-1848.

All bronze proofs, perfect unless contrary is stated.

.50 2290   Taylor, Maj. Gen. Zachary. Bust r. R. Congress for battles of *Palo Alto* and *Resaca de la Palma,* 1846. 40.

.50 2291   Taylor. Same obv. R. Congress for *Monterey,* 1846. 40.

14 2292   Taylor. Fine bust r., by *Wright.* Res. of *Congress,* 1848. R. Minute view of battle of Buena Vista, Feby 22-23, 1847. Splendid medal. 56.

20 - 2293   Taylor. STATE OF LOUISIANA TO MAJ. GEN. ZACHARY TAYLOR Arms of State, pelican feeding her young; above scales JUSTICE, below UNION AND CONFIDENCE. R. The General viewing the battle of BUENA VISTA, at sides PALO ALTO. MONTEREY RESACA DE LA PALMA. Silver. Perfect. Excessively rare, as it must have been one of the few awarded. I do not recall another being offered in this metal, and very seldom even in bronze. 48.

2294   Taylor. As last. Copper. Perfect. Very rare. 48.

Phila.   40. 2295   Taylor. Bust r. R. "A LITTLE MORE GRAPE CAPT. BRAGG" etc. Tin. .55   Holed at top, as always. Perfect. 21.

50 2296   Taylor. Bust l. R. FORT HARRISON. OKEE CHO BEE. PALO-ALTO etc. Tin. Very rare. 20.

WAR OF THE REBELLION, 1861-1865.

2297 BERDAN'S U.S SHARP SHOOTERS. Crossed rifles, etc. Wreath on cross. Bar 1861 * 1865. Ribbon. Bronze. Perfect. Extremely rare. 25.

2298 Berry, Maj. Gen. H. G. Bust r. R. KILLED AT CHANCELLORSVILLE VA . MAY 1863. Silver. Proof. Rare. 17½.

2299 Brooklyn, N. Y. Medal badge presented 1866 by the city to its veterans in War 1861-1865. Bronze. R. Flag suspender and bars. Worn. 21 x 60 over all.

2300 Colored troops. Two colored soldiers charging a fort. FERRO HIS LIBERTAS PERVENIET Below U. S. COLORED TROOPS. R. DISTIN-GUISHED FOR COURAGE (in wreath) CAMPAIGN BEFORE RICHMOND 1864. Bronze. Proof. Very rare. 26.

2301 CUSTER'S 3 CAV. DIV 3 Bust of Gen. Custer. R. THE HISTORY OF THIS WAR—WILL RECORD THE CHIVALROUS DEEDS etc., THE THIRD DIV. CEDAR CREEK. 1864. Tin, struck loop. 23.

2302 Evans, Brig. Gen. N. G. Arms of So. Carolina ANIMIS OPIBUSQUE PARATI. R. AWARDED BY A CONCURRENT RESOLUTION OF THE GEN-ERAL ASSEMBLY OF THE STATE OF SOUTH CAROLINA TO BRIGADIER GENERAL NATHAN GEORGE EVANS, FOR CONSPICUOUS GALLANTRY AT LEESBURG, VA., 1861. Bronze. Perfect. Excessively rare, and I believe the only one I have seen. 36.

2303 Grant, Major General Ulysses S. Grant. Joint resolution of Con-gress, December 17, 1863, for capture of Vicksburg and Chatta-nooga. Bust l. R. View of Vicksburg and Chattanooga; with Mississippi River encircling. Bronze. Perfect. One of the largest medals ever struck. 64.

2304 Grant. Same. Copper. Proof. Very rare. 64.

2305 Grant. Same. Block tin. Slight dents on edge. Probably unique in this metal. Very fine. 64.

2306 Grant. Same. Struck in a composition resembling sole leather (no doubt as Grant was a tanner). Excessively rare, and most remarkable that the Government would strike in such a mate-rial after giving one from same dies to Grant in gold. 64.

2307 Grant. Very fine bust left, by Bovy, of Geneva, Switzerland. R. I INTEND TO FIGHT IT OUT ON THIS LINE IF IT TAKES ALL SUMMER. PATIENT OF TOIL. SERENE AMIDST ALARMS. INFLEXIBLE IN FAITH. INVINCIBLE IN ARMS. Silver. Proof. Very rare in this metal. 38½.

2308   Grant. As last. Bronze. Proof. 38½.

2309   JACKSON—HOPE MEDAL, THE GIFT OF ENGLISH GENTLEMEN Stone-
wall Jackson standing. R. Tablets for names, DISTINGUISHED
GRADUATE VIRGINIA MILITARY INSTITUTE. etc. Tin. Very rare.
29.

2310   McPherson. 1864. Gen. on horseback. R. Society Army of the
Tennessee, Washington City, 1876. Silver. Brass. Copper.
Tin. Proofs. 13.   4 pcs.

2311   Meade, Maj. Gen. G. G. Bust. PRESENTED BY UNION LEAGUE OF
PHILADELPHIA. R. Columbia wreath, Meade's sword, THE VICTOR
AT GETTYSBURG. Splendid medal. Bronze. Case. 50.

2312   Nagle, Gen. H. M. FAIR OAKS 31 MAY 1862 View of the General
leading a charge, his horse shot and falling. R. THE PENINSULA
* CHICKAHOMINY * THE CAROLINAS * TO GEN. H. M. NAGLE A TOKEN
OF ADMIRATION AND RESPECT FOR HIS GALLANT SERVICES. Bronze.
Ex. fine. Excessively rare. 38.

2313   Ohio. Columbia crowning soldier. 1861-1865. R. THE STATE OF
OHIO TO THOS. S. MAXWELL VETERAN CO. G 51$^{T.}$ REGT OHIO VOLUN-
TEER INF. With bar. Bronze. 24.

2314   Reno, Maj. Gen. J. L. Bust l. R. AWARDED TO——. Bronze. Proof.
Rare. 22.

2315   Thomas, Maj. Gen. G. H. TO MAJOR GENERAL GEORGE H. THOMAS
FROM THE STATE OF TENNESSEE. On arm BORREL 1866, below
TIFFANY & CO ED. R. "I WILL HOLD THE TOWN TILL WE STARVE."
The Capitol below. BY JOINT RESOLUTION ADOPTED NOV. 2. 1865.
Bronze. Proof. A splendid medal, and the only example I have
ever seen. 50.

2316   West Virginia. To survivors. Columbia crowning soldier, 1861-
1865. Arms. R. PRESENTED BY THE STATE OF WEST VIRGINIA.
Edge, M. CARROL CO K. 1$^{ST.}$ REGT INF VOL$^{S.}$ Bar, HONORABLY DIS-
CHARGED. Ribbon. Bronze. Very rare. 24.

2317   West Va. To those killed in action. Tomb. R. As last. No name.
No bar. Bronze. Fine. Very rare. 24.

THE MEDAL OF HONOR PRESENTED BY U. S. GOVERNMENT.

2318   Star with Columbia dispelling Rebellion. R. *The Congress to
Enoch A. Simpson Co. C 27th Me. Vol.* Bronze. Ribbon and
bar. In original case. Star 33. Over all 67. Excessively rare
and almost unobtainable, being, as it should be, most highly

cherished by the recipient. This is the only one that I have ever
seen offered for sale.

3   2319   G. A. R. Star with flag suspended edged with orange for the
Cavalry. On the ribbon an extra bar with eagle on blue ground.
Eagle pin at top. Bronze. Perfect. *(/ţau-*

réam 2-   2320   G. A. R. Star with flag suspender and eagle bar. Bronze. Perfect.

FRANCO-AMERICANA COLONIALS.

4aw̄ 605   2321   1670 Fifteen sols or quarter dollar. Silver. Issued in accord-
ance with an edict of Louis XIV, Feby. 19th, 1670, for the pur-
pose of furthering the commercial transactions of La Compagnie des Indes. LUD. XIIII D. G. FR. ET. NAV. REX. (Louis the
fourteenth by the Grace of God, King of France and Navarre).
Splendid bust of the King laureate and draped facing right,
above head sun in splendor, the badge of Louis XIV. R.
GLORIAM . REGNI . TVI . DICENT. 1670 (They shall speak of the
glory of thy Kingdom). Arms of France crowned, beneath A
mint mark of Paris. Above point of crown a castle. Extremely
fine, practically uncirculated. Shows the file marks in the planchet on head. Excessively rare, and one of the finest examples
of about six known. Valued by Mr. Parsons at 5000 francs—
$1,000. Plate. Crosby speaks of it page 133, 134, and illustrates
the 5 sols on his plate III, No. 5. Leroux No. 250, rarity 10,
"almost unique." Breton, No. 501, "One of the rarest Canadian
coins." Hoffman, Pl. XCVI, No. 100. See an interesting article on the 5 sols in the Am. Jo. of Numismatics, Vol. XI, 3, Jan.,
1877.

aut 14,50 2322   1670 5 sols. Same design as last. Fine. Very rare. Breton,
No. 502. Leroux, No. 251. Plate.

3.50 2323   1720 Quarter crown. LUD. XV. D.G. FR. ET. NAV. REX. Dog to
left, 1720. Bust r. R. IMP * CHRS. REGN. VINC. Addorsed L's
crowned, forming a cross, fleur de lis in angles, A, Paris mm, in
center. Extremely fine. Rare. Leroux 254-c.

Lu 4.50 2324   1720 Quarter crown. Same type, slightly different dies. Extremely fine. Rare. Leroux 254-c.

−. 3.50 2325   1720 Quarter crown. Same type, but without dog, and in its
place circle with dot in center. R. K, Bordeaux mm, in center of
cross. Very good. Rare. Leroux 254-c.

2326 1720 Quarter crown. Same type; period after REX. R. II.,
La Rochelle mm, in center of cross. Good. Rare. Leroux 254-c.

2327 1721 Sou. SIT. NOMEN. DOMINI. BENEDICTUM. Crossed L's
crowned. R. COLONIES FRANCOISES 1721. MM H La Rochelle.
Very fine. Well struck and even. Rare so fine. Breton 506.
Leroux 253.

2328 1722 Sou. As last. Obv. very fine. R. Surface corroded.

2329 1723 Company of the Indies. Crowned shields bearing a conical
mountain, allusive to Mont Real, or Montreal, where the Com-
pany had its central house, before the God of the St. Lawrence
River, at either side Indian Princesses; below COMPAGNIE DES
INDES 1723. R. SPEM AUGET OPES QVE PAPAT (It increases hope
and prepares wealth). Ship under full sail to l. Silver.
Original. Fine. Very rare. Plate. Betts, No. 113, p. 57.
Frossard, No. 1, plate I, No. 1.

2330 1738 Marque. Crowned L, fleur de lis. R. Crossed L's Corroded
surface. Good. Scarce. B 508.

2331 1740, '54, '53 (holed), '57. Marques. Good.   4 pcs.

2332 1756 Jeton. Silver. Original. LUD. XV. REX CHRISTIANISS Bare
head of the King, with hair tied by a fillet, beneath F. M. (Fran-
cois Marteau, die cutter, 1720-1749). R. SEDEM NON ANIMUM
MUTANT (They change their seat but not their mind). Exg.
COL. FRANC. DE L'AM 1756. Two bee hives with swarm of bees.
Extremely fine. Leroux obv. 284, rev. 285. Breton 517, but his
lacks the artist's initials. Excessively rare. Plate.

2333 1762 Marque. Uncirculated. Scarce in this condition.

CANADIAN COINS, MEDALS, TOKENS.

Arranged according to Leroux and Breton.

For other medals relating to Canada, see Nos. 2079, 2085, 2086,
2088, 2089, 2138, 2159, 2172, 2278 in this catalogue.

2334 1693 Indian Chief's medal. LVDOVICVS * MAGNVS * REX * CHRIS-
TIANISS Bust in armor, draped r., M. MOLART . F. R. FELICITAS
DOMUS AUGUSTAE Four busts. MDCXCIII. Bronze. Restrike.
Unknown to Leroux and unpublished. Excessively rare. 37.
L., type 300a, but above is by Molart, while this is by Hardy.

2335 1690 Quebec. Head of Louis XIV r., by J. Mauger. R. France
seated on rock, flags, beaver, etc. FRANCIA IN NOVO ORBE VICTRIX,

ex'g KEBECA LIBERATA M.DC.XC. Silver. Perfect. Restrike.
26. L. 306a.

Richards 2/0 2336 1690 Quebec. Same. Bronze. Restrike. 26.

Mild 5—2337 1720 Louisbourg settled. Youthful bust of Louis XV r. R. View
of Louisbourg. Silver. Perfect. Restrike. 26. L. 308.

2.60 2338 1720 Louisbourg. As last. Bronze. Restrike. Perfect. 26.

Wide /3⟩ 2339 1882 New Foundland. 50c. 1882. Very fine. L. 311, B. 946.

2,—2340 1880 New Foundland cent. 1880. Unc. Mostly red. L. 315,
B. 951.

Jenn 2⟩2341 1846 New Foundland. Rutherford Bros. Unc. L. 321, B. 953.

2.—2342 Newfoundland. St. John's Cathedral. Laying of the cornerstone,
1841. View of edifice. R. THE FIRST STONE LAID BY THE R̲ᵀ·
REVᴰ· Dᴿ· FLEMING. VA. 1841. Tin. Holed. Fine. Very rare.
34. L. 323.

Ly .30 2343 1861 New Brunswick cent, 1861. Uncirculated. Part red.
L. 377, B. 907.

Sila 3.60 2344 1861 Nova Scotia cent, 1861. Brilliant proof. Red. Very rare
so fine. L. 432, B. 877.

4. 2345 1864 Nova Scotia half cent, 1864. Unc. Partly red. L. 434,
L. 878.

Hdmy /0 2346 1814 Nova Scotia. Broke. Small bust, more like Lord Nelson.
Ex. fine. L. 835, B. 879.

4. .50 2347 1815 Nova Scotia. Starr & Shannon. Indian and dog. Ex. fine.
L. 432, B. 884.

Harry 2.25 2348 1845 Nova Scotia. Noel. Pres. Con. Church. Communion
token. Tin. Very fine. Rare. L. 463, K., rarity 5!

Mild 2.25 2349 Hudson's Bay Co. Arms. ⅛. Beaver skin. Brass. Unc. Bright,
but has a dark spot on rev. L. 489, B. 929.

Lean 1.75 2350 1815 Magdalen Is. Seal to r. MAGDALEN ISLANDS TOKEN 1815.
R. SUCCESS TO THE FISHERY. ONE PENNY. Split cod. Proof.
Steel, with traces of original color. Slight nick on edge. Very
rare. L. 495, B. 520.

Lead .35 2351 Montreal. Un sou. Bust of man at side. Very fine. L. 509,
B. 716.

2352 Montreal. Un sou. Uncirculated. B. 694.

Jnbn ./. 2353 Montreal. Un sou. Extremely fine. Rare. B. 711.

Lead ./. 2354 Un sous. B., Nos. 670, 674, 678, 679, 680, 682, 684 to 688, 691 to
695, last bent, 697, 699 (holed), 700 to 702, 704, 705, 707, 713
to 716. Good to fine.   28 pcs.

10

2355   Montreal. Front view of bank. Halfpenny, 1844. Bronze. Proof. Rare in such beautiful condition. L. 516, B. 527.

2356   Montreal. Communion token. ST. PAULS CHURCH MONTREAL 1833 E. B. (Edward Black). R. I CORINTHIANS XI 23 29. Hexagon. Fine. Very rare. Pewter. L. 623.

2357   Montreal. Business College Davis & Buie. R. ACTUAL BUSINESS DEPARTMENT 50. Tin. Ex. fine.

2358   Upper Canada. Lesslie & Sons, 1822. Twopence. Covered with light nicks, but very good and very rare. L. 698, B. 717.

2359   Upper Canada. Marriage of WILLIAM DUMMER POWELL AND ANNE MURRAY INTERMARRIED 3RD. OCTOBER 1775. Hands over altar. R. TO CELEBRATE THE FIFTIETH ANNIVERSARY UPPER CANADA 3RD. OCTOBER 1825. Copper. Fine. Very rare. 24. L. 730.

2360   1822 Anchor, crowned. 1/16, ⅛, ¼ dol. Vg. 3 pcs. L. 761-3.

2361   1812 Bust of Geo. III in wreath. R. ONE PENNY TOKEN 1812 Fine. L. 769, B. 959.

2362   1813, '14 Trade & Nav. Penny and ½ p. Vg. 2 pcs. L. 775-77, B. 962-3.

2363   1813 Wellington half p. Bust. Extremely fine. L. 799, B. 969.

2364   Cossack penny. Bust of Wellington. Dented. Good. L. 805, B. 985.

2365   Wellington ½ p. Bust. R. CIUDAD Error. Fine. Rare. L. 810 type, B. 986.

2366   Wellington ½ p. Bust. R. CUIDAD. Uncirculated. L. 810, B. 986.

2367   Canada. 1858 20c., 1858, 1870 10c., 25c., 1872, 1874. Unc. 5 pcs.

2368   Canada. 1870 50c., 10c. semi-proofs, 25c., 5c. Unc. 4 pcs.

2369   Canada. 1871 20c. Plain edge. Brilliant proof. Very rare in this condition.

2370   Canada. 1880 25c., 10c., 5c. Brilliant proofs. Very rare in this condition. 3 pcs.

2371   Canada. Medal awarded to Indian warrior in the War of 1812 against the U. S. VICTORIA REGINA 1848 Head of Victoria. R. The Queen placing a wreath on Wellington, who kneels before her. TO THE BRITISH ARMY. 1793-1814. Edge, SAKSARIE TAWENTSIAKWENTE, WARRIOR. Bar, CHATEAUGUAY. Ribbon. Extremely fine proof and remarkably fine specimen. Extremely rare. L. 929.

2372   Anticosti Island. Bust l. 1870. R. A, ⅛ in wreath. Bright.

2373 Ontario. J. DERBECKER GENERAL MERCHANT NEUSTADT, ONT. R. GOOD FOR 1c IN TRADE. Brass. Very fine. Very rare.

2374 British Columbia. FRANK A. TAMBLYN NELSON, B. C. R. GOOD FOR 5c IN TRADE Brass. Fine. Very rare.

2375 Canada. Confederation, 1867. Bust of Queen Victoria l. R. Britannia and four beautiful females. Superb medal, by *Wyon.* Bronze. Ex. fine. Four slight dents on reverse edge. Rare. 48. L. 1185.

2376 Canada. LORD STANLEY OF PRESTON G. C. B. GOV: GEN: OF CANADA. LADY STANLEY OF PRESTON 1888. Busts l. R. PRESENTED BY HIS EXCELLENCY THE GOVERNOR GENERAL. Elaborate coat of arms. *Silver.* Ex. fine. Very rare. Size 32.

2377 Montreal. PRESBYTERIAN COLLEGE, view of. R. CHRISTIANA PRIZE etc. Bronze. Ex. fine. Rare. L. 1229.

2378 Arms. R. DOMINION OF CANADA. Fame flying r. Silver. Vg. Nicked. L. 1460.

2379 Toronto. Busts of Marquise of Lorne and Princess Louise l. R. Arms of city, etc. INDUSTRIAL EXHIBITION ASSOCIATION OF TORONTO. Silver. Ex. fine. 28. L. 1466.

2380 London. THE WESTERN FAIR ASSOCIATION LONDON CANADA. View of building. R. Attributes of the Arts, etc. Copper. Proof. 38. L. 1474.

2381 London. Same So. Different obverse design. Bronze. 23. L. 1475.

2382 North West. Awarded by the British Government to soldier. Head of Queen Victoria l. R. NORTH WEST CANADA 1885. Edge, S'DT. N. LAMARCHE 65 BAT. Swivel. Very fine. L. 1591.

2383 Military button. CANADA MILITIA Beaver, crown above. R. P. TAIT & CO LIMERICK. Old. German silver. Perfect.

CHINESE SILVER CAST INGOTS.

2384 Helmet-shaped, with two oblong tablets of characters counter-stamped across center. Size 43. Weight, 11 oz. 2 pwt. 22 gr.

2385 Hat-shaped, with two oblong tablets of characters counterstamped lengthwise in center. Size 36. Weight, 11 oz. 21 pwt.

2386 Hat-shaped, with knob in center, at either side are two oblong tablets of characters counterstamped across. 1 small c s in center. Size 38. Wt., 12 oz. 4½ pwt.

2387 Similar to last, but 1 tablet of characters. Size 36. Wt., 11 oz. 16 pwt. 1 gr.

17.   2388   Similar to last, but different counterstamp.   Size 38.   Wt., 11 oz.
18 pwt. 21 gr.

6.25   2389   Round, with central knob and three tablets of characters counterstamped.   Size 29.   Wt., 6 oz. 1 pwt. 1 gr.

6.25   2390   Oval, with central knob and two round counterstamps.   Size 28.
Wt., 5 oz. 14 pwt. 5 gr.

2391   Round, with oblong tablet of characters in center.   Size 16.   Wt.,
1 oz. 5 pwt. 20 gr.

2392   Hat-shaped, with very long ends.   No characters.   Size 20.   Wt.,
10½ pwt.

2393   Hat-shaped, with long ends.   No characters.   Size 16.   Wt., 11
pwt. 16 gr.

2394   Hat-shaped.   No characters.   Size 15.   Wt., 12 pwt. 1 gr.

2395   Helmet-shaped.   No characters.   Size 19.   Wt., 18 pwt. 19 gr.

MALAY PENINSULA.

SULTAN OF PAHANG.

2396   1 ompate, 10=$1.   Hat-shaped.   Square, with deep crown in cen-
ter, border ornamented outside, and on inside covered with
characters.   Lead.   Hole in outer rim, as usual.   Very fine;
remarkably so.   Size 2⅝ inches.

2397   1 dua, 20=$1.   As last.   Very fine, remarkably so.   Size 1¾ in.

2398   1 satu, 30=$1.   As last.   Very fine, remarkably so.   Size 1¼ in.

2399   Set as above, but not so fine, and two have holes where corrosion
has eaten through; however, they are in the condition these rare
old coins come in.   3 pcs.

CUBA.

2400   1897 Souvenir dollars.   Head of Liberty r., in high relief
PATRIA Y LIBERTAD SOUVENIR 1897.   R. REPUBLICA DE CUBA * 900
******FINO*   Milled edge.   Same design in low relief.   Silver
and copper of each.   *The second* impressions from the dies.
Each in fine Morocco case.   Two printed circulars (not
counted).   Exceedingly rare in copper, and the high relief one
rare in silver, too.   4 pcs.

UNITED STATES FRACTIONAL CURRENCY.

All crisp and perfect, unless contrary is stated. One of the finest collections yet offered.

FIRST ISSUE.

Design of the 5c. and 10c Postage Stamps of 1861 issue.

2401 5c., 10c., 25c., 50c. Perforated edges. *A B N Co.* Very rare.
4 pcs.

2402 25c. Perforated edges. *A B N Co.* Dark red-brown. Very rare.

2403 5c. Perforated edges. *Without A B N Co.* Brown color. Very rare.

2404 5c. Perforated edges. *Without A B N Co.* Red-brown color. Very rare.

2405 10c. Perforated edges. *Without A B N Co.* Dark green color. Very rare.

2406 10c. Perforated edges. *Without A B N Co.* Yellow-green. Very rare.

2407 25c. Perforated edges. *Without A B N Co.* Dark brown color. Very rare.

2408 25c. Perforated edges. *Without A B N Co.* Cinnamon-brown. Very rare.

2409 25c. Perforated edges. *Without A B N Co.* Pale lemon yellow-brown color. Exceedingly rare.

2410 50c. Perforated edges. *Without A B N Co.* Dark green. Not quite fresh. Very rare.

2411 50c. Perforated edges, straight end (trimmed). *Without A B N Co.* Yellow-green. Very rare.

2412 5c. Unperforated edges. *Without A B N Co.* Wide margins, showing outer line on two sides. Pale lemon paper. Red-brown color. Very rare.

2413 5c. Unperforated edges. *Without A B N Co.* Light brown. Very rare.

2414 10c. Unperforated edges. *Without A B N Co.* Light green. Rare.

2415 10c. Unperforated edges. *Without A B N Co.* Dark green. Very rare.

2416 25c. Unperforated edges. *Without A B N Co.* Very rare.

2417 50c. Unperforated edges. *Without A B N Co.* Dark green color. Very rare.

2418 50c. Unperforated edges. *Without A B N Co.* Yellow-green. All margins trimmed off. Very rare.

2419 5c. Unperforated edges. *With A B N Co.* Pale lemon, light brown and orange-brown papers. Various shades. Rare lot.
9 pcs.

2420 5c. Unperforated edges. *With A B N Co.* Yellow paper. R. upside down. Creased and worn. Fair. Excessively rare.

2421 10c. Unperforated edges. *With A B N Co.* Pale green face. Back, white paper. Never saw another like it.

2422 10c. Unperforated edges. *With A B N Co.* White paper. Dark green. Cut close on top and end. Rare.

2423 10c. Unperforated edges. *With A B N Co.* Light green shades.
2 pcs.

2424 25c. Unperforated edges. *With A B N Co.* Shades. 3 pcs.

2425 25c. Unperforated edges. *With A B N Co.* Dark brown. Rare.

2426 50c. Unperforated edges. *With A B N Co.* Greenish paper. Cut from a sheet, as it has all the margin up to next notes on every side. Light green. A gem.

2427 50c. Unperforated edges. *With A B N Co.* Plate 27, wide margin on end. Dark green.

2428 50c. Unperforated edges. *With A B N Co.* Shades. 3 pcs.

SECOND ISSUE.

Bust of Washington, with gilt ring.

2429 5c. Silk paper. R. ℞ 1 1863 Brilliant example of this very rare note.

2430 25c. Silk paper. R. ℧ 2 1863 Dark purple. Very rare.

2431 25c. Silk paper. R. ℧ 1 1863 Pale lilac. Trimmed close end and bottom. Rare.

2432 50c. Silk paper. R. ℗ 1 1863 Brilliant example of this extremely rare note.

2433 50c. Silk paper. R. ℞ 2 1863 Cut off on left end. Not quite fresh.

2434 5c. Hard paper, as are following, no letters on back, so are four lots following. Grey paper face—yellow paper back. Very rare.

2435 5c. As last. Gilt ring, badly off center.

2436 5c. As last. Back so uneven that parts of two backs are on this note—the gilt 5, however, is in center. Creased. Worn. Good. Oddity.

2437 5c. White paper. Pale brown back. Cut from a sheet, and shows edge of the adjoining notes on every side; so it has *all* the margin. Perfectly centered. Beauty.

2438 5c. White paper. Dark brown back. Slender 5. Rare.

2439 5c. White paper. R. 1863 clear and blurred. Pale and dark brown of each. 4 pcs.

2440 5c. White paper. R. ❦ 1863. Cinnamon-brown.

2441 5c. As last, but only has ❦ 18, the 63 being omitted!

2442 10c. No letters on back. Cut from a sheet, showing edge of adjoining notes on all sides. Perfectly centered. Matches the 5c. above.

2443 10c. R. O 63 at top. Slightly soiled. I do not remember to have ever seen a duplicate of this.

2444 10c. Grey paper. No letters on back.

2445 10c. Gilt ring printed badly off center. No let. on back.

2446 10c. R. 1 1863. Scarce. Close on top and edge.

2447 10c. R. 1863 clear and blurred. Thin and heavy 10. Shades. 5 pcs.

2448 10c. R. ❦ 1863 Yellow-green back. Rare.

2449 25c. R. A 1863 clear. Dark violet color. Rare.

2450 25c. R. ❦ 1863 clear. Deep purple color. Rare.

2451 25c. R. ❦ 1863 clear. Pale violet color.

2452 25c. R. ❦ 1863 clear. Bluish slate lavender color. Rare.

2453 25c. R. ❦ 1863 clear. Grey lavender color. Rare.

2454 25c. R. 1863 clear. Reddish violet color. Rare.

2455 25c. R. 2 1863 Reddish violet color. Close on top.

2456 25c. R. 1863 clear. Dull violet color.

2457 25c. R. 1863 blurred and no date. Lavender. 2 pcs.

2458 25c. R. *Gilt inverted.* T 2 1863. Worn. Good. Unique?

2459 25c. G. S. A paper. Face and back separate. Sold as 1.

2460 50c. R. 1 1863 clear. Pink color. Wide margins. Perfectly centered. Rare so.

2461 50c. R. A 1863 clear. Pink color. Perfectly centered.

2462 50c. R. A 1863 clear. Slender 50 Vermillion color. Back shows slight pocket-book rubbing.

2463 50c. R. A 1863 blurred. Heavy 50, top of o broken. Gilt ring on obverse off center. Trimmed on end.

THIRD ISSUE.

Various vignettes in center. Green backs, unless contrary stated.

2464 3c. Washington. Light curtain. Cut out of sheet so it has all the margin possible. A gem.

2465 3c. Washington. Light and dark curtain.

2466 5c. Clark. Without and with plate letter *a*.   2 pcs.

2467 5c. Clark. Without plate letter. *Carmine back.* Scarce.

2468 5c. Clark. With plate letter *a*. *Carmine back.* Slight plate stain on back. Scarce.

2469 10c. Washington. *Autograph sigs. Jeffries and Spinner*—think of it the Register and Treasurer of the U. S. *signing* each 10c. note. *Carmine back.* Close on bottom. Very rare.

2470 10c. Washington. *Autograph sigs. of Colby and Spinner. Carmine back.* Rare.

2471 10c. Washington. *Carmine back.* Scarce.

2472 10c. Washington. Plate I. *Carmine back.* Rare.

2473 10c. Washington. With plate I and without.   2 pcs.

2474 25c. Fessenden. Plate *a*. *Carmine back.* Rare.

2475 25c. Fessenden. Without plate letter. *Carmine back.* Rare.

2476 25c. Fessenden. Plate *a* and without *a*.   2 pcs.

2477 25c. Fessenden. Plate *a*. R. M 265. Parchment paper. Brilliant specimen of this rare note.

2478 25c. Fessenden. Without plate letter, otherwise as last. Rare.

2479 50c. Justice. *Autograph sigs. of Colby and Spinner. Carmine back.* A 265. Rare.

2480 50c. Justice. *As last in every way, but without* A 265. Rare.

2481 50c. Justice. Plate I. *Carmine back.* No letter or date. Rare.

2482 50c. Justice. *Carmine back.* No letter or date. Rare.

2483 50c. Justice. Plate I. R. A 265. *Carmine back.* Rare.

2484 50c. Justice. Plate I, the I small. R. *Pale carmine back.* No letter or date.

2485 50c. Justice. As last, but carmine, bright and deep. Rare.

2486 50c. Justice. R. No letter or date. *Carmine back.* Rare.

2487 50c. Justice. Plate I, small I. R. A 265. Scarce.

2488 50c. Justice. Plate I, tall I. R. A 265. Scarce.

2489 50c. Justice. Plate I, very tall I, R. A 265. Rare.

2490 50c. Justice. Plate I*a*. R. A 265. Close on end. Very rare, as there is only 1 note in a sheet with this plate mark.

2491 50c. Justice. Tall I. R. No letter or date. Rare.
2492 50c. Justice. Plate *a*. R. A 265. *Parchment paper.* Very rare.
2493 50c. Justice. Without plate letter. R. A 265. *Parchment paper.*
      Very rare.
2494 50c. Justice. R. A 265. Scarce.
2495 50c. Justice. Plate *a*, minute a. R. A 265. Close on bottom.
      Rare.
2496 50c. Justice. Plate a, large *a*. R. A 265. Back slipped, trifle of
      end off and part of another end on opposite end. Rare.
2497 50c. Justice. Plate *a*. R. No letter or date. Scarce.
2498 50c. Justice. No plate letter or reverse letters or date. Scarce.
2499 50c. Spinner. *Autograph sigs. of Allison and Spinner.* R.
      A 265. *Carmine back.* Very rare.
2500 50c. Spinner. *Autograph sigs. of Colby and Spinner.* R. A 265.
      Carmine back. Rare.
2501 50c. Spinner. Plate I, the I minute. R. A 265. *Carmine back.*
      Very rare.
2502 50c. Spinner. R. A 265. *Carmine back.* Rare.
2503 50c. Spinner. Plate I*a*. R. A 265. *Carmine back.* Very rare.
      Only 1 in a sheet, and it is said only 200 sheets were printed.
2504 50c. Spinner. R. A 265. *Carmine back.* Rare.
2505 50c. Spinner. Plate *a*. R. A 265. *Carmine back.* Very rare.
2506 50c. Spinner. Plate I*a*. R. No letters or date. Very rare, only
      1 in a sheet.
2507 50c. Spinner. Plate *a*. R. No letters or date. Rare.
2508 50c. Spinner. Plate I. R. As last. Rare.
2509 50c. Spinner. Plate *a*. R. A 265. Rare.
2510 50c. Spinner. No plate letter or letter or date on back.
2511 50c. Spinner. Plate I. R. A 265. Runs off on end. Rare.
2512 50c. Spinner. No plate letter. R. A 265. Scarce.
2513 50c. Spinner. Plate I*a*. R. Open back. Fifty Cents, 50 in cen-
      ter, as all following. Very rare, only 1 in a sheet.
2514 50c. Spinner. Plate I. Rare.
2515 50c. Spinner. Plate *a*. Blue face. Rare.
2516 50c. Spinner. Plate *a*. White face. Scarce.
2517 50c. Spinner. No plate number or letter.

FOURTH ISSUE.

2518 10c. Liberty. Large pink seal. Blue end. Scarce.
2519 10c. Liberty. Pale large seal.

2520 10c. Liberty. Small seal, blue fiber end.
2521 15c. Columbia. Large pink seal. Blue end. Rare.
2522 15c. Columbia. Large pink seal. White end.
2523 15c. Columbia. Small pink seal. Blue end.
2524 25c. Washington. Large and small pink seals.   2 pcs.
2525 50c. Lincoln, and one of the best likenesses of him.
2526 50c. Stanton. Very deep blue for half the length.
2527 50c. Stanton. Pale blue end.

FIFTH ISSUE.

2528 10c. Meredith. Green seal. Scarce.
2529 50c. Dexter. Green seal.

SIXTH ISSUE.

2530 10c. Long and short keys, 25c., same way. 50c. Set.   5 pcs.

SHEETS, BLOCKS, ESSAYS, ETC.

2531 1st issue. 25c. Perforated edges. *No A B N Co.* Vertical pair, with wide margin attached at bottom. Dark red-brown color. Very rare.   2 pcs.

2532 1st issue. 5c. Unperforated edges. *A B N Co.* Vertical block, with wide margins on three sides, plate 21. Red-brown color. Slightly crumpled. Rare.   8 pcs.

2533 1st issue. 5c. Unperforated edges. *A B N Co.* Horizontal block. Crumpled and creased. *Plate margin on two sides.* Grey-brown color.   6 pcs.

2534 1st issue. 5c. Unperforated edges. Vertical strip. Plate margin "23rd" on one side. Creased between.   4 pcs.

2535 1st issue. 25c. Unperforated edges. Vertical strip. Plate 21. Margins on three sides. Creased and slightly soiled.   4 pcs.

2536 1st issue. 5c., 10c., 25c., 50c. Face only. On Japan? paper mounted on cards 7 x 5 inches. The 5c., 25c. on a golden brown paper, *unlike any used on regular issue.* Unique item.   4 pcs.

2537 2d issue. 10c. *Inverted 10 on back.* No date or letters. Slightly crumpled or creased in folds, but bright and crisp. Complete sheet of 20 notes! *Unique!* A single note, but with s 1863 and inverted 10, *in Dreer sale sold for $11.* A most valuable item.
                                                         20 pcs.

2538 2d issue. 10c. S 1863. Horizontal strip, creased, 1 small hole, worn, soiled. 5 pcs.

2539 2d issue. 10c. No letter or date. Vertical strip. Lightly folded between. 4 pcs.

2540 2d issue. 5c. No letters or date. Complete sheet. Creased through middle, few slight discoloration spots. 20 pcs.

2541 2d issue. 5c. Blue-grey face. No letter or date. Three 4's, 2 singles in a block. Creased lightly. Most unusual color. 14 pcs.

2542 2d issue. 5c. No date or letters. Complete sheet. Creased in folds. 20 pcs.

2543 2d issue. 5c. No date or letter. Worn in folds, soiled. Some notes a little torn. Block of 12 pcs.

2544 2d issue. 5c. As last. Vertical strip of 3, and then 2 on side. Make nice block of 4. 5 pcs.

2545 2d issue. 5c. As last. Creased, soiled on back. Block. 4 pcs.

2546 2d issue. 5c. As last. Vertical strip. 5 pcs.

2547 2d issue. 5c. Two vertical pairs. Creased between. 4 pcs.

2548 3d issue. 3c. Light curtain. Vertical strip. Uncreased. 5 pcs.

2549 3d issue. 15c. Grant and Sherman. *Autograph sigs. of Jeffries and Spinner. Red back.* ⅛ inch margin, as if note had been issued fully made. Clean. Pasted together. Very rare.

2550 3d issue. 15c. Same as last, but with green back. Very rare.

2551 3d issue. 15c. Columbia. Plate proof, number 1789, on India paper of obverse, with loose margin outside of plate. No seal. Black. A brilliant impression. Probably unique and valuable.

2552 3d issue. 15c. Columbia. Plate proof of obverse only. Same as last, but the India paper is only size of plate, though it has card outside as did last. Black. No seal. A brilliant imp. Probably unique and very valuable.

2553 50c. Die proof in green of *back*—plate 1796—of Lincoln 50c, on India paper on large card. Unique item.

2554 Postal notes, 1st issue for 1c., No. 63, for 2c., No. 666. Phila., Sept. 1890. Crisp. 2 pcs.

2555 "Specimen" notes. As on next lot, but with large margins, and each separate. 3c. note has only 1 face, the dark curtain. The 15c. Grant and Sherman, one has autograph sig's of *Allison and Spinner*, red back (slight tear), the other engraved sig's and green back. The 50c. 1st issue has two small holes. Printed on c. s. a. water-marked paper—a full sheet of which accompanies the lot, but is not counted. 38 pcs., sold as 1 lot.

SHIELD OF CURRENCY.

Issued in this form by the U. S. Government.

2556 U. S. Shield, engraved, printed in black. Seals of Treas. Dept.
Arranged upon it are the notes of the 1st, 2nd, 3rd issues, and
the Grant and Sherman Essays for 15c.—two of them, one with
autograph sigs. of Jeffries and Spinner. The notes are printed
only on one side. Third issue has the carmine backs, and on 3c.
the dark and light curtains. The margin intact. Somewhat
stained and yellowed, and a few trifling abrasions on the surface, but not on the notes. Could be cleaned, no doubt. Unframed. Sold as 1 lot.

COLLECTION OF COINS

OF

RAFAEL H. WOOD, ESQ.

NEW YORK CITY

UNITED STATES COINS.

DOLLARS.

2557 1795 Head. Fine style, lower curl touches first star. Two leaves
under each wing. Extremely fine. Every star sharp. Even impression, with deep milling. A few microscopic nicks on obv.
R. Breast of eagle is not struck up, and shows badly the file
marks in the planchet.

2558 1795 Head. Curl broken by first star. R. Two leaves. Good.
Nick on edge.

2559 1795 Head. Three leaves under each wing. Good.

2560 ʋ1795 Bust in left field. R. Shows light file marks. Very fine.

2561ᶜ 1796 Small date. R. Large letters. Fine. Scarce.

2562 1798 High 8. Sharp imp. Slight edge dent. Very fine.

2563 1798 Close, even date. Very good.

2564 1798 Wide date. 8 touches bust. Good.

2565 1799 Very fine. Sharp imp. Mint lustre.

2566 1799 Very fine. Attempted puncture at top. Another good.
                                                                2 pcs.
2567 1799 Very good.
2568 1840 Liberty seated. 1st year after 1804. Extremely fine, slight
            proof surface. Slight abrasions. Scarce.
2569 1848 Extremely fine. Mint lustre. Scarce.
2570 1853 Very fine. Slight nick on edge of rev.
2571 1873 Trade. Extremely fine. 1st year of coinage.
2572 1875 Trade. Had been a proof. Slightly circulated.
2573 1876 Trade. Extremely fine. Slight edge dent.
2574 1900 Washington and Lafayette. Heads r. R. Monument to
            Lafayette at Paris. Ex. fine.
2575 1900 Washington-Lafayette. As last. Extremely fine.
2576 1900 Washington-Lafayette. As last. Extremely fine.

HALF DOLLARS.

2577 1803 Large 3. Fair.
2578 1805 Over 1804. Very good. Feld slightly polished. Rare.
2579 1807 Bust to right. Small 7. Very good.
2580 1809 Extremely fine; only the high parts show slight wear.
            Sharp.
2581 1814 Over '13. 1817 over '13. Fine.   2 pcs.
2582 1817 Period 181.7. Very good. Scarce.
2583 1822 Proof surface both sides. Frosting before mouth and in
            center of reverse. Unusually fine example.
2584 1827 Over 1826. Very good. Scarce.
2585 1829 29 over or recut. Very fine.
2586 1832 Small letters on rev. Unc. Sharp impression.
2587 1836 Gobrecht's design. R. 50 CENTS. Milled edge. Extremely
            fine. Sharp, even impression, with mint lustre. Rare.
2588 1837 Slight proof surface on both sides. Ex. fine.
2589 1839 Bust. Extremely fine. Slight edge nicks.
2590 1840 O. Mint, o small and high. Very fine.
2591 1850 O. Mint. Extremely fine.
2592 1851 O. Mint. Extremely fine. Mint lustre. Scarce.
2593 1853 Arrow heads and rays. Only year of this type. Ex. fine.
2594 1854, 1856 O. Mint. Uncirculated.   2 pcs.
2595 1862 S. Mint. Medium s. Fine.
2596 1867, '70, '71 Very fine.   3 pcs.

2597   1871   Carson City Mint. Fine. Rare.
2598   1892   Columbian. Bust of Columbus. Uncirculated.
2599   1912 $1/2, $1/4, $1/10, 5c., 1c. Proof set as 1 lot.

QUARTER DOLLARS.

2600   1805   Fine. Weak on clouds.
2601   1806   Over 5. Good. 1818 (2) fine.   3 pcs.
2602   1818, 1819   Fine.   2 pcs.
2603   1825   Over 1823. Extremely fine. Sharp impression.
2604   1893   Isabella. Bust of the Queen, only crowned head on a
               U. S. coin! Unc.
2605   1893   Isabella. As last. Uncirculated.   2 pcs.

TWENTY CENTS. DIMES. HALF DIMES.

2606   1875   20 cents. Dull proof. S. Mint. Unc.   2 pcs.
2607   1875   20 cents. S. Mint. Fine.   3 pcs.
2608   1876   20 cents. Uncirculated. Mint lustre.
2609   1805   Dimes. 4 and 5 berries on laurel. Good.   2 pcs.
2610   1807   Dime. Very good. Pin scratch across rev.
2611   1834, '8, '41, '2 o, '7, '53 to '57, '59. Dimes. Vg.   13 pcs.
2612   1847   Dime. Extremely fine. Two nicks on edge. Scarce.
2613   1794   Half dime. Fair. Rare.
2614   1795   Half dime. Good.
2615   1795   Half dime. 10 pin scratched on head. Good.
2616   1833, '41, '45, '49, '53, '56 to '62, '72. Half dimes. 1861, '2 3c. Vg.
                                                   27 pcs.

CENTS.

2617   1793   Chain. Periods after LIBERTY and date. Obverse pitted by
               corrosion. Poor. Everything shows. Rare.
2618   1794   Hays, No. 21. Very good. Almost invisible pin scratches
               on obv. and rev. Brown color.
2619   1795   Lettered edge. Corroded surface. Fair.
2620   1796   Bust. Deep scratch on rev. Good.
2621   1797   Slender and heavy wreaths. Good. 1 pitted by corrosion,
               another oxidized, as found after long time buried.   3 pcs.
2622   1798   Large date, spur out of back of the 9. Poor.
2623   1801   Very good. Black color.
2624   1802   Very fine. Brown steel color. Nice coin.

2625 1803 Die broken along top of RICA Good.
2626 1808 So-called 12 star var. Very good. Steel color.
2627 1811 Perfect date. Good. Scarce.
2628 1811 Fair. Scarce.
2629 1814 Plain 4. Very fine. Bold impression. Steel color.
2630 1817 Wide dates, spaced thus 18 17 and 1 817 Vg. 2 pcs.
2631 1817 Die cracked for first three stars. 1 before bust. Ex. fine.
2632 1833 Extremely fine. Steel color.
2633 1834 Small date. Very fine. Slight nick on rev.
2634 1835 Large date. Very good. Steel color.
2635 1848, 1849 Very fine. Light olive. 2 pcs.
2636 1850, '1, '3, '6 2 var. Unc. Beautiful light olive. 5 pcs.
2637 (1783) Washington double head cent. One eye knocked out. Good.
2638 Balance of the coll., 1800, '1, '2, '3 (4), '5 (2), '6, '7, '10 (2), '12 (2), '14 (2), '17 to '57. A few poor, but generally good to very good. 98 pcs.
2639 1856 Eagle cent. Worn on eagle. Good. Copper-nickel. Rare.
2640 1858 Small eagle cent. R. Laurel wreath. Copper-nickel. Proof. Rare.
2641 1857, 8 (5 eagle cents), other late common dates. 26 pcs.

HALF CENTS.

2642 1793 Good. Slightly seamed behind head. Rare.
2643 1794 Small bust. Good.
2644 1803, '4, '6, '9, '25, '6, '9, '32-'5, '50, '1, '3,-'5, '7. Good to fine. 1864 2c. 27 pcs.
2645 1804 Crossed 4. Die broken over RTY. R. Stems. Vg.
2646 1829 Uncirculated. Beautiful light olive color.
2647 1832 Uncirculated. Beautiful light olive color.
2648 1833 Slight proof surface. Light olive, traces of red.

ODDITIES OF U. S. COINAGE.

2649 1796 Liberty cap cent. No LIBERTY. R. Has 1796 to left of bow. Very broad milling on both sides. Poor.
2650 1807 Cent. Thin planchet about 4/5 regular diameter (but thin) and not large enough to take in all of die. Good.
2651 1807 Large $\frac{1}{100}$. R. Upside down. Good.

2652   1835, 1853 Cents. Struck ⅛ inch off center. Vg.   2 pcs.
2653   1840 Cent. Large date. R. Cross set. Good.
2654   (1795) Half cent. Across date and on rev. part of die of a cent.
      Poor.
2655   1806 Half cent. R. Cross set. Fair.
2656   1808 Half cent. R. Upside down. Fine. Brown color.
2657   1809 Half cent. R. Cross set. Very fine.
2658   1828 Half cent. 12 s. Badly off center. Very fine.
2659   1865 2c. Die broken on right side. Good.
2660   2c. About 1864. Reverse side very fine. Other side same *incused*.

FOREIGN SILVER COINS AND MEDALS.

2661   1711 Austria. Chas. VI. Bust r. R. Double-headed eagle over
      landscape. Medal. Very fine. 28.
2662   1845 Prussia. F. W. IV. Double and single (1859) thaler. Vf.
                                     2 pcs.
2663   1901 Germany. Centennial, 1701-1901, founding of the Dynasty.
      Busts jugate l. of Fred. I and Wm. II. 2 and 5 marks. Fine.
                                       2 pcs.
2664   1889 Wurtemberg. Karl and Olga. Busts of King and Queen r.
      1864-1889. R. Arms. Ex. fine medal. 24.
2665   1689 England. Wm. and Mary. Busts. ½ crown. Good.
2666   1903 Philippine Is. 5, 10, 20, 50 centavos. 1 peso. Ex. fine.
                                       5 pcs.
2667   Kruger. 6 pence. Franc. Lira. Mex ¼ and smaller. 3 coppers.
      Fine.   18 pcs.
2668   Japan. Low grade bou and silver ¼ b.   2 pcs.
2669   Cuba. Souvenir dollar, 1897. Low relief. Unc.
2670   Roman Imperial denarii. A. D. 79-96 Domitian. 138-161 Ant.
      Pius. 161-180 M. Aurelius. 193-211 Sep. Severus. 197-217
      Caracalla. 211-212 Geta. 235 Julia Mamaea. Very fine. 7 pcs.

COLLECTION OF COINS

OF

H. L. STEVENS, ESQ.

GERMANTOWN, PHILADELPHIA

2671 1722 Wood. 1773 Va. 1783 Nova Const. 1787 Fugio. Conn.,
N. J. Poor. 22 pcs.

2672 1900 Washington-Lafayette dollar. Heads. Ex. fine. ·

2673 1819 $¼. Half dimes 10. 3c. silver 15. Poor. 26 pcs.

2674 1864 to 1872 2c. poor to vg. 21 pcs. 1865 3c. bright. 22 pcs.

2675 1793 to 1857 cents. No 1799, 1804, 1809. Early dates very poor,
but show date. After 1820 poor to very good. 428 pcs.

2676 1801 Cent. $\frac{1}{100}$. Good. Steel color.

2677 1802, 1808, 1812 off center, 1813, 1820 perfect die. Cents. Good.
5 pcs.

2678 1820 Cent. Large date. Cracked die. Unc. Brilliant red.

2679 1820 Cent. Same. Red, light olive, steel colors. Unc. 3 pcs.

2680 1831 Cent. Large letters. 1832 very fine, cleaned, corroded on
back. 2 pcs.

2681 1843 Cent. Type of 1842. Extremely fine. Red. Cleaned?

2682 1843 Cent. As last. Very fine. Slight nicks.

2683 1853, 1855 upright 55. Cents. Uncirculated. Brilliant bright
red. 2 pcs.

2684 1856 Cent. Slanting 5. 1857 large date. Ex. fine. Cleaned.
2 pcs.

2685 1854 Pattern cent. Head of Liberty. Proof. Pin-head speck on
obverse.

2686 1857-'64, '72-'75, '77 (good), '79-'81. 13 later, 2 of s. Mint. Vg.
to proof (3). 29 pcs.

2687 1797 Half cents. Low head. High head. Poor. 2 pcs.

2688 1800 Half cents. Very good. Scarce. 2 pcs.

2689 1803 Half cent. Wide $\frac{1}{100}$. Uncirculated. Dull red and steel
color. Bold impression. Beautiful specimen, and very rare in
this condition.

11

2690   1803 to 1811 inclusive, 1825, '6, '8, '9, '32-'5, '49-'51,-'53-'7. Half
       cents. Poor to unc.   31 pcs.

2691   1806 Half cent. Large 6. Ends to stems. Very fine. Light
       olive.

2692   1828 Half cent. 13 stars. Brilliant bright red. Part of reverse
       steel color.

2693   1909 10c., 5c., 1c. Lincoln. Proofs.   3 pcs.

2694   1903 Philippine Is. 50c., 20c., 10c., 5c. (nickel), 1c., ½c. Dull
       proofs.   6 pcs.

2695   1859 Cent. Oak wreath, narrow shield. Uncirculated.

2696   1857-8 Eagle cents 54. Indian head nickel cents 69, 1905-'11 26.
       Poor to good. Last lot unc.   149 pcs.

2697   Cents. Very poor, a few holed, 36. Foreign coppers. Rubbish.
                                                        111 pcs.

2698   1837-41 Hard Times Tokens, etc. Good (1 slave damaged) to
       ex. fine.   19 pcs.

2699   Rebellion Cards and Tokens. Good lot.   85 pcs.

2700   Slave kneeling AM I NOT A MAN (2). Similar obv. R. WHATSO-
       EVER etc. Tin. Slave trade abolished 1807. British General
       and slave. Very fine.

2701   1792 Coventry ½ p. Lady Godiva nude on horse. Good.

2702   Guernsey. 1, 2, 4, 8, doubles, 1885-'9. North Borneo ½c., 1c.,
       1891. Bright red.   6 pcs.

2703   1719 England. Geo. I. Farthing. Uncirculated. Light olive.
       Broad milling.

2704   Washington. Bust l. R. Headquarters. Lovett's series com-
       plete. Copper. Proofs. 16.   10 pcs.

2705   Lincoln. Bust r., by *Key*. R. SHALL BE THEN, THENCE FORWARD,
       AND FOREVER FREE" EMANCIPATION. Silver. Proof. 14.

2706   Tilden. 1876. "THE GREAT FRAUD." Satirical medal. 1897 Nash-
       ville. 1901 Buffalo Exp. 1907 Jamestown. 1909 Seattle,
       Alaska, Yukon Exp. Percie Kirk (restrike), Yucatan. Bronze.
       Copper. Tin. 16-26. Perfect.   7 pcs.

CONFEDERATE STATES OF AMERICA.

2707 1861 Cent. CONFEDERATE STATES OF AMERICA 1861. Undraped bust of Liberty, wearing cap with 5 stars facing left. R. 1 CENT in a wreath of cotton, sugar cane, etc., tied by a ribbon, and with a bale of cotton below on which L for LOVETT. Nickel. *Original.* Not restruck in this metal. Uncirculated. Extremely rare, probably about five known. Plate.

2708 1861 Half dollar. Obverse regular U. S. coinage. R. CONFEDERATE STATES OF AMERICA HALF DOLL., in center C. S. A. shield, liberty cap above, between branch of cotton and sugar cane. Silver. Restrike—made by using U. S. $½, smoothing off back and striking the C. S. A. die upon it. Splendid impression. Uncirculated. Rare. Plate.

2709 1861 "Dime." JEFFERSON DAVIS. Fine bust, undraped l., below C. R. R. C S A FIRST PRESIDENT In olive wreath 1861. Uncirculated. Excessively rare, probably about 3 known. Plate.

2710 1863, '4 Almanacs. Vicksburg, with bust of Davis. Mobile.
2 pcs.

2711 1864 50c., $1, $2, $5, $10, $20, $50, $100, $500. Notes. Set. Crisp.   9 pcs.

U. S. MINOR PROOF SETS.

Sold so much a set. Fine, bright sets.

2712 1864 1c. nickel, 1c. copper, 2c. Very rare as a set.
2713 1865 1c., 2c., 3c. Rare as a set.
2714 1866 1c., 2c., 3c., 5c. rays. Scarce.
2715 1867 1c., 2c., 3c., 5c. no rays. Scarce.
2716 1868 1c., 2c., 3c., 5c. Scarce.
2717 1869 1c., 2c., 3c., 5c. Scarce.
2718 1870 1c., 2c., 3c., 5c. Scarce.
2719 1871 1c., 2c., 3c., 5c. Scarce.
2720 1872 1c., 2c., 3c., 5c. Very scarce.
2721 1872 1c., 2c., 3c., 5c. Rather dull. Very scarce.
2722 1873 1c., 2c., 3c., 5c. Very rare.
2723 1874 1c., 3c., 5c.
2724 1875 1c., 3c., 5c.

2725   1876   1c., 3c., 5c.

5.— 2726   1877   1c., 3c., 5c.   Very rare.

2. 2727   1878   1c., 3c., 5c.   Rare.

.16 2728   1879 to 1914. 1883 complete with three 3c. 1887 both 3c. over and
perfect dates. 1909 Indian and Lincoln. Splendid line of sets.
                                                      36 sets.

5€ 2729   1909, 1910, 1911, 1912, 1913. Cents. S. Mint. Unc.   5 pcs.

THE PROPERTY OF THE ESTATE

OF THE LATE

CHARLES STEIGERWALT

/2.50 2730   U. S. Currency Shield. Issued by U. S. Gov. U. S. Shield, engraved, printed in black. Seals of Trea's Dep't. Arranged upon
it are the notes of the 1st, 2nd and 3rd issues—only printed on
one side, but having both carmine and green backs; dark and
light curtain 3c. Also has the two 15c. Grant and Sherman, one
of them and two others with autographs of Jeffries and Spinner.
Unusually fine and clear. Rare. Unframed. Sold as one lot.

/2. 2731   Same as last, but slightly yellowed with age and matted down to *faded*
size and shape of shield. Ready for framing. Sold as 1 lot.

.15 2732   U. S. Fractional Currency. 5c. 1st issue, without *A B N Co.* on
back. Perforated edges on two sides, trimmed off on others.
Crisp.

/6 2733   1st issue. Perforated edges. 10c. With *A B N Co.* Crisp, but
not quite fresh.   .   2 pcs.

6a 2734   3rd issue. 10c. Autograph signatures of Colby and Spinner.
Carmine back. Crisp. Rare.

2735   3rd issue. 10c. (3), 25c., 50c. Spinner, both trimmed on one side.
Crisp.   5 pcs.

/.50 2736   3rd issue. 50c. Spinner. Carmine back. A 265. Crisp.

.7 2737   3rd issue. 50c. Spinner. Plate 1a. Only one in a sheet. R. Open
back. Crisp. Rare.

2738 3rd issue. 50c. Spinner. R. Open back. Crisp.

2739 3rd issue. 10c. Large and small seals, and pink face. Crisp. 4 pcs.

2740 3rd issue. 50c. Lincoln. Plain wk'd pp. Ex. fine.

2741 3rd issue. 50c. Stanton. Various blue ends. Crisp. 4 pcs.

2742 5th issue. 50c. Dexter (2), 10c. green seal. Crisp. 3 pcs.

2743 6th issue. 50c. Crawford. Crisp. 1 faded. 5 pcs.

2744 Soiled currency. 5c., 10c. (3), 25c. Canada. Lot.

2745 C. S. A. $1,000 Bond, 1864, with 59 coupons (1 off). Fine.

2746 C. S. A. and Southern notes issued during Rebellion. 5c. to $500. Av. Good. 3 counterfeits. 41 pcs.

2747 Chicago. P. Palmer & Co. Unsigned notes for 50c. (49), 25c. (38). In colors. Issued during War 1861-65. 87 pcs.

2748 Rebellion envelopes. Clean. In colors. Few, if any, dups. 240 pcs.

2749 Stock notes, period 1837. Blanks and unsigned. Some with head of Washington. 6 sheets of 6 notes each. Sold as 1 lot.

2750 Electrotype. Cuts of Colonial and other coins used by Mr. Steigerwalt in the publication of his book on U. S. Coins, etc. About 150 pieces (5 cigar boxes full). As 1 lot.

2751 Germany, Austria. Old notes. 7 pcs.

MASSACHUSETTS.

2752 1652 Shilling. Oak tree with two shrubs. MASATHVSETS . IN. R. NEW ENGLAND . AN DOM 1652 XII. Very fine. Evenly struck, remarkably so for this variety, which is generally much clipped. Very rare. Plate. C. 7-B.

2753 1652 Sixpence. Oak tree, bushy, and with two shrubs. MASATHVSETS . IN. R. NEW ENGLAND . ANO. 1652 VI. Uncirculated. obverse all on, but not quite even. R. Perfectly even. Slightly bent, which is probably done in the striking. A wonderful example of this very rare coin, and probably the finest known. Plate. C. 1ᵇ-D.

2754 1652 Threepence. Oak tree, open trunk. MASATHVSETS R. NEW ENGLAND 1652 III. Very good. Very rare. Plate. C. 3-A².

2755 1662 Twopence. Bushy oak tree. Fine. Plate. C. 1-A¹.

2756 1652 Shilling. Pine tree, with heavy formal branches. A few letters at top do not show, otherwise very good. Rare. C. 14-R.

PLATE I

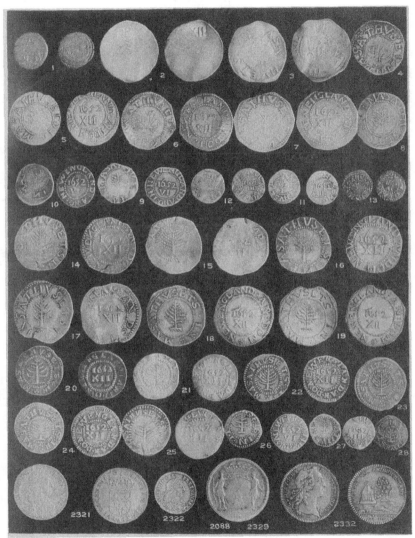

HON. GEORGE M. PARSONS COLLECTION
CATALOGUED BY HENRY CHAPMAN
SOLD AT AUCTION, PHILADELPHIA, JUNE 24-27, 1914

PLATE II

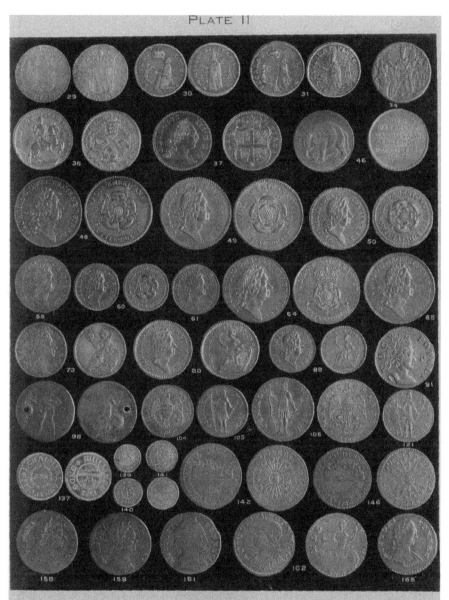

PLATE III

PLATE IV

HON. GEORGE M. PARSONS COLLECTION
CATALOGUED BY HENRY CHAPMAN
SOLD AT AUCTION, PHILADELPHIA, JUNE 24-27, 1914

PLATE V

HON. GEORGE M. PARSONS COLLECTION
CATALOGUED BY HENRY CHAPMAN
SOLD AT AUCTION, PHILADELPHIA, JUNE 24-27, 1914

PLATE VI

HON. GEORGE M. PARSONS COLLECTION
CATALOGUED BY HENRY CHAPMAN
SOLD AT AUCTION, PHILADELPHIA, JUNE 24-27, 1914

PLATE VII

HON. GEORGE M. PARSONS COLLECTION
CATALOGUED BY HENRY CHAPMAN
SOLD AT AUCTION, PHILADELPHIA, JUNE 24-27, 1914

PLATE VIII

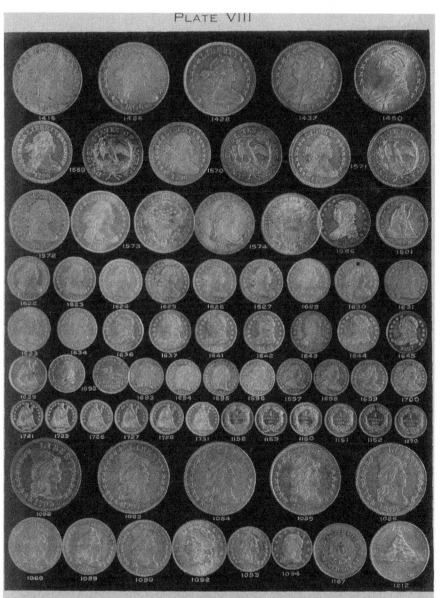

HON. GEORGE M. PARSONS COLLECTION
CATALOGUED BY HENRY CHAPMAN
SOLD AT AUCTION, PHILADELPHIA, JUNE 24-27, 1914

PLATE IX

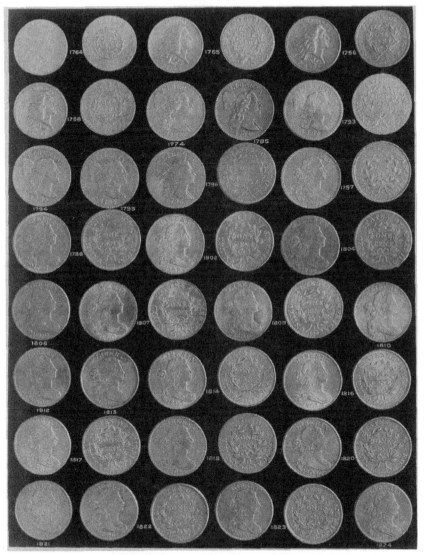

HON. GEORGE M. PARSONS COLLECTION
CATALOGUED BY HENRY CHAPMAN
SOLD AT AUCTION, PHILADELPHIA, JUNE 24-27, 1914

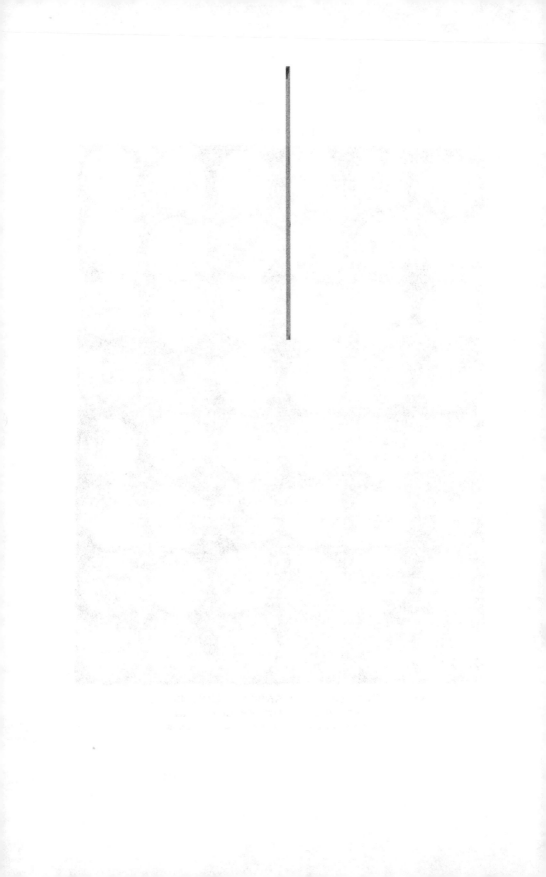

PLATE X

HON. GEORGE M. PARSONS COLLECTION
CATALOGUED BY HENRY CHAPMAN
SOLD AT AUCTION, PHILADELPHIA, JUNE 24-27, 1914

PLATE XI

HON. GEORGE M. PARSONS COLLECTION
CATALOGUED BY HENRY CHAPMAN
SOLD AT AUCTION PHILADELPHIA, JUNE 24-27, 1914

PLATE XII

HON. GEORGE M. PARSONS COLLECTION
CATALOGUED BY HENRY CHAPMAN
SOLD AT AUCTION. PHILADELPHIA. JUNE 24-27. 1914

PLATE XIII

HON. GEORGE M. PARSONS COLLECTION
CATALOGUED BY HENRY CHAPMAN
SOLD AT AUCTION. PHILADELPHIA. JUNE 24-27, 1914

L Friday
JITU Hereford
send Danbury 1857 KG